ALPHONSE

BY

LÉON DAUDET

TO WHICH IS ADDED

THE DAUDET FAMILY

("Mon Frère et Moi")

BY

ERNEST DAUDET

TRANSLATED BY CHARLES DE KAY

BOSTON

LITTLE, BROWN, AND COMPANY

1898

MEMOIRS OF

ALPHONSE DAUDET

University Press:

John Wilson and Son, Cambridge, U.S.A.

DEDICATION

I dedicate this book, in all piety, to Madame
Alphonse Daudet, my dearly beloved mother —
my mother who discreetly aided and encouraged
her husband in all his good as well as wretched
hours and created about him that atmosphere
of tender reflection in which he was able to live,
work and die under the protection of a pure,
pensive and restful soul.

LÉON DAUDET.

PARIS, January, 1898.

PREFACE.

HIS tomb is hardly closed and I set myself to write these words. I do it with a brave heart, but broken by a frightful sorrow, for the one of whom I shall speak was not only a father and husband of the most exemplary sort, he was also my teacher, my counsellor and my great friend. There was not a line written by me which I did not read to him while the ink was wet; there was not a thought of mine, the true value of which I did not beg him to state: there was not one of my feelings, the power or the origin of which I concealed from him.

This life which I owe to him, the beauty, dignity and importance of which he caused me every day to perceive; this life, burning with admiration for his intellectual and moral beauty; this life which he scrupulously and jealously guided and which he filled with pride at the example offered by his own — I presented this life to him as it proceeded in order that he might judge and strengthen it.

And now, although he, my darling one! exists no longer, as I march onward through this sor-

rowfully dark night toward him, the beacon, yet
do I persevere in my endeavor, guided by the
sound of his voice and the tender fire of his look.

My heart overflows; I shall open it wide. So
many noble and grand things which he has said to
me tremble within me and seek an exit! I shall
permit them to be scattered before the feet of his
numberless admirers. The latter have nothing to
fear; their gentle consoler was without a blot. If I
turn my eyes backward over the path of my existence, already harsh, though brief, I see him standing calm and smiling despite his torments, showing
an indulgence which at certain critical hours has
thrown me trembling with admiration at his feet.

But it is not only for what he was in regard to
myself, or to my brother, my sister or my mother
that I love him; it is also, and beyond everything
else, for his humanity which shone within him with
so profound and serene a splendor; for his vast
and sympathetic comprehension of all kinds of
things and all sorts of people! Surely seldom has
such a character been known here below and never
in a more splendid form.

I write for you, young people, and for you also,
old men, adults male or female, and for you by
preference, ye disinherited ones whom the world
repulses — vagabonds, luckless ones and the misunderstood! The extraordinary thing about this
writer was that he preferred the humble and the
disinherited of fortune to all others. It is with the
pale flowers of their lives that he wove his great

crown; it was by relieving their distress with words or with a discreet action that he closed the circuit of hearts, and, as it were, created a new kind of comprehension in his harsh day and generation.

Oh, most generous circulation of blood! I have never seen my father angry except when justice was defrauded. He never swerved from justice save when carried away by pity. And, to make an end, his schooling was obtained through the pain which he heroically supported for the love of his family and the honor of human life.

Muddle nothing, ruin nothing, was his usual motto. I draw inspiration from his tomb, but I should not be the only one to benefit by his experience, I should not be the only one to direct his life according to his example. I believe that I am imitating him to-day when I draw aside the dark veil which falls about a deathbed, permitting that life-work only to shine with brilliancy. Moreover, that work emanated from him like his breath and gesture. So, in order that you may know him better, in order that you may love him more — I mean all of you, big and little, whose unhappiness he alleviated as by enchantment — I abandon to you in part my filial privilege and am about to allow those voices to be heard through which the heredity and the paternal affection have spoken that are the occupants of my respectful soul.

CONTENTS.

APPENDIX.

THE DAUDET FAMILY.

ALPHONSE DAUDET.

I.

LAST MOMENTS.

IT is a fact that my father was ill for many long years, but he supported his sufferings so bravely, he accepted his restricted life with such a smiling resignation, that we had come to the point — we, meaning my mother, my brother and myself — of divesting ourselves a little of the anxiety we all felt at the time his sufferings began.

All the same, walking supported by one of us and resting his weight on his silver-headed cane — in regard to which he told our little sister and his grandson so many marvellous legends — all the same, with head erect and eyes bright and hand held out toward the friend who visited him, he was the joy and life of the house. This family which he cherished and brightened with his most tender looks was kept close about him; he guarded it by that moral force of his — immense, always in full power and ever increasing as he lived. On all about him he breathed an atmosphere of kindness and of confidence which the coldest and most reserved could not evade.

For the truth of this I call to witness the innumerable friends and literary comrades and strangers who came to make the author a visit; without exception they found him ready with counsel and help, ready with those precious words which elicit confidences and calm and heal the soul.

No one understood as he did the path to hearts. He himself had had hardships in the beginning and his extraordinary sensitiveness, which I shall presently attempt to analyze, caused him to place vividly before his own mind all the difficulties and rebuffs and shames others might have met, and with unexampled sharpness and vigor in particulars. When a man stood before him with his face in a strong light he divined him and summed him up with a precision which was like magic; but he was chary of words and only used his eyes, so soft, veiled and yet so penetrating! "The look out of his eyes warmed one" — that was the phrase which I caught from so many lips during those days of mourning; and I admired the justice of the expression. Moreover, confession — that balm for souls which indignation or disdain has closely imprisoned, that consolation of the afflicted, of the abandoned and those in revolt — confession came true and sincere from the hearts of the rudest people; yes, the ears of my beloved father have had to hear strange avowals!

I believe also that in him people divined a veritable ferment of indulgence; his love of pardon and of sacrifice belonged to his Catholic blood. He believed that every crime could be forgiven and that nothing was absolutely irreparable when confronted by a sincere repentance. So many luckless ones are captives of the evil which they themselves have caused and only begin their crimes over again through distress! My father had a final argument; he pointed out to them how he himself had been struck by illness in his mid career, and how, by the force of his will, he could offer himself now as an example. His strength of argument was such that very few resisted him.

And then, what an intimate eloquence was his! His words and his very intonations remain in my memory quite intact. The tone was not the same when he was telling some story in lively, splendid and precise words, as when he took my sufferings in hand. In the latter case he employed words which were vague enough at first and rather murmured than spoken, accompanied by gestures gently persuasive. By little and little, and with infinite precaution and delicacy, this speech became more definite and connected; it wove about one's being a thousand little tangible and intangible bonds, a fine and delicate cobweb for the heart, in which the heart very soon was beating warm. That is the way he employed strategy; but what I cannot express in words was the spontaneity and irresistible grace of his manœuvres, half methodical, half inexplicable, the net result of which was the solace of unhappiness.

He expected silence to do a great deal; in this silence the last words he had uttered vibrated and

thus grew in grandeur. I can still see certain
people standing erect before his table with moist
eyes and trembling hands. I can see others seated,
turning toward him with a movement of thanks,
astonished by so much wisdom as his. I can see
the frightened ones and the stutterers, to whom he
knew how to give confidence by means of a smile.
Or else, while waiting for the result of his counsel,
he would pretend to look up a piece of paper or
his pen, his pipe or his eye-glass, somewhere about
his always cluttered table.

A depositary of so many confidences and secrets, my father kept them to himself; he has
carried them with him into his tomb; very often I
guessed at certain things, but when I put him
questions, he gently evaded me and teased me for
my curiosity.

Far, far back, at the very beginning of my
youngest childhood, I can perceive the kindness
of my father. That kindness shows itself in
caresses, he draws me close to him, he tells me
wonderful stories, we walk together through the
streets of Paris and everything seems to have the
appearance of a festival. I perceive the warmth
of the sun and then another warmth, softer and
nearer to me, which is transmitted by the dear,
strong hand. In my narrow little breast I feel
something tangible and exquisite, for the sake
of which my breathing is quicker, something
which I have already learned to call *happiness*,
and as I walk along I repeat to myself *I am very
happy to-day*. My father talks to me; for me he

has neither features nor face; he is not a marvellous man, but just simply *my father.* I often
call him Papa, Papa, just for the simple pleasure
which that word gives me, because attached to it
seem all the germs of brilliant and noteworthy ideas.
I ask him questions about everything around us, in
order to hear the sound of his voice, which appears
to me like the most beautiful music and seems to
sound in exact accord with the happiness and
brilliancy of all my hopes.

We pass through squares full of people and
enter grand mansions; those who greet us are
jovial and Papa always makes them laugh. I am
wonderfully quick to perceive that there is something in him which is greater than that which exists
in others. They turn toward him, they address
themselves to him.

We are in the working-room, he, my mother,
and I; at that time we inhabited the old Hôtel
Lamoignon, 24 Pavée Street in the Marais; this
time there is sunshine, too, in the shape of a big
yellow streak which lengthens the designs of the
carpet, a streak which I insist upon trying to polish
by rubbing it with my hand. My mother is seated
and writes; my father also writes, but standing
up, using a little plank screwed to the wall. Now
and then he stops, turns about and puts a question
to my mother. From the way in which they look
at each other I divine that they are very happy.
Now and then he quits his place, strolls up and
down with long steps, repeating in a low tone
phrases which I know are his "work."

These conversations of my father with himself when he "plunges into work," form part of my childhood's atmosphere. This expression of plunging into work often makes me pensive, but the most violent labor does not prevent him from raising me in his arms when he passes near me, or of kissing me, or of standing me upright on an armchair or on a table, — a dangerous but delightful exercise, during which I feel perfect confidence as to his strength.

Of all my comrades he it is who knows how to play the best. In a corner we have a great mass of paper balls, in order to have a snowball fight; we have a corner of the drawing-room where two armchairs placed together form an actual cabin, in which we do not fear the attacks of savages and where all the fruits of the Fortunate Isles grow in abundance. When winter's cold groups us about the fire, Robinson Crusoe's shelter is between the thin knees of my father; as to the roof of the cabin, that is his inevitable laprug which has been known to take on the strangest forms and reach the most unexpected destinations. The situation in my mind is twofold; I know perfectly well that my father draws on his fancy and holds the thread of the plot; nevertheless I believe in my own *rôle* and I inhabit with him a lonely country which a very terrifying conflagration ever lights up.

Here is a painful matter: later, very much later, it must be a year and a half ago, when I had that typhoid fever and my father watched me every night; my vague and floating brain revived those distant remembrances. As in the case of a weakened convalescent, my memory went back to pluck these flowers of my extreme youth. I trod again the pathway of the heaped-up years and with an inexpressible tenderness looked upon the handsome face of my beloved, turned toward me under the rays of the lamp; he did not seem to be changed at all.

Often, as he recalled it to me later, were our walks in the fields of Champrosay, roads given over to filial love, roads of my heart! At that time I was hardly four years old and my father held me by the hand. I had an idea that I was leading him and constantly called out "Look out, Papa, beware of the little stones!"

Since that time, O Destiny, he has had need of my grown man's arm! We passed again over the same paths, becoming gently melancholy the while. We called back again those fragile hours in the meadows and autumnal plains, the splendor of which he would celebrate in familiar brief phrases, and once more in the footpaths among the broom and common herbs the past touched the present. Our silence was filled with regret, for we had formed the most beautiful dreams of trips together, travels on foot yielding all the emotions and all the surprises which my friend knew how to extract from the slightest episodes; but his malady made all these things impossible!

"Do you know, Léon, under what guise the roads appear to me? As escapes from my pain! O, to flee away and disappear behind a bend of the road! How beautiful they are, those long pink turnpikes of France which I would have so liked to tread with you and your brother!" He raised his black eyes with a great sigh, and I felt my love for him augmented by an immense pity.

At the end of my childhood my father stands before me proud and valiant and ready for his growing fame. I know that he writes fine books, for his friends compliment him about them, his big friends whom I call *the giants,* who come to dine in the house — *M. Flaubert, M. de Goncourt!* I am very fond of M. Flaubert; he kisses me with a loud laugh. He speaks in a very high voice and a very strong one, while he beats with his fists upon the table.

When they are gone we talk about them with admiration.

Then my education begins; my father and mother undertake it all; I shall talk about this later. At present simply a few recollections:

We are in the country in Provence at the house of a friend. On a delightful morning filled with fragrances and the hum of bees my companion takes his copy of Virgil, his lap-rug and his short pipe. We settle down on the brink of a river; the horizon, where lines of gold and rose are trembling, is of a divine purity and is heightened by the slender dark cypresses. My father explains the *Georgics* to me. Thus does poetry show itself to me! All of a sudden, at a single stroke, the beauty of the verses and the rhythm of the singing voice and the harmony of the landscape — penetrate my heart. An immense beatitude invades me, I feel myself ready to weep, and as he knows what is passing within me, he draws me to his breast, increases the charm and shares in my enthusiasm; I am fairly drunk with beauty.

This time it is the evening. I come back from college after several courses in philosophy: with incomparable power Burdeau, our master, has just been analyzing Schopenhauer for us. Gloomy images have torn my soul; positively, in that lecture I have eaten of the fruit of death and pain. Through what disproportion of things have the words of that sombre thinker completely conquered me and won such an actual power in my impressionable brain? My father understands my terror; I hardly say a word to him, but he sees something has been born within my look which is too hard for a growing boy. Then he goes about it as before. He approaches me tenderly and he who is already filled with sombre presages about himself celebrates for my sake the glory of life in unforgettable terms.

He talks of labor that ennobles everything; of goodness radiating happiness; of the sense of pity which provides an asylum for the sad; finally of love, the only consoler for death, love, which I only knew by name, but which was soon to be revealed to me and was to overwhelm me with happiness. How strong and pressing are his words! He makes a radiant picture of that life on which I am embarking. Before his eloquence the arguments of the philosopher fall one by one; he

repulses triumphantly this first and decided attack
of metaphysics.

Do not smile, ye who read me; to-day I understand the importance of that little family drama.
Since that unforgettable evening I have gorged
myself with metaphysics and I know that in that
way a subtle poison has slipped into my brain as
into those of my contemporaries. It is not
through its pessimism that this philosophy is
perilous, but because it carries people aside from
life and overwhelms humanity in us. Bitterly do I
regret that I did not jot down the lecture my father
gave; it would have been in many ways a great
comfort.

Thus I reach the final years, only stopping at
the brighter points of that life of filial piety on
which my whole being depends. If I speak of
myself, still it is always he round whom the matter
runs, because I was his field of trial — a field, alas,
very often ungrateful and without a harvest.

My father would have liked me to have entered
the literary career in the line of instruction. It
seemed to him that the finest of all duties was the
education of young minds to the point of understanding ideas, following them step by step, forming in them a character and developing in them
the power of feeling. He admired all those in our
epoch who have, as he was wont to say "taken
charge of souls," and he showed a sympathy and
respect to my masters at Louis le Grand College
which most of them unquestionably will recall.
By what way and wherefore did destiny at first

drag me toward medicine? That is something of which I shall speak in another place. His own maladies and the visits of celebrated doctors unquestionably had a good deal to do with it, so impressionable is youth!

But the very day on which that career repulsed me, the day I grew disgusted with the charnel house, its examinations and its competitions, he respected my evolution. My first literary essays, which I read to him at the Baths of Lamalou, were resolutely encouraged by him; and from that very moment, entering into the estate on which he planted and caused to grow such magnificent trees, I profited every day by his counsel and experience.

In the rare old copy of Montaigne that never left him, which carries on its yellow and green pages the traces of visits to many a noted thermal bath—in this book wherein he found every kind of instruction and every sort of comfort, I find that famous chapter on *The Resemblance of Children to Their Fathers* marked and annotated with special care. Unquestionably, he had realized for several years past that there had been roused in me, and almost without my knowledge, that strange literary demon from whom it is not possible to escape.

When I confessed to him this new zeal which had filled me, he gave me a fine lecture which I remember perfectly. It took place in a vulgar and bare hotel room; by some unusual chance my mother had been forced to stay in Paris with my brother Lucien and my sister Edmée who was then very young. He spoke to me with a gravity full of emotion, coming after his usual manner very near to my heart and my intelligence. He represented to me the troubles of the profession of a man-of-letters, in which no one has a right to be an artist in the highest sense, because one remains always responsible for those who, reading one's books, might be troubled in mind thereby. He did not conceal from me the many and varied difficulties which I would meet upon my way — even admitting that success would favor me, "which is very rare!" To this he added some very simple rules, but so true! — rules for sincerity and effect in style, the part played by observation and imagination, the building up of a work, its method, and the relief to be given therein to the actors and their temperaments.

I listened in a religious spirit. Well I understood that he was pouring forth to me, there, the accumulated result of his hard work and the finest crystallization of his mind. At about that time we were in the habit of reading Pascal of an evening in a loud voice from chamber to chamber and from bed to bed. He presented this sublime master of style to me along with his beloved Montaigne, not as if he were too lofty an example, but like a constant stimulus. He also spoke to me of his own sufferings, but in a manner almost like that of a philosopher in order not to make me sad; and he insinuated that, for a number of souls who have not expressed themselves, literature was a solace and relief, such persons finding in it a

mirror and a guide. He showed me the near-
est examples in Flaubert and the de Goncourt
brothers. He closed with a eulogy upon life in all
its forms, even the most painful.

The light was failing, but still lit up his proud
and delicate face. Filled with a sort of holy confidence, I traced his words back to their original
meaning, back to those deep motives concerning
which he was silent. Between us two there was
some happiness but a great deal of anxiety. As I
evoke them, I make them live again, decisive
hours that they were!

From that day onward till his last hour he never
ceased to counsel and instruct and guide me; we
got in the habit of such a way of talk that I was
able to translate his silences, so that a single word
from him was equivalent to long phrases. From
that time forth, without a variation or truce, he was
my impartial and tender critic.

During his last years the fear of losing him grew
upon me, but owing to that sorrowful privilege of
mine it made me attentive to his slightest word.
That has made it possible for me to write this
book. I lived as it were in a cave where shone a
perpetual flame; our garden at Champrosay and
his working room are crammed with the memories
of conversations in which I limited myself to questions concerning all the great problems of humanity. I shall try to give some idea of his curt,
elliptical and picturesque language, which really
approached a human look, owing to its intensity,
rapidity and the crowding of images. Of a surety

the novelist was a power and the future will show him to have been one still more ; but the man behind the novelist had not his equal for the treasures of experience and truth, which, like minted money, he poured forth from dawn to night.

His friends knew his power of divination well; he analyzed the most distant and varied events with an almost infallible acuteness. His rare mistakes became for him so many causes for new observations of himself. His pitying, charitable nature was lightened by playful and ironical phrases in which tears seemed to mix with smiles. At our family table in the presence of my grandmother, whom he adored, his wife, whom he loved more than anything else, his baby daughter and two sons — at our delightful table which his departure has left so empty and silent, he took as much trouble in conversation as he would at a reunion of his friends.

There indeed it was that death came to seize him on the 16th of December, 1897. It was during dinner. I had come in somewhat late and found our little family met together as was usual in his working-room. I gave him my arm into the dining-room and seated him in his big armchair. Whilst taking his soup, he began to converse ; neither in his movements nor his way of acting was there anything to announce such a disaster; when, all of a sudden, during a short and terrible silence, I heard that frightful noise which one never forgets — a veiled rattle in the throat followed by another rattle. As my mother cried out we rushed toward him.

He had thrown his head backward; that beautiful head of his was already covered with an icy sweat and his arms were hanging inert along his body.

With infinite precautions my brother and I lifted him up and laid him on the carpet; in one second, behold the horror of death fallen upon our unhappy house! Ah, the groans and lamentations and all the useless prayers addressed to one who had known how to give us everything, except just one little bit more of himself! The doctors came quickly. Dr. Potain, who loved him, tried everything possible and impossible. O frightful and heart-rending spectacle of the body which had given life to us and from which life had fled in a lightning flash! So much kindness, gentleness and beauty, so much sympathy, so many generous enthusiasms, all are nothing more than a remembrance for us!

An hour later, amid repressed sobs, he lies upon his bed as beautiful in the motionless gleam of the candles as his image in my heart. The bonds which attach us to him shall be broken only by our death, but now they are being lost in the darkness. Our memories have become the tombs where lie his motions and his words, his looks and his tender deeds. Here below love will keep no one from that path. Virtue keeps no one, genius keeps no one back. But as, broken and despairing, I bent over his most pure and lovely brow, it seemed to me that I heard these words: "Be of good cheer, the example remains!"

LIFE AND LITERATURE.

MY father never separated life from literature; that was the secret of his influence. In his view art was accomplishment. To create types of humanity and free the souls of men, that before all else is what he longed to do.

Many a time has he told me how his youth was devoured by that same love of life and how it was due to my mother, "his devoted, his sweet and tireless comrade in work," that he did not foolishly dissipate those gifts received from nature which at a later moment he employed in such a splendid way. He hardly thought of fame for a moment and let the important question of the future which awaits the works of dead men stand aside unquestioned.

One day I read him a sentence by Lamartine from the *Cours de Littérature* which struck him; he asked me to repeat it, as he usually did when sowing new seeds in his memory. The poet speaks of "that marvellous shiver of sensibility, a forecast of genius, if the genius do not come to shipwreck from the passions." That shiver of sensibility was considered by my father the source of every work which was to last.

In certain obituary articles, otherwise very well meant, I have read this sentence, which has caused me to smile : " Alphonse Daudet was not a thinker." No, certainly he was not and never was a thinker in pedantic fashion, a maker of abstractions and a juggler with obscure phrases ; that he was not !

But here on my table I have his books of notes where, every day, without wearying and with an incredible scrupulousness and patience, he wrote down the incessant workings of his brain. Every sort of thing is found here in these little books bound in black moleskin, all their pages rumpled, scratched and scribbled up and down and from side to side.

At first one gets the impression of a tumult and a buzzing, a kind of regular trembling. That fine mind, I fancy, is completely awake in those notes, awake with all its revulsions and whirlwind changes, its comings and goings, its quick-dying flames and its fiery spaces.

Then, after a great deal of attention, I pick out a kind of rhythm, the harmonious movement of his mind which had its origin in feeling; it multiplies itself, inspires itself with picturesque views, visions of travel, dreams and reminiscences, and traverses those colored and rosy regions where the miracle of art takes place; where through the mystery of birth a vivid impression becomes the starting-point for a book or an essay.

Then the tone rises; it remains living and clear, but becomes more precise and closely set; phrases crammed with experience of the world

appear placed side by side, without apparent
bonds. Nevertheless they appear to belong together like colors and brush strokes in some sketch
by Velasquez or Rembrandt, phrases which contain
a realism that is sometimes cruel and as if shudder-
ing with anguish and sincerity, phrases which, like
countenances modelled by the heart and the senses
of man, arouse innumerable reflections.

And in this abridged way and from this vibrating cohesion and out of this tissue of flesh and
nerves spring astonishing formulas, brilliant witnesses to his own soul, in generalizations far
grander than those detached ideas of the human
mind in which metaphysics lose themselves.

To sum up in a word, this perpetual work of
analysis, done with a sincerity which reaches the
verge of crying aloud, reveals in the author's
thought a constant ascension and purification; it
shows a zeal to carry the torch into the fogs and
cobwebby corners of the human spirit and it ex-
hibits, as it were, a patience pushed to the ideal
point.

There is more than passion alone, there is also
the spirit of sacrifice. Sometimes I used to say
laughingly to my father: "How you do derive
from the Catholic blood!" At the last analysis
these notebooks reveal to us a soul in a complete
state of sensitiveness where without doubt dogma
has been obscured, but where religion has left its
imprint on whatsoever religion offers that is at
once touching and implacable. He is certain to
examine himself without cessation. He is sure to

write down without delay whatsoever people have
felt, whatsoever people have suffered. The joys
of life and of death, the slow crumbling of our
tissues, the unfolding of our hopes and disillusions
are a terror for the greater part of mankind; but
the last and greatest terror is *ourselves*. This terror
it is, this secret need of paltering with our conscience which makes somnambulists of us and
causes us to hesitate before the confession which
our heart makes to our heart through the long
silence of the nights and days, even as we carry on
our unseen and obscure existence!

The most powerful souls remain children rocked
in the cradle of an ignorance which they voluntarily
render denser and deeper, an ignorance which they
keep tongueless and dark with shadows.

Montaigne, Pascal and Rousseau were the three
chief and violent admirations of my father. He
himself was a member of that mighty family. He
was never without his Montaigne. He annotated
Pascal and defended Rousseau against the honorable reproaches of those who are ashamed of
shameful deeds and turn aside in disgust from
things of the flesh. Without a moment's rest he
entered into the abodes of these powerful models, wandered through their crypts and pondered
over those redoubtable silences which lie between
their confessions. He took to himself one of their
thoughts and lived with it as with a lady-love, or
some forgotten sister whose resemblances and dissimilar traits he was examining — all with that
scrupulous earnestness which he brought to bear

upon matters of feeling. He put questions to the people about him, or to those who are on the wing, and even to the facts which happen every day. He loved the sincerity of those three geniuses, so ripe and so vast and so big. He proposed them as examples for himself. He was thoroughly saturated with their substance through having conversed with them so long. Was not that the work of a thinker?

Well, of all the great books that lie open, that one which he studied more than any other was the book of life. Impressionable as we know him to be, his youthful days must have been extraordinarily crowded with sensations and things of all kinds that attack the nerves, things which he was able to classify in his old age. But here is one of his most surprising characteristics: maturity did not show itself in his case either as a drying-up or a stoppage of development; to the very end of his life, and only through suffering, he preserved intact the faculty of being moved.

In our talks we used to compare that precious and most rare faculty to a constant sore on the spot through which force circulates, flooding over from the human being to nature and rising from nature to the human being. I remember that he likened it to the wound given by the Holy Spear that pierced the side of Christ.

"Listen," said he to me one day, "listen to one of my visions! Our Lord hangs on the cross; it is dawn, a cold and biting dawn. There is the martyr so in love with life that he is willing to lose it after it has poured forth upon every one its charity and redemption, and toward the Master are rising the sounds of the city which is awaking to a new day — sounds and odors from perfumes and from kitchen hearths, noises of mighty crowds; and then, much nearer, the groans and long lamentations at the foot of the cross. He drinks this all in through every pore and the taste of the vinegar becomes less bitter whilst the torture of the nails, of the crucifixion and of the lance wound becomes less keen. . . ."

He went no farther, but he laid a certain weight upon the last words, so that I might follow him on to the sequel. He did not insist upon particulars in these beautiful dreams, but left the care of completing them to his listener, knowing that he who adds a little of himself understands better than if he be told all.

This delicacy of feeling, often so acute that it reached the point of the inexpressible, remained perfectly straightforward notwithstanding, and never attacked the right and proper rule. That rule, which was perfectly simple and lucid, remained in him as a boundary not to be transcended. My father detested the "perversity" of certain minds, those unwholesome games played with the conscience in which it has pleased certain remarkable men to indulge.

This delicacy of feeling was alway on the alert. In his little note-books he talks of the hours *without grace*, in which the priest finds that his faith has left him, or in which the lover, horrified by the

discovery, questions himself concerning the depth
of his love. One of his preoccupations was never
to harden himself in pain, but to remain accessible
to all the emotions. For my part I have never
known him to have any hours " without grace."

In telling a story he had a way which belonged
to him alone, one his friends will never forget,
nor indeed others who merely heard him once.
The description followed close upon his memory
of the affair and adapted itself to it like a wet
garment. In their proper order he reproduced
the facts and sensations necessary to the story,
suppressing the intermediate ones and leaving, as
he was wont to say, only "the dominant ones."

"The dominant ones"—that word was always
on his lips. By that he understood the essential
and indispensable parts, the pinnacles of the book
or the novel. "It is on these points," he used to
add. "that it is necessary to let the light
play."

He used also to repeat: "Things have a sense
and a side by which they can be grasped," and in
that vague term " things " he understood what is
animate as well as what is inanimate, whatever
moves and expresses itself, as well as whatever
agitates or weighs itself.

In that way we penetrate the secret of his simple
method which at first blush seems by no means
simple and indeed is one which demands in a
writer those natural gifts that were his.

A lover of real things and of truth, he never
ceased that search of his. As long as he was able

to leave the house he went about in the greatest variety of places, never neglecting a chance and particularly never despising any human being. Most remarkable was it how he detested disdain as one of the forms of ignorance. Whether the person in question was a clubman in the drawing-room, or an artist, or a sick man, whether it was a pauper on the turnpike, or a forester, or a passer-by, or some workman met by chance, my father took advantage of his own prodigious turn for sociability or of his charmingly delicate kindness in order to break through that vulgar region where only hypocrisies are exchanged, thus penetrating to the soul of the person.

He inspired in people that extraordinary confidence which springs from the delight of being understood and is doubled in pleasure by compassion; and that compassion was not a *rôle* assumed for effect. I have seen very different kinds of people surrender their confidence to him with rapture. How many people suffer from recoil! How many people feel themselves quite alone upon the earth, finding everywhere nothing but misfortune!

I have used the word method; it has a false sound when applied to activity like his which is so human. Before everything else my father followed his own inclination, which was that of loving his neighbor and sorrowing and rejoicing with him. My mother, my brother and myself indulged in tender pleasantries over the wrath which boiled up in him on hearing of some act of injustice, or

over the personal interest which he took in affairs
as far as possible separated from him.

When a cruel malady drew limits to his earlier
modes of life — limits in a certain way less griev-
ous, it is true, than people have stated — he opened
his portals wide. He welcomed all misfortunes
and listened patiently to the recital of every kind
of distress. Never did one hear him complain of
having his work interrupted in order to soothe an
actual pain. Very few people duped or abused his
confidence, for he knew how to uncover lies with
extraordinary sagacity; but even that did not
irritate him: "The poor wretch," he often said to
us with his delightful smile, "the poor wretch
thought that he was deceiving me; but I read
falsehood on his face and divined it from the trembling of a little muscle down there in the corner of
the mouth which I know very well; it was made
known to me also by the 'winkiness' of his eyes;
there was a moment when I was on the point of
betraying myself. Pshaw! he's an unhappy creature all the same."

When the man was gone he would note down
whatever in the conversation seemed to him peculiar and worthy of memory. And his memory,
besides, was infinite, for, notwithstanding his bad
sight, he could recall a name, a figure, a gesture,
an odd habitual motion or a form of speech after
several years had gone by. He suddenly asked
one of his old fellow pupils of Lyons College, whom
he had not seen for thirty years:

"Why, you still have it there on the nail of your

thumb, I do believe! That little blood-red mark that used to astonish me when you wrote!"

His most vivid recollections comprised one of the emotions of the past which he reconstructed for us with complete fidelity to fact. I still have ringing in my ears an account of a conflagration in which the flames were still crackling, and through which the outlines of firemen and half-nude women ran helter-skelter. He appeared on the scene of the combat pouring water himself and having water poured on him, holding a lance in his hand. He had attained the age of ten years! "Stay there, boy!" one of the life-savers said to him. He did stay there until the flames came and burned off his eyelashes and licked at his hands. And he had never forgotten the cries, or the cracking of beams, or the flares of light, or the terror on the countenances, or his own particular emotion mixed with joy. And how he did tell us all that! With what exact and striking strokes of the brush!

Another time it was an inundation from a sudden freshet in the Rhône, with the strokes like a battering ram in the cellars delivered by the running water; this he recalled, adding detail to detail, while his thought turned back to the past. Then the crashing boats and that very boat on which he stood, and the drunken feeling of danger he had; then the people invaded by the flood, perched in clusters on the roofs of houses, and again, the moaning gulfs and whirlpools, the *irresistible* quality of the waters.

The peculiarity of a mind like his is this: it

makes a sort of tapestry out of so many different
kinds of images, groups everything and classifies
everything unconsciously through the slow labor of
perfection. From the natural tendency of images
to come together, through that movement of impressions which have been received, which brings
them into contact the one with the other, it thus
forms the complete bundle of impressions. The
peculiarity of a mind of that kind is that it makes
use of the slightest touches in its incessant labor
in order to compare things, deduce and amplify
them without deforming them, just as naturally as
the heart beats and the lungs inhale.

Take the works of the great writers. Note with
care the dominant points; it will be very surprising
if you do not notice two or three fixed and well
defined pictures among the most varied and rich
descriptions; they return periodically but they are
painted in new colors. Among the wealth of characters created by Balzac, Goethe or Dickens or
Tolstoy, there are certain primordial turns of character, certain basic elements in nature which are
central and marking points. Life has given them
into the hand of genius. Genius has returned them
to life while decking them with all its own prestige.

Thus it was with my father. I can well remember his astonishment when, having begged his
friend Gustave Toudouze to make a selection from
his works in which only examples of materialistic
love should be found, the latter pointed out in the
long line of his novels and dramas a constant return
to the motive of " the mother," who is herself the

sum and entirety of human tenderness. Without his knowing it, the figure of her who conceives us, bears, nourishes and educates us, suffers with our sufferings and becomes radiant with our own happiness, and ceaselessly sacrifices herself for us, that admirable and spotless figure had taken possession of him. In his eyes she was the grandest and deepest problem of the heart, and, without his having noticed it, this problem had ever harassed him under all its forms.

He attached an enormous value to the emotions which open up our lives. "There is a period," he cried, "when one has *finished printing*. After that come the second editions." And often I have found him occupied by this other thought, subsidiary to the last: "In the human being there is a centre, a nucleus which never changes and never takes on wrinkles; whence our astonishment at the swift flight of the years and the functional and physical modifications that befall us."

When one of these statements caught hold of him he was not satisfied with a formula, however clear-cut and well-defined. In the first place a formula scared him. He saw in a formula the image of death, he wished to nourish it with examples. He believed that on the day when the formula would no longer apply directly to life it would lose its sincerity and become a dead leaf. "Humanity," that is the grand word which includes all those tendencies which I am now piously unravelling here, a word full of blood and nerves, which was the motto of my tender friend.

During those last years we often went out together. As long as he was able to choose his
carriage at the station, it was always the most forbidding and dilapidated he took, a carriage which
he thought nobody else would accept. I remember a very old coachman, driving with great difficulty a very old horse and seated on the tottering
box of one of those fantastic cabs such as one may
find waiting for the night trains. My father had
adopted this wretched team as his own and as
soon as we turned the corner of Bellechasse Street
we were sure to see it jogging toward us. On his
part the old fellow had fallen in love with this easy-
going customer, who never found fault with his
slowness and his lack of cleanliness. One of the
last times that we took him, before he went to
complete wreck among the shadows of Paris, what
did he think of but a plan of writing large, in big
red letters, on the panels and on the glasses of the
cab, the initials A. D., thus calling attention and
announcing himself as the property of the person
who had taken compassion upon him!

A crowd of little reminiscences of this sort fly
about my heart. I do not hesitate to jot some of
them down, so that when you read his great books,
dripping with emotion and sweetness, you may
know that they were the fruit of a sincere soul, as
splendid in his slighter movements as in his long
and patient efforts.

Naturally our outings were but little varied. We
caused ourselves to be driven along the Champs-
Élysées as far as the Arc de Triomphe. My father

loved that splendid sloping way, which recalled to him so many memories, recollections that I followed in his expressive eyes, eyes always turned toward the picturesque, seizing upon and defining humanity with a fabulous quickness. If he felt himself more than usually melancholy, we went to Béthune Quay, where the history of Paris vibrates from the ancient stones as they warm beneath a pale autumnal sun.

Beloved sun, how my father did adore you! Though meagre and pale, that sun recalled to him his balmy Provence, the very name of which would cause his face to change and would bring back color to his pallid cheek. " Primeval joy: to cook one's back in the sun ! " ' Oh, for a good cagnard[1] down there toward the Durance ! " he would say, resting gently on my arm and looking into the whirling water of the Seine. Whereupon, as if given wings by his dream, he would start off on his voyage toward one of those mirages which made a perpetual enchantment of his slightest conversation.

It might start with some trivial remark: a ray of light on the forged iron of a balcony, a pane of glass lit with the sun, a reflection flung up from the river. Stimulated by some nice parallel — and no one loved exact nicety so much — he would squeeze my arm a little and his imagination would rouse itself. The merely picturesque tired him quickly. It was necessary that something

---

[1] A little shelter from the wind made of reeds in which to lie and sun oneself.

human should intervene. All he needed was a half-opened shutter to cause him to picture the entire interior with the poetical decision of the old masters of Holland. It might be an anxious old woman's outline, an old man drinking in his last sip of sunlight, or some mark of tenderness in the people — childhood or decrepitude; he divined their meaning, combined and evoked their story, glad at his own discoveries; and so ever with a gay and easy air he scattered abroad his energy and verbal treasures: "We are still playing Robinson Crusoe, my boy," said he, "just as we did in the old times under the lap-rug. Every one of these good people is living on his own narrow island, very zealous indeed on the subject of his nourishment and the satisfaction of his interests!"

During a terrible summer's heat on that very Béthune Quay we saw a workman stripped to the waist who was laughing under the spout of a watering-cart which was being vigorously played upon him. That powerful torso, that masculine attitude, those swollen muscles, his powerful short neck and erect head, these formed a departing point for a magical improvisation. How he gloried in the robustness and simplicity of the man! What splendid things he said concerning sculpture and muscles played upon by the sun, concerning sweat and water, the caryatids carved by Puget, and that antique vision which appeared round the corner of a Parisian street!

There! I can see his quick and generous smile, I can hear his laugh. For, notwithstanding his

sufferings, he preserved his gayety and took
advantage of the slightest respite; fun sprang
spontaneously and irresistibly from a character so
in love with nature, so ready to seize upon amusing thoughts at the very moment that they were
making him sad. We never knew one of his rare
fits of wrath which could not be disarmed by a
droll turn of words. Then it was delightful to see
how his severe face changed, how he yielded with
delight, only too glad to return to the usual
sweetness of his nature.

It was when he happened to be with his old
friend Frédéric Mistral, whom he loved and
cherished, it was at that charming table of his
where genius sat enthroned, or else it was at the
house of the Parrocels, likewise in Provence, that
I have seen him oftenest the cause and starting-
point of tumultuous fun. His inherited race characteristics, his surroundings and contact with his
compatriots roused in him vivid, unexpected, impromptu dramatic power. He imitated the different accents in the dialects between Valence and
Marseilles, the very attitudes and gestures of the
people. He gave us the benefit of the *two* voices
in the same narrator — that voice which claims all
the advantages, counsels, lays down the law and
defines things, as well as that voice which starts
contradictions, stutters and goes all to pieces.

He gave us the worthy citizen, the " Cato in
very low relief," the sententious man, libidinous
and longfaced, whom the boarding-school teachers
fear. He played the politician with dishevelled

hair, slipping in the vehemence of his speech into
the most dangerous metaphors. Then we would
get "dear old Father Oily," or the godly woman
confessing herself in the confessional box and the
same woman cursing a station master: or, again, a
customs officer, a servant, a child who clamors
for his orange, the crowd collected at a bull-
fight.

In one of our first trips down South we were in
a waiting room of the tavern while the rain fell
without; the presence of his dear friends Aubanel,
Mistral and Félix Gras who were drinking with us
and the giddy joy of "showing them off" to his
wife, his Parisian girl, roused in him memories of
his most turbulent youth. The round table of
poets grew wildly excited. There were songs
from the countryside, old Christmas waits in which
tears were mixed with smiles, rich ballads from
Îles d'Or and passionate cries from the *Grenade
Entr'ouverte.* The correct and warm voice of my
father dominated the noise and showed me its
beauty by its rhythm. Enthusiasm was seen on
every face; the real sun of Provence was shining
there in that tavern!

It is that frantic fun, it is that flashing of gayety
which make *Tartarin* and *Roumestan* such rare
and charming books, true products of the soil,
warm and savory, juicy and brilliant. But the fine
characteristics in my father's nature sparkled all
through his life before they came to ornament his
books. When I open one of them I hear his sweet
and quiet accent; how is it possible to separate

that memory from the part which the future will
find to admire in him?

As a matter of fact his celebrated irony was
really the fine flower of his tenderness. By means
of that irony he escaped from the commonplace
and avoided the bitterness of comparisons. By
means of it he brushed artifice aside. Gifted with
so spontaneous a talent, he escaped vulgar
comedy; endowed with a sensitiveness which was
sharp and even cruel, he softened its effect with
smiles and appeased its acridity with those twists
and turns which leave the soul of the reader trembling and impressed, instead of overwhelmed with
gall.

This irony, purely Latin in its genius, has been
compared to the sarcasm of Henri Heine. Such
parallels are almost always false. Heine was an
exquisite poet but an exile and a nomad, having
no connection with his own soil and suffering from
the fact that he could not find a surrounding
nature. He makes the whole world responsible
for his disquiet. Hardly has he excited emotion,
when he puts us to the rout with a bitter grin. He
sneers at our hearts and at his own heart. Gifted
with a nature of marvellous harmony, he throws all
his sensations into disorder, and when one approaches him to sympathize, he escapes from us
with a grimace. My father knew well the beaten
footpaths of his own friendships.

He used to speak of a ballad from the north of
France in which a woman who sees her husband
again after a long absence begins to weep. This

same ballad in its Southern version makes her keep
herself from smiling. In that little allegory he was
defining his own character.

In his little note-books I read a reproach addressed to the husband who relates to his young
wife all the love adventures of his past: " Idiot,
you 'll find out later " is the end of the note.
Under that simple form, behold the irony. It is a
mask for pity. The picture in *Jack* of the men
have " missed fire," the supper of the Old Guard
in *Sappho* and one page or other of *L'Immortel*,
are further examples of that tendency he had
to move his readers by taking the slant road, if
the direct path seemed too much trodden. That
is the resource for a warm heart which has a certain bashfulness with regard to over-vivid and too-
apparent sensations.

In this manner the author of *Femmes d'Artistes*
and of *Tartarin*, of *Le Nabab* and of *L'Immortel*
rose to the height of lofty satire, which is nothing
else but an inverted lyricism and constitutes the
revenge of generous souls. Irritated and wounded,
the poet causes the brazen string to vibrate; but
there is never anything too harsh, even amid the
most bitter assaults! " Implacability," that word
made him ponder. Every fault seemed to him
capable of correction and every vice capable of
remedy; he sought for some excuse for every
crime. I have found the finest arguments in favor
of human liberty and of the resources offered by
the moral world in that same life of his, so simple
and open to the day.

The man who has been reproached in so silly a way for never having given forth metaphysical ideas seemed to me on the contrary ever troubled with those great problems of the world within us, which are now the mirage of inspiration and now the mainspring of our actions.

Among philosophers he admired Descartes and Spinoza, as much for their lucidity of mind as for their minute and anxious researches into the play of human passions. If his love of life drew back before the extra-terrestrial form of those mathematical formulas applied to flesh and spirit; if he preferred Montaigne's method, he also loved, as he said, to "inhale a breath upon the lofty heights" of Spinoza's *Ethics.* He often said that it would have been singularly interesting if some Claude Bernard should annotate these commentaries on the movements of the soul.

For Schopenhauer he had a very pronounced taste. That combination of incisive humor and power of dialectics, that tissue woven of the blackest arguments and picturesque aphorisms delighted him. I read aloud long extracts from Schopenhauer; having taken them thoroughly in, he pondered over these readings, and took them up again on the morrow, enriching them with subtle remarks.

We used to talk everywhere and at all times. He delighted in shutting himself up with me in his dressing room; I can see him now interrupting himself to discuss a point, a comb or a brush in his hand, and then, when our ideas began to get into a fog, thrusting his head down into the basin "in order to clear up our ideas." "My boy, the action of fresh water on the brain in the morning is a grand problem all of itself! The man who, having made a night of it, has not washed himself or made his toilet, is capable of performing the most frightful follies, and is incapable of the meanest train of argument."

Incidentally I have spoken of his conscientiousness. He returned always to the same subject without ostentation and without dulness, as long as anything which was obscure remained. He would not take words for coin. "Sellers of phrases"—that is what he called those hardskulled reasoners who would like to run the moral world by mathematics and in accordance with fixed laws. "I do detest the automatic point of view!" he would also cry, when considering some icy and involved analysis; and as to this "automatic point of view" he showed how it killed off every kind of frankness and all original impulse, down to the simple happiness that comes from creation.

Suffering, which is so relaxing and persuasive, has periodical phases. The song of the nightingale is capable of inspiring in us disgust for a delicate machine. What poetry there is in the fall of the leaves, the retardation of waters as they turn to ice, if at the same time one thinks of the alternation of the seasons!

Unless I am mistaken, metaphysics themselves, having finally taken up the consideration of the feelings, will take account in the near future of those very arguments which are called reasoning from feeling, which so profoundly correspond with our need of liberty for the mind. Unless I am mistaken, the grand philosophical system that we shall have to-morrow will put emotion in the first rank and will subordinate all else to it.

Possessed of an absolutely honest intellectual process and ever a prey to constant scruples, my father never hesitated to acknowledge himself ignorant of anything: "I do not know — Why, I did not know that!" His eye would brighten at once. Filled with the delight of learning, he would forget other people and busy himself only with that person who could bring to him a novel point of view or a story full of useful results.

His knowledge was vast and accurate. Moreover he surprised me sometimes, when our talk fell upon some scientific or social subject, by the truth of his information and the largeness of his views. He read enormously and with method, and assimilated difficult questions to his mind with marvellous quickness. He demonstrated the strength and the weakness of an argument and called attention to the paradox. His love of truth was of use to him there as always, since it freed him from prejudice and refreshed his logical strength. Long-winded theories bothered him: "Let us get forward to the picture." I can see the movement of his hand sweeping aside mere words.

He had a real and abiding love for Latin and Greek. Because he admired education, he made

of education one of the grand mainsprings of
humanity and was up in arms against the new
pedagogues who try to restrict the study of dead
languages:

"Certain men and women," cried he, "who possess the innate gift of style, have instinctively the
taste and the tact to choose the words which
they employ. A woman of that kind was the
much-to-be-admired Sévigné. But that sort of
mind is a great exception. Most people get from
classical study a benefit which nothing else can
replace. The mind which feels the beauty of
Tacitus, Lucretius or Virgil is very near being
that of a writer."

Tacitus was always to be found upon his table
by the side of Montaigne. He read from him a
little at a time, only a page or two, and then translated him after a style which I have found in very
few masters. Besides, he had already shown a
proof of his cleverness in that line by his translation into French of the admirable Provençal prose
of Baptiste Bonnet. And as far as the *Annals*
are concerned, I have seen him for hours at a time
feverishly hunting for a faithful and correct expression, as anxious to fulfil the poetic rights of the ear
as those of the mind.

Difficulties delighted him. How often, whilst I
was making my studies, when too arid and close a
text had brought me to a stop, did I leave the
book on his table of an evening; the next morning early I would find it there with the French
translation opposite. My professors complimented

me and gave out my work as examples to the class. At the general competitions for rhetoric I remember a sentence which had shipwrecked the strongest of us. The line has remained in my memory, it is such a model of a Chinese puzzle.

"Ut cortina sonet celeri distincta meatu."

My father took the accursed page, and, whilst he walked once round the garden, translated it for me without hesitating into words quite as strong, robust and brilliant as those of the author; and he added, in order to console me:

"Certain pages, and those by no means the least beautiful, of my dear de Goncourt will certainly prove as difficult for the college boys to come as that line is."

He broke me into my Latin by reading the verses or fragments of examples in prose with which Montaigne interlarded his *Essays:*

"As for us people of the South, the classic phrase has never died out amongst us. Just look at this Gascon of the sixteenth century! He delights in manuscripts ever opened and reopened. Parchments preserved in monasteries and libraries have the authority of oracles to him, of messages from the past. He clothes his modern arguments in toga and buskins. He grafts the sibylline leaves upon his thick-leaved tree. The 'Renaissance,' my dear boy — have you ever comprehended the entire meaning of that splendid word? It is Pan the Great restored to life. Rising from out old dusty scrolls, a tremendous shudder ran through

souls alive with beauty. 'Why, then, let Gascon
words fill the gap,' said Montaigne, 'if French will
not do!' But there was Latin also and Greek
besides. 'Let beauty show, let plainness hide its
head,' as our own Mistral sings.

"Don't you see him, that happy Michel who
shows us Michel himself and recognizes in him the
nature of all men, don't you see him in his library,
trembling with enthusiasm before the grandeur of
nature, gesticulating, like the regular Southerner
he is, at the memory of some line from Lucretius
which delights him and corroborates his thought?
Antiquity pulses through his heart. Thirst for
learning consumes him. And over everything else
stands the necessity of expansiveness, of telling all
about himself, which is so active in modern characters as they are still found among us."

Such bits of talk as this have remained in my
intellectual treasury. Alas, I have just perceived
that there is lacking to it the warm Southern
accent, the "monster" itself. And, as happens in
meetings constantly renewed, we were apt to return
to the same subjects; but each time my father
added something. Until the day of his death his
life was a perpetual seeking.

Some few friends are able to recall the memory
of a page from Rabelais read aloud by him. He
had found a good many bushes and fronds and
flowers from the South in that forest of Gargantua
and of Pantagruel. The author's long stay at
Montpellier explains these reminiscences in Rabelais. At the end of his own copy my father has

noted down the chief localisms; naturally they greatly stirred his lively soul. He mimicked for us the entire tempest scene or else the adventures of Gargantua, booming up his voice to the diapason of frenzy, laughing at himself at the same time, throwing back his hair, sticking his eyeglass into his eye, fairly drunk with the power of words the while.

Another day it would be Diderot whom he would take up and celebrate by declaiming his most brilliant pages, the most vibrating of those in *Ceci n'est pas un conte, Maintes lettres à Mademoiselle Volland*, or else *Le Neveu de Rameau*. At another time it would be Chateaubriand, in whom he admired his long deep breath and his rhythm like the tremendous swing of billows. In his verses he pointed out that epic tone which is applied to familiar reminiscences, that splendor of a soul which never weakens, though always melancholy and as it were draped in the classic folds of mourning for its lost illusions.

I would have to pass the entire French literature in review in order to cite the literary gods my father adored and invoked, from whom in his sorrowful hours he demanded comfort. O the miracles wrought by poetry! Our friend and parent is wrapped in gloom; he is suffering. We hesitate to speak to him, knowing too well what his answer will be. All of a sudden a name or a quotation uttered by one of us brings life back to his look, as if it were the coming of a friend or a well-known air of music. In a moment he asks

what is going on and is all excitement. He must
have the book and the page! Lucien or I run
to the library. Oftener it is my mother who takes
the trouble, because she has a clear and soft voice
and never hurries. Here are the *Confessions* or
the *Mémoires d'Outre-Tombe.* At the first words
uttered my father is no longer the same man. He
approves and degustates, his head inclined forward
in the attitude of meditation as he stuffs his little
English pipe. He interrupts. He asks us to go
on again. He questions the author and discusses
a matter with him. Enthusiasm has driven out
suffering and moroseness and started up again the
fires of youth.

Now it is our turn to listen, and the hours pass
as in a dream, and those magnificent phrases of
a past generation live once more a pallid life at the
touch of a wand from a magician such as he was.
So, across the ages, do those who love and seek out
beauty begin their lives anew.

Since the love of research is universal in a mind
of that kind, I would hardly know how to tell its
depth and width. The misfortune of a study of
this sort is that of necessity one is limited. One
of the virtues in the model I have before me was
exactly that continuity of his, his harmoniousness,
or, if one may so express it, the architecture of his
joys and sorrows. So it was that, being a connoisseur of words and always surrounded by dictiona-
ries of the first class, such as that compiled by
Mistral, he loved to examine the débris and
metamorphoses of a word. Thence derive his

exactness and the beautiful clearness of his style.

Every one of those noble feelings was a guide and torch to his feet. He judged of a word by his ear which in him possessed delicacy and a supreme wisdom; and by his eye, because in spite of his short sight, he was a seer. He weighed the word and rolled it on his tongue like a connoisseur; for there is more than one noun which will evoke an entire period for us, more than one adjective whose historical importance is greater than that of a manuscript or a suit of armor.

He avoided the exceptional and precious, knowing well that there is often a rare quality in some word of seemingly common appearance; he left its true meaning to every term, being an enemy of the torturing of language, because he understood its structure so well. It is one of the follies of our time to believe that limpid transparency cannot exist along with depth. There are rivers whose pebbly bottoms gleam as if they lay just beneath the surface — but a giant may drown himself therein!

He reiterated: "I hate monsters!" The conversations of Eckermann and Goethe which for a long time were his breviary (for he changed his intellectual loves and only showed a continuous fidelity to Montaigne) are confirmation of several stages in that thought. My father sided with Goethe, whose motto " Reality and Poetry " seemed to him to sum up the wisdom of mankind. He was also wont to say: " Nothing in excess! " and in truth sanity of mind and a hatred of that too-much, which one finds unfortunately among most Southerners, were brought to their highest expression in him.

"On Goethe's side against Jean-Paul" — how often have we not held discussions concerning tendencies. "Art" was one objection he made "is not merely the expression of one's own character; the man who does not drive the monsters out of his own soul is very soon devoured by them."

When we were discussing this question we would often glide quickly to composition and the architecture of a work, to which he accorded capital importance; according to him it was the condition of its durability: "Every book is an organism. If its organs are not in place, it must die and its corpse become a nuisance."

And since he had given great thought to the putting of order and rule into his novels and dramas, he also wished to make his interior and outward life harmonious. For this work a great mass of knowledge and of studies seemed to him necessary.

In his library, beside all the great masters, the stories of life and adventure were found on the main shelves. He stated that the love he bore for men of action had been developed in his case by the necessity of a sedentary life: "I accomplish through imagination whatever my body does not allow me to do."

He knew in detail all the campaigns of his hero

Napoleon and the journeys of his other hero Stanley, as well as expeditions to the North Pole. When people talked to him of the nineteenth century, so restless and full of tumult and perhaps more covered with incomplete monuments than any other, he defined it with two names: " Hamlet and Bonaparte; one the prince, not only of Denmark, but of the life of man within; the other, a source of the grandest deeds and of the entire gamut of gesticulation."

As for Stanley, he did not boggle at comparing him to the victor of Austerlitz. The works of this distinguished man never left him. He read them on, without wearying. During a recent touch of typhoid fever which befell me and which I shall have reason to mention often as one of the luminous summits of paternal tenderness, when I was lying inert for hours with scarcely a bit of memory or intelligence remaining, he tried to bring my wandering faculties back by reading to me some pages from *Through Darkest Africa*, or from *Five Years on the Congo*. He sat close to my bed toward the end of day on one of those sultry days near the close of May which are so troublesome to a convalescent. He held the big book in his weak hands; he wanted to carry me far, far away (using the remedy which was a solace to his own sufferings) in the wake of the intrepid traveller, overwhelmed by a much heavier fever than mine, through that land of dangerous plants, and beneath the shadowy dome of leaves.

" His only hope was in his companions, Jephson,

whom you saw at our house, a brave boy with ruddy cheeks, and that delightful Dr. Clark. And notwithstanding his delirium he retained his feeling of responsibility. He remained the chief in the midst of all his sufferings. What an extraordinary reservoir of energy! "

Every Thursday he explained to our guests that Stanley was not a cruel man, as envious people have insinuated, but that on the contrary he was the most humane and least ferocious of conquerors; that he was as just as he was firm.

In London, during a journey which to-day is precious for its slightest episode, where we met the man whom he so much venerated, when he had him beside him on a little low sofa it was one of the most touching spectacles in the world to see the affectionate relationship of two souls which understood one another so well. I state again: the man for whom my father had such a real and tangible friendship is not a bad man; in him one may admire one of the finest types of the Anglo-Saxon race, but one who belongs to all the races through the discovery of a continent, through a lucidity of mind equal to his courage and a clear and unhypocritical judgment.

At the time of that very jaunt abroad which made it possible for my father to understand England, he also had the delight of visiting " Hamlet " at the same time that he met " Napoleon." I allude to George Meredith, that extraordinary novelist whose fame is brilliant on the heights, on the very noblest summits of the mind, and will come down some

day to delight the crowd whenever the torches take
up the march. What a delightful visit to that
green country about Box-Hill all decked with trees
and waters, where the author of *The Egoist* and
Modern Love and of twenty masterpieces welcomed at one and the same time his comrade in
letters and the family of that comrade with a tender
and spontaneous charm!

How I cherished you that day, O master of the
bitterest thought, of the most robust and liberal
thought! I understood you to the verge of tears!
What things passed that day between the looks
you gave forth and those that emanated from your
brother in intellect! What hours worthy of you
and of your power of analysis were passed in that
cottage where lights and shades played about your
aureole. O, vast and subtle heart, and friend of the
French to the point of having defended them in
1870 with a piece of verse unique in its generosity!
You are the genius whose brain devours him and
who with a subtle smile rails upon evil! Hamlet?
yes, you were Hamlet for Alphonse Daudet and his
following, a mirror as it were of Shakespeare on that
spring afternoon when nature herself became moral, when the black pine-trees were trembling like
so many human bodies, when the lawns themselves
seemed to have the softness of human flesh!

Above and beyond love there is another love
and it was that you gave as a gift to your comrade,
a man as ardent as you are for life and just as
yearning for beauty. I ponder over you in these
sombre hours as a holder of those secrets which

people who are detached from this world hug to their breasts, or as those raisers of ghosts who pursue phantom shades. The image of your magnificent and pure features shall never be separated from the one for whom I weep because they have lost their perishable shape.

As far as Napoleon Bonaparte is concerned, one man satisfied the passion that my father felt for him, namely, our friend Frédéric Masson. For many years he clamored for those books in which the life of his military god was followed day by day, in which the author unravelled the motives, the character and the adventures of Napoleon. When Masson's books appeared he could not leave them; he boasted of their worth to every person who came in; he declared that the task which he himself had so often dreamed was now accomplished, — namely, to reconstitute the man in his completeness, further the love of him and rouse the whole race. The author of that final and definitive work will hardly deny the statement if I affirm that he met with the greatest encouragements in his " dear Daudet."

He was not only in love with the heroes of action, my father also celebrated the lives of the obscure and devoted ones, those who were sacrificed to glory; from Rossel " a reversed Bonaparte," "a starless one " whose name returns more than fifty times in the little note-books, down to the bold hero of Port-Breton, down to Blanqui whom Gustave Geffroy has made famous, down to Rimbaud the prodigious and the Marquis de

Morès — in fact all those who nourished tremendous plans, men, as he often repeated, following the striking formula of Baudelaire, for whom action " has never been the sister of their imagination."

His shelves were filled with a multitude of pamphlets referring to the works and deeds of these knights-errant, these men of imagination, these deserters from an existence according to the code, who risked their lives without hope of return, railed at and tempted destiny, throwing their bodies as food to the ravens and the future, men who opened up new paths and disdained death. "That scorn of death which makes man invincible"— he placed that above everything. He was tremendously interested in the Trappists, whom he had visited in Algiers, and in the Foreign Legion and in the fits of desire for revolution and in outbursts of unemployed energy seen among those boiling courages which are confined without enough breathable air by our false-faced society, courages which are lamed by the tight boots of the law.

Enthusiasm of this sort brought in play two sides of his nature, his taste for risks and his love for humble folk. For weeks at a time he was haunted by the defence of Tuyen-Quan by Dominé and Bobillot. His fantastic faculty of turning himself into others, which I shall examine in detail, permitted him to take on himself the *rôle* of every one and follow his blunders and weaknesses and recoveries. "You who love philosophy so, why don't you make two monographs, one on Scruple

4

and the other on Risk, and show the points where they meet? Give powerful examples, don't fear to lay it on thick! Your old father will supply you with the images."

On my return from a trip to the Alpine Club a month before his death I told him that I had made the acquaintance of Capt. Camps, one of the defenders of Tuyen-Quan; his delight was endless: " I am sure you did not know how to make him talk! What did they eat? When did they sleep? The cries of the Chinese during the night! And the battles following one another! Tell me, tell me!" Alas, I have not his power of glancing through a man as through a book.

That last expression always delighted him, for it justified his method; one of his last happinesses was the dedication to Grosclaude at the beginning of the book on Madagascar. "Grosclaude, a Parisian, a witty talker, and a subtle artist. He is all energy and does not know his own powers. O the admirable French race!"

The war of 1870 was a revelation to him; it made a man of him. He realized this one evening when on guard in the snow; at the same time he had his first attack of pain and of remorse for the indolence which permitted him to sing and write light verses and current prose without a serious or durable life-work. He adored all military trappings; the music of regimental bands set him aglow "like a colonel's horse;" an officer's title opened wide his door and his heart: "Those who have formally made a sacrifice of their life

stand on a higher plane than all other people."
One of the few questions in which he would admit
of no alternative view was the question of patriotism. I intend some day to tell in a pamphlet, a
special pamphlet furnished with documents, what
his conduct was during the Terrible Year; according to him that year was marked by not only a
change in himself, but a complete metamorphosis
of the nation — customs, prejudices and culture.

If I spoke well of a German, he lauded the literature of Germany and murmured in a melancholy
way "Oh, our little fellows in their defeat!" He
felt more keenly than anybody the disorder shown
in everything during that tragic epoch. Owing
to our lack of reminiscences he desired that my
brother and I should be exactly informed, so he
surrounded himself with all the French and foreign
works which speak of the Franco-German war.
During our sojourn at Champrosay this very summer he related to us in detail his impressions and
his anguish; in a way it was his patriotic last will;
he desired that the account of the defence at
Châteaudun should be read and re-read in the common schools.

His powers of persuasion were such that he
fashioned me after his own mind, and I saw that he
was happy therein. I believe that he loved his
sons as much as anybody, but without a shadow
of hesitation he would have devoted us to the flag.
I made it a reproach to him to have never put in
black and white that analysis of our disasters
which he alone was capable of writing; but he

shook his head: "One cannot elevate souls by
such a story; for a warlike country like our own
it is necessary to sound the clarions of victory."

One admirable thing about him — this man who
had done his entire duty always modestly held his
tongue about it; but the wound never healed.
When Madame Adam came to see him the talk fell
naturally enough upon revenge; my dear patroness
and he were not afraid of anything. He was
proud to learn that our army on the first line
seemed absolutely ready: "I have never doubted
the right intentions of any one. Our governors are
in error when they accept humiliations. And yet,
after all is said . . . who knows? . . . There's the
grand mystery. . . . Where is the leader? . . ."

I can say that his last days were darkened by
the Dreyfus affair. "I saw Bazaine," he repeated,
anguish in his face, "I saw Fort Montrouge after
the treason, the distress and sad horror of the
brave men who caused themselves to be killed next
day." Eager as he was in favor of justice, anxious
as he was that every creature should have his
rights and clever as he was to unravel the threads
of intrigue, he could never reconcile himself to the
idea that a nation might be disorganized intentionally, certainly not without immediate and striking
proofs. The man who sells his own country
seemed to him unworthy of any pity whatever.
On the morning of the catastrophe I promised him
that Rochefort would come in person to confirm
him in his certainty. The idea of the visit delighted him, because he much admired the great

pamphleteer and recognized in him a unique gift
of observation analogous to the divining power of
Drumont.

"Unquestionably that comes from his long exile.
He looks at and judges things from afar, but he
has scented the needs of our interests."

He had that power of scenting things out, himself, although he disdained the actual politics of
social clowns and phrasemongers. His opinion
on this question is expressed in a chapter of his
last novel *Soutien de Famille:* "It is through
the lobbies of the Chamber of Deputies that the
blood of France is being lost." But what irritated
him more than anything else was the bad faith
shown by parties and their universal hypocrisy.

No one better than he has described "the platform effects and gestures and rhetoric of second-
class actors," all that macaronic verbiage which
makes up the conjugation of the word "to govern."
If there ever was a man in the world who loved the
populace with a real and *unaffected* love, it was he.
I recall our walks in Paris on the first national fes-
tivals of the 14th of July (we were then living in
the Marais), his happiness at the sight of the banners and women in their Sunday clothes and
radiant men carrying their boys on their shoulders.
He fraternized with everybody, offered people
drinks, extolled the good looks of the children
"whom his long hair caused to laugh." "Do you
see that gown?" said one of them, "for a month
now father has been talking about it with mother;
they have cut into the money for the household

and quarrelled with the old parents; you may just believe it is a big thing!"

He was touched by their round-eyed looks of greed before the shop fronts. He emptied his purse in buying toys; the value of the gift was increased a hundredfold by the adroitness of its presentation and by his charm.

One of his dreams was to write an anecdotal history of the Commune, all the more impartial because he made excuses for the madness of that day: "I partook of that madness" said he; "I left Paris when they wanted to put me in the ranks and when the crazy leaders exasperated me. I reached Versailles; but there again I found, in an inverted way, once more the same cruel delirium, the same injustice, the same eyes of hate — but without the excuse of misery and hunger. I understood then that, at the risk of death, it would be necessary to hold oneself apart from each one of those camps."

During those terrible years how often did we have ourselves taken to the outskirts of the city! He was excited by the movement of the crowd of an evening toward Belleville, by the sparkling eating houses, the push-carts, the quick succession of faces and of attitudes of people at work. One of his most perfect satisfactions consisted in that popular edition of his works which his friend and former school comrade Fayard made an actuality. He trembled with delight while turning over the leaves of the little pamphlets for two sous apiece, which placed his works within reach of those common folk whose wretchedness he understood so well.

Just here I wish to insist upon one of the finest qualities in my father. Though favored by success he never sought it in a vulgar fashion; "big editions" surprised him, but did not turn his head. I have never known any one who disdained money as much as he. Extremely and uncommonly plain in his daily life, an enemy of luxury and show, touchingly simple in his dress, his household and his manners, he considered wealth the most dangerous trap so far as morals are concerned, a well of corruption at which he who drinks poisons himself, and the usual cause for the breaking up of families and for hatreds among relations and in society.

"The infamy of gold;" it was described and foretold by Balzac the sublime, whose literary work, constantly overheated and overstrained, appears to me as the poem of Covetousness. It is true that he has not made use of either gnomes or giants as Wagner has in order to express the power of the precious metal; but he shows none the less its legendary force when he generalizes the tortures and shames and infamies that spring from it, when he makes special mention of the faces and grimaces, noting those words which are sharply defined and carved upon the live flesh. "Gold cannot give *any* of the radical happinesses, those which are primordial and true; no, not one! On the contrary it controverts nature, carves wrinkles and digs bogs; it tears to pieces and corrupts.

Economists state that gold circulates — yes, like alcohol and opium, making the one it may inspire cowardly or crazy, bringing him whom it raises up low in the mire, heaping itself up only in order to bring ruin, and accumulating itself only in the interest of vice.

"Power and interest, and how they trouble human passions — that is the Hell of the Magician to whom we owe so many masterpieces. As if it were an alcohol distilled from gold, it makes us drunk, drowning out heart and brain.

"Whenever I pass by some magnificent mansion, a residence or castle, a park with gleaming waters, I ask myself what sorrow and what unhappiness all that may conceal." He believed that in literature a quick success and money are bad things, leading the artist aside from his true path, which is to perfect himself according to his individual nature in response to his own conscience, without any prospect of pecuniary gain.

But this is what preoccupied him before everything else: the author's responsibility. "Our period is playing in a terrible manner with the forces of print, which are worse than explosives." One day I discovered in one of his little notebooks a list of the social injustices, the principal wrongs which should be fought against. "I drew it up," he confessed to me, "with an idea to supply subjects for books. Now if there is one thing which is consoling, it is that over against every wrong there rises up a feeble — true, a very feeble, attempt at reparation. Now it is a threat, now a simple outcry. Notwithstanding the universality of egotism, there are ears for the greater part of scandals which grow too great. Unfortunately pitying humanity is possessed of narrow resources and cannot be present everywhere at the same time."

Then he came back to the policy of "phrasemongers," who, instead of taking up their time solely in making social wrongs less severe, interest themselves in nothing except the ballot-box. "Some one little improvement every day " — that ought to be their motto! But little do they occupy themselves with such works!

So you may easily guess that he was a liberal and indeed the most liberal of minds, although still ever attached to tradition. But a parliamentary label would have been just as insupportable to him as a literary label. Only he did show indignation when people accused him of having smutched the memory of his former patron, the Duc de Morny: "I had no connection at all with public affairs, I simply occupied a sinecure as a man of letters. I am certain that I never wrote one line in *Le Nabab* which could have been disliked by the duke during his lifetime."

As a matter of fact *Le Nabab* is a historical novel without coarse colors and without invective. The outline of Mora is drawn with discretion and no little grandeur. When he dealt with him, my father always represented that statesman with all his elegant and sinuous grace, respecting in him the "connoisseur of men." "At that period I was quite as careless and fantastic of brain as the greater part of my contemporaries. Though it was merely a suspicion of the terrible and grim things which were preparing, I had nothing more than a poet's shudder when listening to *La Belle Hélène* in which the insulted gods of Olympus and the shrill sound of Offenbach's violin bow seemed to me a forecast of the catastrophe.

"But what catastrophe? I did not know. Yet I went back to my room troubled and anxious, as one feels when leaving some unwholesome atmosphere. A few months later I understood."

I have heard many conversations concerning those most significant times. The most striking were talks with Auguste Brachet, author of *L'Italie qu'on voit et l'Italie qu'on ne voit pas*, one of those men for whom my father felt the very liveliest esteem. "I may be able to see individuals and discern the motives for their action, but Brachet judges the masses, nations and national events with an unrivalled sagacity. Listen attentively to him and profit by him! You have before you one of the finest brains of modern times!"

I did listen, and profited. This took place at the Lamalou Baths where Brachet was taking the waters for neuralgic pains. The two friends were never apart. The links in the chain of memories were evoked one after the other. Those were wonderful hours! The author of *L'Italie*, which was a prophetic work in its way and roused so many hatreds, had in preparation a great work, which ought to be near publication, on the *Com-*

parative Psychology of the Europeans. He "talked" the main chapters in our presence with a glow like that of Diderot, with a lucidity, power and erudition that dazzled us. He was a teacher of the Empress Eugénie and "showed up" the Tuileries and society, the actors and their surroundings in sharpest relief after the manner of Hogarth.

I hope that from all these details, which are often difficult to classify, the reader extracts this clear idea — that Alphonse Daudet wrote his books with the very sap of the human tree.

A form of foolishness one constantly meets is to compare realism to photography. Every organism has its own angle of refraction which is much more complicated than that of an objective glass; my father's organism was one of the most delicate and most impressionable materials in which the outer world could possibly refract itself.

His ear had a delicacy and correctness most exquisite. At a dinner-table with twenty present he could make out conversations though they were held in a low voice. He caught even the silly talk of children. The slightest noises in nature impressed themselves upon him and delighted him. Thence came his passion for music which was made an aid and assistance to his labors.

He sits at his table in his working room. My mother is at the piano in the next room and the music of Mozart, Beethoven, Schumann or Schubert follows, one after the other, and excites or calms the imagination of the writer. "Music is another planet." "I adore all music, the commonest as well as the loftiest." But no man could analyze and understand better the masters of harmony, no man lauded the genius of Wagner in more splendid terms or more brilliant images: ".The conquest by Wagner and the philosophers."

When he went to a concert his eyes were wet with tears, so lively was his emotion. I could feel him trembling from head to foot. His auditory memory had no limits. With what a delicate and penetrating voice did he not hum the airs of his own country and of all countries!

Beautiful lines made more beautiful by sounds induced in him a gentle melancholy. In former years Raoul Pugno, Bizet, Massenet, men whom he admired and cherished, and during the later years Hahn, were real enchanters for him. The melodies by his " little Hahn " which he caused to be played three times in succession — Hahn, so precocious in genius, so learned and so free from pettiness, so lucid and gently sensual — positively put him in an ecstasy. Seated in his big armchair he half closed his eyes while his nervous hand clasped the knob of his cane; his half-opened lips seemed to drink in the sound.

I perceive him farther back in my memory at the Exposition of 1878, listening to the gypsies, a glass of Tokay before him, encouraging the cries of " bravo " that resounded in their honor and quite carried away by the music! Then it is Venice. The lapping of the water, the sound of violins and human voices rise from the dusky canal. He himself is no longer with us; he is off travelling through the land of imagination in company with his youth and manly vigor and hopes. When that music ceases, another begins — music which proceeds from him and celebrates the games of the wave and of the night, and those polished marbles which live again in memory.

And so always in the hours of intimate intercourse he seems to me the same person, whether he may be asking questions of his learned friend Léon Pillaut on violins and old refrains, on the guimbarde, the alto and the hautbois, or listening in a grassy plain of Provence to the mystery of the pastoral pipe, making the passers-by stop their carts, or else enjoying in the garden at Champrosay the endless gamut of bird-notes, which regulated for him the hours of spring.

His eyes, which short-sightedness really sharpened, though he pretended that they were no good for painting or the plastic arts, perceived color and form with the greatest liveliness notwithstanding. He was one of the very first to appreciate the Impressionists.

As to masters of painting, naturally his preferences went out to the realists, to the Hollanders and notably to Rembrandt, and to the French school made famous by Troyon, Rousseau, Millet and a score of others. He liked to recall delightful hours passed with his friends Bague and Gouvet. The picture-seller Bague delighted him with his robust merry-making eloquence, in which true touches of artistic fervor played hither and thither, all warmed up with slang. I remember one entire day passed in turning over Goya's etchings; he uttered at the time many radical truths concerning sincerity, the excess and paroxysm of which become cruelty; on the combination of grandeur and minuteness which is a distinctive feature in the bull-fight series; on the crude power of shadow and of light; on the particular disorder in military and artistic matters during that epoch; on the morbid drying-up, the Etruscan angles and the "voluptuous twist" found in Spain. As it was a matter of the South, it was easy for him to read these Spanish riddles; at first sight he deciphered for us the fantastic "Proverbs" and "Dreams."

The conversation ended with a picture of that frenzy which is particular to the peoples of the lands of the sun — the sun, "that alcohol of the South!"

During our stay in London he remained for many hours seated in the British Museum before the Furies and the Friezes of the Parthenon:

"Don't you find that a magnificent music disengages itself from these groups? 'Reality and poetry' — of a truth there is nothing else beside. Those old peoples copied nature. Nature was dancing in that blue air. No separation between the exterior world and the world within; no one shaken by desire; never a lack of harmony! Whenever there is a rhythm anywhere it seems there must have also been some happy inspiration."

"And how as to sorrow, father?"

"Sorrow did not put discord into the human

being. The latter did not raise a revolution against it. It did not foment disorder."

The idea that the figures on these friezes might become violent like true daughters of the North, might become Valkyrs, brought him to talk of Wagner's brain, in which two forms of beauty fought for empire. One, to a certain degree immovable and in equilibrium, having very gentle waves, being near of kin to the ideal of the Greeks; the other having a furious form, the boiling wellspring of the Saxon race.

It is mere laziness of the imagination to divide intellectual men into classes of analysts and syntheticists according to their works or their speech. Alphonse Daudet was in search of original causes and he triumphed in giving details, but instinct warned him of the exact place where too great division would have dissolved and ruined everything. Work offered itself to him as a whole; he admired it in the mass. A lover of right proportions and of exact measure (he himself used as a motto for himself: *Ne quid nimis*) there was nothing of the miniaturist about him. He saw things in a big way, nor did he reason or discuss matters for the mere pleasure of so doing. He respected deeply every kind of emotion. Quarrels over words wearied him, just as those oratorical games in which each participant decides a matter according to his particular temperament without the slightest regard to the opinions of others. Whatever superficial critics, led astray by his monocle and his conscientiousness, may say in this regard, he had no use for the microscope in his work.

The best proof of this is a hatred of what people have agreed to call " art for art's sake." He repeated this formula with a look of astonishment on his face, for there was no one who was less ready to admit catch-words in conversation Insincerity made him yawn; " whatever has not roots in actuality is dead. Heavens, I know well enough the apology they make for artifice! Baudelaire invented that to use as a weapon, out of pure hatred for fools and fat citizens. Nothing ages so, nothing loses its grip so quickly as what is unusual. '*Les fleurs du mal,*' '*Les petit poèmes en prose*' are marvels and the quintessence of truth; they are precious poems plucked from the very depths of the moral soil. But the imitators of a fad were foolish enough to imagine that they also could build and inhabit the '*kiosque en marqueterie*' of which Sainte-Beuve speaks. What an error!"

If he loved to put himself in contact with poems, if he excelled in the faculty of *reading* the most lowly characters and classifying all the movements of the mind, all habits and functional "creases," yet did he also delight in solitude: "Where the form of observation, the vision of the poet and the nicety of mind in the author concentrate and purify themselves." In his agitated youth when he began to be anxious concerning his spiritual and physical health he made some veritable "retreats." He went and shut himself up in a *mas* of the Camargue, a big farm, and even went to stay in the lighthouse on the Sanguinaires: "The two lighthouse men, forced to live side by side, loathed each other; one copy of Plutarch all marked up by their great clumsy fingers constituted the library, O Shakespeare! and filled these simple imaginations with the murmur of battles and of heroism similar to that of the moaning sea. The useful shine of the revolving lantern in the tower lured thither reckless birds which dashed their brains out against the enormous glass lens. The keepers made soup of their bodies. If a storm did not 'bellow,' the revictualling boat would bring us once a week ancient news and fresh preserves. Fine hours have I passed there — sometimes, 't is true, slow, sorrowful and anguished; but they were hours in which I took stock of myself and judged myself, and listened there to other storms beside those of the ocean. Lucky are they whom necessity suddenly separates from the social gulf and who find themselves in the presence of their own self! People will never know how much exile added to the greatness of Hugo and Voltaire, how the prison of Blanqui increased and enlarged his dream!"

After a silence he added: "And, going into that solitude, which one of the men of a single book, *unius libri*, which would I carry with me? Montaigne or Pascal? Or would I cheat and take an anthology of the masters of prose, or the sublime literature of Taine, or the Plutarch of my lighthouse men? A constant interchange of thought goes on between that one book of his

5

and the isolated man who is a thinker. It forms
a library, an encyclopedia, which the movements
of the solitary one's soul engraft upon what is
printed; and the soul boils up again because of
that which is printed. Double offspring, starting
from the germ of the story of *Hamlet!* slender
pamphlet for a bookseller and for *Hamlet's*
author! When I was living with the *Essays*
as my Bible there was not one of my dreams for
which I did not get from them an answer and
comfort."

As head of the family he was forced to renounce
his love of solitude, for we never parted from each
other; but my mother always did something to
satisfy that love of the country which he kept so
vividly alive down to his last moments.

That delightful valley of Champrosay which
played such a great rôle in our life stretches in
reality from Juvisy to Corbeil along the curvings
of the Seine and the corresponding caprice of the
woods of Sénart. We inhabited successively three
houses on the right bank, one of which had belonged to Eugène Delacroix. It is the village
and forest bank open like a cornice to the sun,
warm and healthful, and moreover sown with
historical castles, Soisy-sous-Étiolles, Lagrange,
Grosbois, which recall the 17th century, the Revolution and the Empire. The left bank, toward
Montlhéry and Étampes, traversed by the acque-
duct of the Vanne, brings back memories partly
similar, partly much older. Some villages belong
to the 12th century.

Formerly my father loved to boat with his neighbors, Gustave Droz and Léon Pillaut, with his friends Gonzague Privot and Armand Sylvestre, particularly with his brother-in-law Allard; he passed his life on the Seine and frequented the taverns of coachmen and carters, rowing up those pretty by-streams which lose themselves in private properties, shady parks, or factories: "Once we came to so narrow a little branch and so shallow that we had to disembark and carry the 'Arlésienne' on my shoulders; lo and behold, we are in a garden; a young girl, very much surprised, raises her head from her book and sees us both before her, your uncle and me, very much like the red Indians of Fenimore Cooper, loaded down with the boat and rudder, the oars and the boat-hook."

At that time, too, he was wont to scour the woods for mushrooms and chestnuts. He was proud of knowing the proper sort and distinguishing the good mushrooms with ends like *tulle*. He pranced about through the bushes with me on his shoulders, dragging my mother after him. In the evening we devoured the gleanings of our harvest.

He told us how during a wrestling match with the sculptor Zachary Astruc, whose independence and robust talent he admired, he had broken his leg. He was carried home groaning and feverish and particularly preoccupied with a fear that his comrade would be blamed. That very summer's night, which was heavy and stormy, the newspapers brought a terrible piece of news: declara-

tion of the Franco-German war. He had but one
idea after that : get himself healed as soon as possible and be in shape to help his country. " Horrible and stupefying period, during which every
courier announced a defeat and the countenances
of the peasants reflected fear and meanness."
Finally he was on his feet again, capable of holding a gun !

Later on the state of his health no longer permitted him anything more than walks down the
alleys of that great park which all our friends
know. There is not a bench, there is not a slope
which lacks a memory of my beloved. On my
arm or on that of my brother his gait was alert and
rapid. He would not stop except to light his little
pipe, as clever as a herdsman of the Camargue
plains to get the better of wind and dust, delighting
in "nice little warm shelters," interesting himself
in flowers, in garden plots, in vegetables, happy of
the slightest embellishment and delighted to show
off " his domain."

It was there one should have seen and heard
him, excited by the great "out-of-doors," watching the play of light, listening to the songs of
birds, the singing of the cricket and the rustling
of the leaves. He improvised extraordinary
stories for my very young son, his little Charles,
and for my sister Edmée, stories in which everything about us played its part — magical, delightful tales which placed the beauty of things in
nature on a level with those budding intellects,
moved them and held them attentive to the point

of closing their eyes in order to enjoy the feast all the more.

There is the secret pulsation of his genius: In a few exact and a few simple images, the objects corresponding to which are near to us, he touches our soul. There is the word and there lies the object. Even grains of sand and sticks of wood and bark he rendered animate. He would say that that insect had carried off the end of his story and in order to pursue the robber he would stick his glass in his eye. In these little games thus organized, while little hands pressed his hands and the " Thank you, Papa," " Thank you, Grandpapa," resounded — in these homelike and fairylike pictures one finds again his subtle and simple art with its thousand delicate shades, like to one of those flowers whose fragrance lends balminess to the air.

When the heat of the day lessened we would take a drive in the family landau. My mother has a pronounced taste for things of the past. She points out many an ancient residence such as that home of Mme. de Beaumont at Savigny which the grass and mosses are slowly invading. Autumn is the finest season here; across the broad plain one sees the fires of the rubbish heaps. My father expresses his longing for happiness: "An old mansion broad and somewhat low, with an extension consisting of farmhouse and poultry yard. In the hearths the crackling wood of the pruned vines. A few selected friends and the snow outside. Absolute and tender con-

fidence among all present. Chats and delightful
readings aloud. The old people are not morose,
the young are neither pedantic nor bitter. Life is
one delight."

In one of his last letters received at Grenoble
whilst I was serving with the Alpine regiment he
wrote to me: "Fancy to yourself one of those
delightful 'artist consolers,' such as I have
dreamed of being myself, dwelling in some old
property near the gates of a little town with ram-
parts and mall, passing two months in Paris, a
few weeks on the Nile or in Spitzbergen, but at
last getting tired of running about and then finding his completest pleasure in a few roomfuls of
friends, crowded on the traditional days of the
calendar year — Christmas, New Year's, St. John's
Day, Thanksgiving Day. Such a man as that
might print a book consisting of numberless
volumes embodying our very best society. He
could put at the close of the last volume published 'to continue' and then the 'Book of Life,'
or the 'Science of Life' would be under way."

In the chapter entitled "The Vendor of Happiness," I shall show what it was he meant by
those words "The Science of Life."

The intervals in the little note-books are delightful and stunning landscape pieces. In such
cases, as in others, he only noted the dominant points; things that strike and trouble us in
some spectacle of nature are hit off in a few
precise, clear and vibrating words, as quick and
sharp as the impression of the spectacle itself.

One day I was turning over the leaves of these masterpieces and said to him: "You recall old Hokusaï to me — old '*Crazy-for-drawing*,' who at the end of his life stated that he almost understood the form of living creatures and could almost fix line and point as they should be."

He answered: "I have not reached that point. How bitter it is to me, this gap between that which my pen sets down and that which my soul has perceived! I suffer from the torture of not expressing myself. How can one render and express that swifter pulsation in our veins which comes when one looks upon the evening star rendered golden by the autumn, or a little lake upon which the sunlight separates itself into its component parts, or an horizon with beautifully pure lines, or a stormy sky, copper-colored and black, a dusky abyss in the midst of the blue heavens? How express the way in which a memory palpitates at a given hour, or tell what part of us it is that lingers in things, what it is in us which weeps and smiles in accord with them? Through my lips how many impressions have escaped which are rebellious to verbal forms!"

Still, if ever methods of work were submitted to the rules of natural law they were his. In his turbulent youth he never seated himself at his writing-table except when fired by his subject. He stated that a talent was an "intensity" of life; and his stories are a proof of that formula.

Later on, through the happy influence of his "direct collaboration" he made channels for and

regulated his wonderful faculty as an improvisor.
He got the habit of daily work and, as usually
happens, his brain became more supple in response to the appeal and submitted to the discipline. *Fromont Jeune et Risler Aîné, Jack,
Le Nabab, Les Rois en Exil, L'Évangéliste* were
so many continuous and unbending efforts. Summer or winter he rose at an early hour and
went at once to work on his task without other
means of excitement than a dip in cold water;
then he covered page after page with that little
close-set, nervous and elegant handwriting of his
which his illness made still more delicate without taking from it any of its attributes. Many
a time have I remarked upon the likeness of his
" graphic type " to that of Jean-Jacques Rousseau.
There are the same excessively minute distinctions,
the same intervals between letters and words, the
same care in punctuation and the same sharpness
in the handwriting. The similarities are very
evident between the handwriting of my father and
the manuscript of the *Nouvelle Héloïse*, which I
was able to examine one evening at the Château
des Crêtes, thanks to the kindness of Mme. Arnaud
de l'Ariège.

He erased with courage and frequently; at the
first blush a mere sketch served as it were for a
canvas. My mother and he then took this "monster" up again, expending the greatest pains on
its style and bringing into relationship that harmoniousness and that need to be real which were
always the writer's care. "Without my wife I

should have given myself up to my facility for writing. It was only later that perfection tormented me."

After that slow and disagreeable proving, the third and finished copy was made. Those whose imaginations are in the state of flame may readily understand the peculiar merit in sacrificing " go " to exactness and making enthusiasm perfect. In my father's soul the word itself was that which called the idea forth. In the case of a formalist like Baudelaire, for instance, the word curtails and reins in the lyrical results, it limits in place of rousing up; in the case of Alphonse Daudet, however, the word excited an entire world of sensation and form. Thus, the man whom the " word " renders drunk can never know the delight of achievement. My father was a Latin genius and was the possessor of a sense of proportion and of measure.

Without entering into the critic's domain, a thing which would hardly suit my actual part, it may be permitted me to note the constant evolution of a temperament like my father's, a temperament so virile and so lucid. His first works, burning and super-abounding as they are, give signs of less anxious care than those that came after, so far as nicety of language and of equilibrium are concerned. They spring rather from temperament than from character.

The traits which particularly belong to my father are a conciseness in rendering picturesque motives, an intimate blending of nature moral with nature physical, and a disdain of useless ornaments, to a degree which no one has shown at a higher point, not even the greatest of writers. Human beings are characterized according as they absorb sensations, think and act; each type is completed by its own passions; no outside traits are added to overload the picture. Every brush-mark tells its story and is harmonious with the whole. A book by him is of such a kind that in memory it follows the very movements of life. Firm and solid in its expository parts, uplifted as regards the chief matter, it is turbulent in critical passages and calm after the close of a crisis.

Every person in the book has his or her own atmosphere, every scene has its own culminating point; the whole hurries toward a common goal. The central model is embellished by a multitude of particular examples. Next comes that classic power which his contemporaries themselves have noted, that elegant and sustained vigor which preserves the work from any sudden labelling of naturalistic or realistic, and attaches it to national tradition, to the deep-seated and harmonious literary heritage of our race.

The fact is that labor does not begin at the moment when the artist takes his pen. It begins in sustained reflection and in the thought which accumulates images and sifts them, garners and winnows them out and compels life to keep control over imagination, and imagination to expand and enlarge life. The heroes of those romances and dramas of his, the words of the conversations

they hold and the places they frequent, are not
products of a super-heated imagination, not parts
of the mind of their creator which are, as so often
happens, terribly enlarged and diversified — the
bold impressions of one and the same man imagining himself possessed of opposite passions.
Alphonse Daudet was always a portal wide open
and tremendously alive to the entrance of natural
phenomena. His senses transmitted to his brain
the most exact, the most generous and the truest
observations. His brain made a choice among
them and organized from them their marshalling.

He lived with the persons of his book as with
friends. He put them questions on all sorts of
topics and listened to their answers. He tempted
them with vices and virtues and followed the
working of these ideas in their minds until he
obtained complete figures and reached the mysterious limits of the laughable and the impenetrable.
He would rather cause them to act than to argue,
being by no means ignorant that a truthful gesture is the immediate ruin of a thousand theories
and that a sudden change of face is more powerful than the most subtle discussion. He knew that
characters betrayed themselves through typical
phrases — that hybrid individuals with an oval
and undetermined physiognomy, who have as it
were enfeebled our epoch, nevertheless do have
special moments of a brilliant and determined
life.

So he granted to cowards occasional pluckings-
up of courage; to the bold, periods of weakness;

to the weak, moments of strength, and to liars,
impulses of truth; to hypocrites, times when masks
fall; to chatterers, spells of silence; to hidebound persons, singular relaxations; to chaste
people, low dreams, and to the vicious, ideas of
chastity. He had cross-examined woman and
placed her in the confessional in her various *rôles*
as mother, wife and lover; in her generosities, her
perverse actions, her ordinary tastes; in her faults,
terrors and anguish. He knew the taste of every
sort of tear, he held the key to every sort of sorrow. No intricate path of remorse or of regret
escaped him.

He did not fail even to study the mirror-like
and complex souls of children. And over all his
conversations, over his patient research and his
precise knowledge he cast the merciful cloak
of a philosopher whom no dreadful spectacle has
hardened and no human horror has disgusted —
one who has not grown weary of mankind.

We often used to laugh among ourselves at the
ease with which some men treated him amicably
as a "locust," or "cicada," men who sum up the
entire South of France with a single emblem. In
many an obituary note, otherwise sympathetic or
enthusiastic, I have met with these suggestions
of "enchanter" or "troubadour" or "light poet."
Nothing could be more false than such an idea.
It is true my father was realist enough to admit
that " gayety " and " charm " have also a place in
existence; since nothing is uniformly black and
cruel; but that harsh labor in his own mind is

badly expressed by a suggestion of legs scratching wings, of a rattling in the sunlight.

When we come to publish in their entirety the thoughts jotted down in his notebooks, people will see with what zeal he studied out for us those ideas of forms which are more tangible and human. An admirably gifted poet, he was as suspicious of metaphors as any philologist or biologist, just as he was suspicious of the slightest cause for error in other respects.

He finds in life an episode, a striking trait. With a few clear words he fixes it, and then continues the task begun. The first noting of it overwhelms him with parallels. It may be that it is the germ and the beginning of a book; but this book itself offers itself to him from several points of view in a way which I cannot express better than as the attitudes of a living man. So, then, it becomes a series of sketches and more or less intense and exact drawings, in which the large constructive lines are already strongly marked.

As ideas are thus associated, the moral elements approach each other and come together in intimate union. Now the high lights can be distinguished; types, situations, portraits and conversations spring from two distinct origins, one of them basic and primordial, the other fragmentary, altering day by day, and always subject to the changes of fact. It forms a *mulatière* [1] of reminiscence and improvised additions. The being thus

---

[1] Name of a suburb of Lyon, but here it probably stands for *mulassière* or " hybrid."

metamorphosed comes slowly toward the author through the mist. What joy when he feels that he has his model thoroughly there and needs to work only upon secondary parts and improvements! Nevertheless the last selection is always a subtle and laborious one.

Alphonse Daudet's mind was of such a sort that details of his work offer an abridged resemblance of the whole. That is why his novel affects us like an hallucination and makes every reader a witness to the drama.

Take Delobelle as he appears to us. From one end of his biography to the other he remains exactly in accord with his outline; you will never see the hand or the arm of the author. It is the same thing with the Nabob, Numa, Bompard, Paul Astier and the others. This extraordinary continuousness in a figure proves a complete assimilation of the author with the character created. His imagination has no jumps and bounds which interfere with observation and subtract whatever may be gained by lyrical liveliness from truthfulness to the fact.

That explains how there comes to be, alongside of the Daudet who writes, a Daudet who lives and talks; it is necessary to leave the picture of him incomplete, such as I trace it here. That which my father did not put in his book, the overflow of his brain which he would have feared to use as surplus matter, all this unemployed force was found again in his conversation and his acts. The tree, it is true, has left immortal fruit, but at the same time sap was running through its branches and out to their extremest points, to the stems of the leaves and flowers.

I have said that he worked with tremendous vigor; nevertheless no amount of work prevented him from receiving a friend, aiding a comrade, or giving counsel to a young man. My sudden runnings into the room did not irritate him. He would welcome us with a kind word or a joke. He took an interest in the whole house, in the sense that every hour was good, as far as he was concerned. He had no regular hours. From the time he ceased to go out he passed his life at his table, reading or taking notes; summer or winter he got up at half-past seven and went to bed at eleven o'clock, except on Thursday, when we kept a longer watch.

For Thursday was his day of recreation. His uncommon amicability was the reason for the great pleasure he took in those simple but most interesting receptions, at which we saw in active play the most splendid intelligences belonging to our time. My father enlivened everything, started and kept up discussions, warmed the timid, soothed the angry ones, put a truce to hostilities, softened rancors and strengthened sympathies.

In the miserable drivel of a poor broken-down symbolist, a man, besides, who never knew him, I have read this strange statement: that Alphonse Daudet could never forgive! In the first place he did not know of most of those attacks with which the young bald-heads of the small reviews

did not fail to regale him; and for the very
good reason that he did not read them; besides,
even had he read them, they would at most
have brought to his lips an indulgent smile, so
entirely indifferent did such appreciations leave
him. But several of his enemies who became his
sincere friends might bear witness to the kindliness
and ease of forgetting things which he always
showed in literary discussions.

"Most of the time people don't understand each
other. Ferocious and time-honored antipathies
do not stand a moment before a few minutes'
contact."

And although there was a constellation of the
"arrived" and of the "illustrious" at those Thursday reunions, there was also no lack of beginners, because he had a warm interest in new
talents. Uncertain of himself, he did not disdain
those obscure powers which announce themselves
in some writer of the future and issue out in overwhelming or paradoxical words, in a frenzy of
criticism or of blind enthusiasm. A great number
of those who to-day hold the first rank were in
their days of beginning encouraged and sustained
by him. What a host of letters to editors, to
managers of newspapers and theatres, what a lot
of recommendations and notes of introduction!
"Alas," said he, "I can no longer use my actual
presence!" He knew very well the power of his
own speech and what the most eloquent letter
lacks in persuasive gestures and accents of sincerity.

That love of youth, even in its faults and vanities, was part of his eager desire to know: he wished to *see and understand.* An attitude, a grasp of the hand, a look, a word from a person revealed more to him than a piece of verse or a picture. He adored Plutarch, who in his biographies followed the sensible rule which adds to the portrait of a great man his way of eating, drinking and walking, his preferences and even his hobbies. He approved absolutely certain decisive pages which Marcel Schwob wrote on this subject at the beginning of his *Vies Imaginaires.* Details which are small in appearance are in fact serious channels through which we penetrate to the clearer view of ancient times and thread the labyrinth of dead souls.

Opinions are "things of the word," transitory and insignificant things ; that is the reason that the life of political people is generally so wretched and commonplace. The market-place, the pretorian tribune, the ante-chambers of sovereigns, federal chambers and legislatures, as well as the conversations there taking place, are no better than ghosts, phantoms and masks. This or that habit, this vice, that peculiarity of speech or of costume, this touch of gluttony or luxury in Talleyrand or Napoleon the Great becomes in our eyes extremely important and takes on the lively air of a confession. This it is that is called by pedants *bonhomie,* but more correctly by others "humanity."

Now what interests us in such notes as these in

history is that quality whereby they differ from other things, whatever may be the differences themselves.

When he was creating my father *saw* what he created. When he was writing *he heard.* A certain number of physicians belonging to the new school came to interview him on this point and in pedantic words they have simplified a natural and complete method. Ever since the celebrated "Schema" of Charcot, people keep repeating indefinitely the old scholastic distinction between "auditives" and "rituals," categories which have nothing absolute in them, and are of no use except as an hypothesis. And if he heard he also spoke. He practised the sound of his dialogues and tried the harmony of his descriptions. Fear of wordiness, which was always on the increase with him, caused him to use, especially in his last works, a picturesque brevity in which every sensation is like a lightning flash; reflection does not come to the surface but silently emanates from the characters. He has been reproached, but very foolishly, for his curt and nervous phrases which are as near the actuality as possible, since every word plays a trick with us and deceives us as to its duration.

I have forgotten none of the fine regulations which he scrupulously applied: "Whether the question is a book or an article, whether a direct creation or a criticism, never take up the pen *unless you have something to say.*" If the literary mania continues to develop itself, very soon there will not be a single Frenchman who has not got out his own book.

"Setting, ideas, situations, characters, all these are not right until a very slow and instructive digestion has been gone through with, in which all nature, gifted in the least of its component parts, collaborates with the writer. We are like women in a hopeful situation; people can see it in our very faces. We have the pregnant woman's mask.'

"Style is a state of intensity. The greatest number of things in the fewest number of words. Don't fear to repeat yourself, according to Pascal's counsel. There are no synonyms.

"Push always toward clearness and concise lucidity. Our tongue has its own moral laws. Whoever attempts to avoid them will not last. Our tongue is suppler than any other, as intellectual as it is logical, more closely ranged than declamatory and has quick and short reflections in very precise forms. It is not favorable to antique terms or phrases. It appeals more to the mind than the ear. There are very few shades which it does not express, very few true distinctions which it does not define. It is especially triumphant when expressing ideas suggested.

"Descendants of the Latins, who were a constructive people, we have a taste for solid things. Harmony also is indispensable, even for picturing the passions where disorder is a beauty. Let that same disorder only be a seeming one: let us be aware of a profound rule and order underneath!

That will always be in conformity with the truth; the worst of tempests submits to its own laws.

"Description of a character carried on to its final completion should not be made except little by little, according as the character reveals itself and according as life reacts upon it.

"Society, landscape and circumstances, all that environs us, have a share in our state of mind. You must enter into the person you are describing, *into his very skin*, and see the world through his eyes and feel it through his senses. Direct intervention on the part of the writer is an error.

"On the other hand the theory of impassiveness is exaggerated. He who tells a story has the right to be moved, himself; but with discretion, and as it were behind the scenes, by the affairs of heroes and heroines, but without doing harm to that illusion which makes the charm. All the live forces of the author are taken up by the expression of reality. Lyricism, realism and even frenzy, all these may unite and produce power. Beauty has no label. Sincerity includes everything.

"It is necessary to have respect for the reader: An author has morally a guardianship over souls. Sure of his means and being able to corrupt, he is culpable if he abuses his trust, if he ruins vital nobility, if he does not go from below upward, which is the direction of an honest conscience. Intellectually, too, he should have respect for the reader and insist only upon the essential things, not falsify enthusiasm but keep his scrupulousness simple and pure.

"Truth is a perfect union of soul between the author and that which surrounds him, between that which he conceives and perceives and that which he expresses. The realm of imagination itself has its truth. There are lies on Mount Parnassus as well as in the street.

"Art consists of more than mere selection. It includes decision and boldness besides. No hypocrisy, no fraud! The roadways of life lie open. It is not permitted to deviate from them nor to halt by the way.

"There is the courage of the author to be considered, which consists in accomplishing his mission to the very end. The bold are always victorious. The timid ones always remain incomplete. It is not necessary to help on one's work; because it goes of itself. No obstacle, however frank and powerful, will prevent its triumphing.

"There is danger in thinking about pleasing. Another danger is to wish to astonish. Notoriety flies always from those who seek it through low means."

A very incomplete enumeration. I shall rectify it as I go on. My father presented the same principles in the richest and most multitudinous forms. But the foundation remains unchanged.

These few profound and solid rules, which he laid down whilst we were talking in private, gave

him the chance to use a delightful variety of images
and of impressions for all the rest, for the transitory affairs of life.   Just as in conversation he was
never caught napping when a reply was due from
him, for he uttered it quickly, brilliantly and in
winged words, in the same way the small affairs of
daily intercourse and the most trivial episodes
could never take him unawares. We had gradually
formed such a habit of these delightful and charming conversations during which the hours slipped
by over our books, that an elliptical language had
gradually grown up between us for our own special
use.   Each one filled out the other's thought and
then prolonged the idea by a remark, the sense of
which he indicated in the fewest words, where only
the essential was uttered.

That you will find again in his work; it is a
faithful mold of his mind. The largest good sense,
that masterly gift in comparison with which the
most brilliant qualities are worth but little, animates the whole of his work with a deathless breath
— that good sense which Descartes called "least
common to man." So fruitful is its action that
it no longer expresses itself but leaves the field
clear to the imagination, which thereafter becomes
as free as any goddess, smiling, fleeing and clad
in curtal robe.

The reader is ever close behind the author and
the author inspires him with confidence. Take
for example some poet, Carlyle, we will say, a rain
of stars and of metaphors which play across the
sky and the veiled night. Notwithstanding all his

genius, why has Carlyle only a very narrow place
in human imaginings? It is because he lacks that
intimate harmony which souls ecstatic over fancied
images unconsciously demand. He has never conquered our confidence. A word from the lips, a
slightest word from the lips of him who has completely conquered us by his wisdom takes on a
magical value. Whither he ascends, thither we
follow. We fraternize through enthusiasm. A
sympathy is set up between the most magnificent
genius and the reader. We are astonished, we are
astonished, but we are not conquered.

What I have attempted to express as well as I
could in these words was carved into my mind by
my father in clear and marvellously exact terms.
I myself was one of his works. He desired to
finish me in every part as he did the others. Alas,
poor stuff that it was! If you have not been able
to profit by his teaching, at any rate pass on his
fertile words! Be exact and truthful! Perhaps
another will be found for whom this torch, piously
relit, may show the way. Many a time while
listening to my friend have I thought:

"If I am destined to survive him, I shall call
upon my memory for a grand effort of revival. I
shall impose upon myself the task of putting down
in writing those fugitive beauties, often as impossible to transmit as words of love which lack the
time and the countenances of the lovers." And
ye who read, be indulgent to me, for I bring
hither my entire conscience. A witness of a most
noble spectacle, I have tried to retain phrases,

gestures, intonations and play of features. My
father loved the truth. I wish to serve truth in
my turn down to the most intimate scenes, guided
by him and encouraged by the lofty recollection
of his character.

III.

AS FATHER AND AS HUSBAND — THE VENDOR OF HAPPINESS.

MY father was often wont to repeat: "When my task is finished I should like to establish myself as a Vendor of Happiness; my profits would consist in my success."

Then he would add: "There are so many men who are somnambulists and pass through existance without seeing where they are, stumbling against obstacles and bruising their brows against walls which it would be easy for them to circumvent! I have put this phrase in the mouth of one of my characters: 'All things in life have a side or a meaning through which they can be grasped.' But that is no metaphor."

Then he would toss his head with an indulgent half smile and a sigh: "There is no such thing as commonplace in the world; it only exists in people's minds. Renan is a little sad because Gavroche is as learned as he is. But Gavroche is a parrot. In his brain words have no value at all. Suppose a young person talks about death. It is very rarely the case that one notices in him the existence of that black gulf which this terrible syllable at once opens in the soul of an old man.

You know the emotion which all of a sudden comes upon us at sight of some noun or verb which we had been carelessly repeating up to the day on which the true and deep-seated meaning appeared to us. Revelations of that sort are the result of the teaching of years.

"I am not boasting, I was a precocious mind. At an early age I understood, *in my very bones*, the actual value of many of the words which youth employs with the utmost carelessness and ease. Disease and sorrow produce another sort of maturity. They lend truthfulness to language. In such cases people live *on their capital* instead of living on their interest; for it cannot be ignored that emotions and even a somewhat burning thought represent a loss of substance, the *one step farther on.* Oh, the wisdom of the very sick! Oh, eyes too brilliant and too well informed! In the public gardens, dragged about in sick chairs, I meet people whose looks frighten me."

"Then, father, the vendor of happiness . . . ?"

"I mean no allegory; the vendor would go to the sick and to every one; by tenderness he would gain their confidence; like a patient and gentle physician he would examine the moral wound, mark its extent and progress and reassure the sick man through the spectacle of his fellows; that is the argument of egoism which never faileth! From that point he would gradually rise toward the picture of a restricted but still a noble destiny, if only the patient knows how to employ himself by drying the tears about him and consoling others while consoling himself. To put one's goal beyond oneself, to place one's ideal outside of oneself — that is to escape from Fate to a certain extent."

How many a time, entering unexpectedly his study, have I not caught sight of attitudes of anguish in his visitors and interrupted confidences which I felt were grave and pressing! If secrecy had not been asked my friend would then show the situation to me, and all the difficulties whose simplest and most "humane" solution he was seeking.

But when I said to him: "Be vendor of happiness to yourself!" he answered: "My existence is a mere matter of effort from day to day. I have the greatest confidence in those little efforts of the will which bind me down to some fixed hour, such as to seat myself at the table notwithstanding my sufferings, to disdain and affront my illness. Imagine the torture of the circular wall which little by little grows smaller, the torture of one impossibility after the other! How true it is, that phrase repeated by the coquette in front of her looking-glass: *To think that I shall regret all that to-morrow!* Well, the never-ending cares of the father of a family, the anxieties as to my household are a great resource for me. The feeling of responsibility is enough to keep a man on his legs after his strength has given out. Then I think about my fellow-men. If financial want is added to their sufferings, if they have not the resources of fire and of food and of wine and of warm affection — why then I consider myself still happier.

"I keep my pitifulness fresh by repeating to myself that there are far worse sorrows than mine, and so I do not use up all my pity on myself. You know that a good many philosophers banish pity from their republic as if it were a weakness or degradation, or as if it were a lack of energy.

"The vendor of happiness would preach the religion of active pity and not of useless fears. To him who suffers, suffering is always new. But to witnesses thereof, even tender and energetic ones, suffering grows old and becomes a mere habit. I tell a sick person: 'Give yourself distractions and through your spirit wrestle to the very end; do not weary and harass the people about you.'"

"The Stoics long ago discovered the pleasure which people find in the constant exercise of energy. I could suggest a thousand tricks to a patient who is gifted with imagination. I would advise a person who is not able to mix laughter with actualities to place his sufferings before him on a grand scale until he reaches the point when the beauty of the struggle makes its appearance and gives grandeur to the whole. That is a particular kind of intoxication which makes the least subtle person strangely intelligent; *it is one of the keys of human nature.*

"And, to start with, everything takes its place and falls into its natural plane. Little trivial sorrows which increase for us our enjoyments and moral laziness recoil toward the background and reach their proper level. Had it not been for

my sickness, perhaps I might have been an
'author,' a prey to the sillinesses of the profession,
trembling at criticism, off my head through praise
and duped by empty triumphs. Of course I have
weaknesses . . . nevertheless I have been purified. . . At the Lamalou Baths I have met 'So-
sies[1] of suffering' in the shape of men belonging
to the most varied professions. They were all
transcendental and 'above themselves,' lighted
up by swift gleams which traversed their flesh and
penetrated their very souls.

"Among the confessions which I have received,
those made me by the damned ones *down there*
seem to show a special kind of harshness and
frankness. The very words they use have more
breadth and more relief."

The notes taken by my father in regard to this
subject during his stay at hot baths are very
typical and fine. Such observations on the part
of a man of letters astonished the physicians,
because they were more complete and subtle than
those which might have been collected by a
scientist. Without preconceived ideas and inter-
mingled theories, they possessed the clearness of a
cross-examination put on paper. The most frightful shames, the secret wretchednesses of men,
women and aged men are stated there discreetly
with the wisdom of a physician-poet. Most of
our neighbors in the hotel, some of them strangers from America, Spain and Russia, arranged

---

[1] Character in the *Amphitryon* of Plautus, whose semblance
was taken by Mercury; Molière used him in one of his plays.

their hours so as to made their treatment coincide
with that of the novelist. He reassured them and
quieted their spirits, thus completing the work of
the physician. Many of them confided to him
with that zeal in giving details, that ardor and
extraordinary pride which are common to people
who possess a grave and still undefined malady.
He noted down, classified and compared the most
peculiar nervous troubles, manias, fears, chronic
or recurrent disorders; these deviations from the
course of nature often aided him in understanding nature; they would light up some obscure
region and thus do service to his constant search
after knowledge.

"Evil in the family and society," such modifications as it makes in characters, temperaments
and trades, the ingeniousness shown by egotists,
rich or poor, these are the questions which inflamed him and warmed his blood; these he collected at every moment with a methodicalness and
conscientiousness most uncommon.

There are entire lives which are summed up in
a few lines: " Misers turned to spendthrifts "—
" violent men become timorous " — " chaste people tormented by passions they dare not avow."
Initials call back to me names and faces and sorrowful outlines. A word is enough to bring up
a whole personality; "ruined careers " — there is
one like the title for a chapter. Frightful odds
and ends of a dialogue: " Sir, what I fear the
most is the moment when I do not suffer. This
evening my imagination shudders. . . I see all my

hopes dashed to the ground — love, future, . . ah ! . . "

Sometimes a smile or a funny phrase lights up these frightful pictures. *A give-away phrase!* Like to lightning which for an instant illuminates the landscape, such a phrase lights up the hidden depths of a being, that labyrinth into which even the most intimate observation penetrates in vain.

It was owing to such facts as these that my father perceived this idea which he has so often expressed: " No matter how much of a realist one may be, a writer recoils before the reality. Discourses that one gets off, vanities that one shows off, passions in which one wallows, all that is so much parade before the multitude.

" Beside this there is an abyss which no one dares to stir, mud which does not belong to our being, a thick and miry mud in which are the half-formed models for all vices and all crimes such as do not even reach the priest's confessional. Would it be possible a single time to plunge down there? That is what I have often asked myself. Let us imagine, then, some dark and secret place, for example a hospital for maladies of the eyes, in which people, lying near each other side by side in absolute black darkness, ignoring each other's names and age, and almost each other's sex, moreover never intending to see each other again, should freely express themselves and avow what torments them, whispering as it were gropingly from bed to bed."

He applied to his sorrows the celebrated axiom:

"Poetry is deliverance;" whence that sketch for
a book called *La Doulou* whose elements he
had collected, which he did not publish, however,
owing to our insistence. Here it is before me,
that terrible and implacable breviary! Certainly
it did need a fine courage "to deliver oneself"
after such a fashion; but have I not already indicated the fierce necessity of confessing himself
which my father showed?

In our days science has taken on pretentious
airs. Science has believed that she could conquer
the spirit. Alphonse Daudet was too sagacious to
believe in the labels called psychology, physiology, pathology — labels which the wind blows
away and the rain defaces.

Auguste Comte's dogma had never secured any
hold upon his imagination, always so clear and
always in action, one that never accepted fine
words for facts. We used to amuse ourselves together over that impudence shown in explaining
and systematizing everything which is the mark
of the modern pedant: "the husk of words for
the grain of things" according to Leibnitz. He
had had long conversations with powerful and
lucid Charcot, with Brown-Séquard, tormented by
his genius, with Potain, the master of masters, in
whom pity went on increasing as his knowledge
grew. So he did not fail to know all there was
to know upon that other side of the human riddle
which bears different mottos and teaches us by
two very different ways. There as elsewhere his
power of comprehension had served him well.

But by the power of his thought he kept himself at the point where art, which differentiates and individualizes, crosses the path of science, which classifies and generalizes; so that it has often happened to me to say to him laughingly: " You are creating a new method."

That which is scientifically known concerning pain could be put in a few pages. That which one obtains metaphysically by induction concerning pain can be expressed in a few lines. That which a poet and observer obtains for his harvest through the study of pain among individuals is infinite. The metaphysician and the scientist, yes, even the mystic, ought to draw from that treasury if they wish to enrich their facts at a single stroke. Not only did my father suffer, but he has seen others suffer. In that way he was able to recognize certain domains in the realm of evil where the ignorance of to-day, drawing from the sources of the old biographers, is still putting the old inscription " tigers and lions " on the map, that is to say, hollow formulas !

One day when I was explaining to him the crossing of the new fibres in the brain and spinal cord, he cried out: " Plato's team ! " Thus was imagination in touch with reality. That is the tendency which I remark in all his notes on suffering. In one place he compares those whom paralysis has stricken to satyrs changed into trees or to petrified dryads. In another place he sighs: " I might date the beginning of my pain as that delightful Mlle. Lespinasse dated her love — from

every instant of my life!" Or else it might happen
that he said with gentle irony: "For hypochon-
dria read ignorance on the part of doctors."

What becomes of pride in the person who
suffers, what become of tenderness and of charity,
whither go the lively passions, luxuriousness and
hatred? How does the life of a family change its
aspects, the relations between the married people,
beween father and children and friends? How
do people habituate themselves to evil and resign
themselves? or what revolt is there against it, and
what form does that revolt take? and in consequence of what efforts? These are just so many
troublesome questions which he answers with an
absolute frankness in accordance with his hard
experience or which he allows to remain in doubt,
if that is his mood. The variations themselves in
this same mood he passes in review with a resigned philosophy all his own, and it is wonderful
to see how through his will power he resists and
opposes to every attack all the resources of a
hard-headed morality.

I can still see him seated in the little garden of
the Hôtel Mas at Lamalou surrounded by sick
people, preaching energy to them, reassuring the
nervous ones, taking pains with the despairing and
giving them glimpses of some possible holding-off
or drawing-back of their fate: "The doctors don't
know any more than we; they know even less
than we do, because their knowledge is made up
of an average drawn from observations which are
generally hasty and incomplete, and because every

case is a new and peculiar one. You, Sir, have
this symptom, you yonder have another. It would
be necessary to join you both to Madame here,
in order to obtain something which resembles
somewhat my own martyrdom. There are a great
many different kinds of instruments belonging to
the hangman; if they do not scare you too much,
examine them carefully. It is with our tortures
as with shadows. Attention clears them up and
drives them off. Let us change a bit the beautiful
verses by Hugo:

" ' Il n'est point de *douleur*, comme il n'est point d'algèbre
  Qui résiste au milieu des *êtres* ou des cieux
  A la fixité calme et profonde des yeux.' "

"Come now, just watch me; I am talking; I
say oh! ah! ow! and my talk is a great solace to
myself. While warming others I warm myself. . . .
It is all right — since those among you who have a
family which they love consider their disease as a
sort of lightning-rod. Destiny has satisfied its
hatred in them. Avoid egotism; it increases
suffering; it renders suffering atrocious and more
unbearable. Don't open those big books; you will
never get anything out of them except terror, for
they never treat of any but extreme cases. The
frightened face of Diafoirus will be enough if you
present to him some unpublished symptom 'which
cannot be found in the dictionary.' The surprise
on the part of the doctor is so amusing to me that
I would like to invent such words. But it will not
do to push the thing too far, for then they treat

you as a 'malade imaginaire' and they cease to
feel sorry for you. Now we people of the South
who are here in a majority, we like to be worried
over; Molière saw that very clearly when he came
to Pézénas.

"Argan is Orgon pronounced in the Provençal
way, and Orgon is found in the character of Tar-
tuffe. They ought to play the *Malade Imaginaire* with the accent of the South; that would
furnish an irresistibly comic spectacle."

With such discourses and many others and with
his own example and courage my father was wont
to enliven the wretched people in that sorrowful
country which, when he retired to his room, he
compared to the inferno of Dante, because one
could find there specimens of every kind of punishment. And that action in a twofold way of the
observer and consoler is a faithful image of his
nature.

One can readily understand that he was interested in famous sufferers of former days. He knew
fundamentally the maladies of Pascal and of Rousseau and of Montaigne as well as that of Henri
Heine nearer his day. But he was very careful
not to take up wild hypotheses like those which
our psychologists have seized upon; for example,
the likening of genius to madness made him shrug
his shoulders.

A continued theme with him was the alliance
between pity and pain: "He who has never felt
hunger and never been cold, he who has never
suffered can talk neither about the cold, nor hunger,

nor suffering. He does not even know very well
what bread is, nor what is fire, nor what is resignation. In the first part of my life I made the acquaintance of misery; in the second, of pain.
Thus my senses became sharpened — if I should
say to what point sharpened, no one would believe
me. A single face in distress at the corner of the
street has upset my soul and will never leave my
memory. There are certain intonations which I
avoid recalling lest I should cry like a fool. Oh,
those actors! What genius is necessary to them
in order to reproduce that which they have experienced. No trembling, no exaggeration . . . and
then the right accent — that wonderful right accent
— which comes from the vitals ! "

Moreover any false note in an intonation, every
attempt at second-rate pathos, every philanthropi-
cal masquerade — all "honored ladies" and "worthy
sirs" uttered in what he called a "throaty" voice
exasperated him. I have seen tactless persons who
knew he was charitable boasting in his presence of
sacrifices and imaginary benefactions. Irony began
to stir in his eyes which suddenly became black
and brilliant. He cut the hypocrite short by some
disconcerting exclamation, or else he expressed
his disbelief with a malignant sweetness which
delighted every one.

Readers of his books need only recall the portraits of Argenton, Madame Hautmann and of
Astier Réhu, but, as he said, the most complete
figures of romance lack the "moisture of reality."

We are in the landau. The sky is clear. On

the edge of the turnpike sits a ragged fellow with a mean face, no linen, eyes full of anger and weariness. The magnificence of nature sparkles and gleams about this vagabond as if to exasperate his distress. Willy-nilly, we must stop; my father is not able to get out of the carriage, but he talks to the man whilst I hand over the alms of the "rich gentleman." And he asks questions in a familiar way, with a kindliness and so clear an expression of a wish to excuse the disproportion of things, that the hollow face softens and relaxes.

We go on. Then says my gentle friend: " These horses, the coachman, the carriage, everything is arranged so that one can pass quickly; everything combats charity, everything is in a state of virtuous indignation against the tramp. There it is, that is fortune! One cannot see the poor from the cushions of the landau; they form part of another world, and those favored by fortune turn their heads aside. But in the glare of the unfortunate one hatred accumulates. . . . Nothing is lost in this world . . . just as in chemistry."

Among the works he had in preparation one of the most important, for which he had many fragments and a general plan, was *La Caravane*. The thread of the book is a journey in a trap made by two couples who are friends, men and women of opposite character and lively intelligence, between whom a drama of passion and jealousy unrolls itself whilst they are traversing the finest landscapes of France. My father knew and admired the principal sections of our land in all their diversity. He always insisted upon the influence of the soil and local habits; a devotee of tradition in his soul, although a revolutionist on other sides, he extolled in conversation the marvellous views of Brittany, Normandy, Touraine, Alsatia, the Ardèche, the Lyonnais, Bourgogne, Provence and Languedoc. He had made a profound study of characters according to district.

His first question of a stranger or a beginner was: "Where were you born?" As soon as he was informed he sought through his vast memory for the dominating points of the region. From having made researches into his own origin he had constructed a method. Changes of temperament along a given river or a given valley excited his curiosity to the highest degree: "The Norman is the Gascon of the North." —"Lorraine finesse is a clear and sometimes dry observation of men and events." —" You must not confound Provence with the stony South, the Hérault and Languedoc. Provence has a touch of Italy, but Hérault and Languedoc prepare one for Spain." — " The logical imagination of the Touraine country (Rabelais, Descartes) differs profoundly from the intellectual wine of Bourgogne and from the Mediterranean flash-in-the-pan." — " Anger of a woman, anger of the Mediterranean; all on the surface. Ten feet of calm water under one foot of foam!" — " Panurge, the type of the Parisian, has not changed since *Gargantua*. I have him, exactly like himself, in at least ten of my comrades!" — " The lie in the North, heavy, tenacious and

gloomy, is very different from *our* lie, which runs
about, changes a subject, laughs, gesticulates —
and ends all of a sudden in sincerity."

He had a very significant "schedule" for the
city of Lyons which he saw much of in his youth
and for the Lyons temperament: "The two
banks — Fourvières and Croix-Rousse — the two
rivers, the Saône and the Rhône, mystics and *canuts*
(silk-weavers). A tendency to general ideas on the
one side: Ballanche, Blanc-Saint-Bonnet; and on
the other the taste for jewelry: Joséphine Soulary.
On this side Puvis de Chavannes, on the other
Meissonier. This parallel might be carried on
among the scientific minds."

"Instead of losing themselves in volumes of
verse which no one reads, why do not sincere men,
who are friends of the real, carefully write the history of the corner which they inhabit and enjoy.
The novel form lends itself admirably to this.
Customs, legends, that which strikes the infant
mind, the part which forest, mountain or village
play in the popular imagination, or that of childhood; that which remains from ancient times;
that which has not yet been absolutely levelled. I
do not ask that every village shall have its Mistral;
the great poet is rare. But conscientious souls are
not lacking who might do this admirable business.
We should be stupefied at the intellectual and
moral riches of France. They form a treasure
which is wasted, all these customs, dialects and
stories. Oh, how fine are the Gascon tales by
Blasi!

A book of that kind on the Périgord country compactly enough written delighted him; it was recommended to him by his friend Senator Dussolier. I can no longer remember the title; it was something like *Le Moulin du Frau.* He praised it to all his friends. He lent it to me. It is a complete work in which the author gives himself up completely and relates all about his little country with a prodigious care for the truth.

"Why don't they imitate him?" cried my father. "I follow with delight the consequences of the impulsion which our Mistral gave. And if Mistral has wrought in the poetical domain, Drumont has wrought in the social domain. The profound feeling of his boldness is of the same kind. A return to tradition! That is what may save us in this contemporary dissolution of things. I have always had the instinct for things of this sort; but they have not appeared to me clearly until within a few years, thanks to the efforts of my great friends. It is bad to lose one's roots entirely and forget one's village.

"That life Maillane led, what an ideal! Not only to cultivate one's garden and vine, but to celebrate them also, and add to legendry by glory, renewing the linked chain of friendships. It is very singular that poetry only attaches itself to objects that have come from a distance or are of very long usage. That which people call progress — a vague and very doubtful word — rouses or excites the lower parts of the intelligence. The higher parts vibrate better to that which has

touched and inflamed a long series of imaginations that have issued one from the other and
are strengthened by the sight of the same landscapes, the smell of the same fragrances, the touch
of the same polished furniture.

"Very old impressions settle down to the very
bottom of an obscure memory, that memory of
the race which the crowd of individual memories
weave together. The old impressions unite themselves with all the efforts of laborers, vineyard
tenders and foresters. It is with them as with
the roots which worm their way along and mix
themselves with the nourishing earth, twist themselves together and mix their juices. Didactic
poems on steam, electricity and the X-rays are
not poems at all. Oh, I guess already the exception which will be objected; the singer of the
future will be mentioned, the sublime American,
lyrical Walt Whitman! But he belongs to the
country without ancestors."

That was one of his habitual themes. He developed it with a vigor and richness of images
quite incomparable, for all his feelings were
brought into play. The love of "his Provence"
rose to his lips.

"Léon, I'd have you know that I am the vendor of happiness myself. When some young man
comes to see me in his arrogant or timid way,
with his little volume in his hand, I say to him:
'From what part of the country?' 'From ———,
Sir.' 'A long time since you have left your
house and the old people?' 'About so long.'

'Are you thinking of returning?' 'I don't know.'
'But why not right away, now that you have had
a taste of Paris? Are they poor?' 'Oh, no, Sir,
they are comfortably off.' 'Then, hapless one,
flee! I see you there, undecided, young and
impressionable. I do not believe that there is
actually in you that energy of Balzac which boiled
up and fermented in his garret. Listen to my
counsel and later you will thank me. Return to
your home. Make a solitude to yourself in some
corner of the house or the farm. Stroll back
through your memories; recollections of childhood are the living and unpoisoned source for all
those who have not the master's power of evoking
thought. Besides, you will see. You have plenty
of time. Make the people who are about you
talk, the hunters and village girls, the old men
and vagabonds, and let all that gradually settle in
your mind. Then, if you have any talent, you
will write a personal book which will have your
own mark on it and will, in the first place, interest
your comrades and then the public, if you are
able, or if you have the chance, to find some odd
piece of intrigue, well carried out, to put inside
this frame.'"

"But, father, it must be very seldom that the
young man will listen to you! He thinks that
you are jealous of his future glory; he has his
answer ready: 'But you yourself, Sir, never acted
in this manner, and you have not fared very
badly.'"

He smiled, thought a moment, knocked the

ashes from his pipe, and answered: "Some of
them have listened to me. The example of Baptiste Bonnet may be cited, the author of that *Vie
d'Enfant*, which will be continued in two more
volumes and I hope as successfully as the first.
Bonnet has shown himself an admirable poet
merely by recounting what he found right before
his eyes; his eyes are those of an observant
lyrical talent. Imagine what the sketch of a novel
or poem in French would have been from his
hand, in French, which he understands very badly,
and moreover on a subject which did not spring
from his own heart! Yes, I can cite Bonnet and
many others. The vendor of happiness is not an
obstinate fellow carried away by theory. From
those who have had the pleasure of travel and
sojourn in foreign lands he asks an account of
their impressions. Profit by the inestimable op-
portunity which has filled your mind with new
sounds and colors and odors! There is poor little
Boissière, now dead, whose thought, in his only
book, *Fumeurs d'Opium*, gave warrant of a great
mind.

"Bonnetain too has known how to take advantage of his trip round the globe. It is quite true
that Loti is an author of great talent, but he has
not closed the path for other navigators and
dreamers. And as to those who glorify the land
of their birth, here is Rodenbach, the most exquisite and refined of poets and prose writers,
moist and dripping with his Flemish fogs, a
writer whose sentence has the tender effect of

belfries against the sky and the soft golden hue of reliquaries and stained-glass windows.

"There is Pouvillon, to whom we owe the complete description of the Montalban district, so full of charm. Examples are numberless. Whether nomadic or stationary, let them all make their work conform to their own likings and let them chant that which has enchanted them."

"We are not far off from *La Caravane.* Such conversations make the days of travellers a delight; they are held at the bend of the road before the grounds of some old château while twilight lends to nature restfulness and calm and the servants prepare the meal. According to his own character each person in the party becomes the sponsor for some theory in conformity with his own moral nature. The subjects of conversation are brought in by the chance sight of things without, as it happens when we allow our thoughts to run delightfully hither and thither.

"But," added my father, "I would not permit them to philosophize long and fatigue the reader; their opinions must follow the same curve as their adventures. I do not want any puppets crammed with phrases and stories; the blood must circulate."

When by chance the vendor of happiness talked about politics, he made a grand argument concerning the underhand but constant warfare between Paris and the Provinces. Some years ago Mme. Adam, my dear "patroness," for whom my father entertained a warm gratitude

because of her kindness in my regard, had an
idea of transforming the *Nouvelle Revue.* My
father admired her greatly for her "divining
qualities," her gift of prophecy, her ardent patriotism and those many and lofty qualities which
place her in the first rank of Frenchwomen.

Knowing the sagacity of her friend Daudet with
regard to everything connected with periodicals
and newspapers, she addressed herself to him.
He was categorical in his reply:

"My dear and illustrious friend, I myself
have pondered long the idea of establishing a
Revue de Champrosay, in the management of
which I think I should have the necessary tact to
distribute the work according to the powers of
each one who contributed.

"You cannot be unaware that one of the gravest
contemporary questions is the latent antagonism
between France and the Provinces. That showed
itself very energetically in 1870; and after the war
the enmity of the village churches toward Nôtre-
Dame, the memories of the siege and that strange
and memorable separation between the heart and
the blood-vessels, all these rancors were continued.
You can still perceive certain echoes of this in the
polemics of the provincial press, that press which
has been ruined by the telegraph and the quick
distribution of news."

I can recall very well the turn of the conversation
and the general sense of the interview, but I am
powerless to reproduce the picturesque army of
arguments, the lightning flash from his eyes, his

charming smile and the elaborate gestures made
by the hand which still held his pen.

"It is not necessary to inform you, dear friend,
what very considerable resources the Provinces
contain, material and moral resources, if I may
talk like a Deputy; but what we both of us feel
much more vividly than any parliament man you
please is the necessity of giving a little air and
life to the members which the *head* is by way of
fatiguing and ruining.

"Decentralization is one of those big words which
say nothing to the mind. Armed with your idea,
you have a weapon at hand. The professors of the
universities, those well-taught and well-informed
journalists whom one finds on the actual press of
the provinces will answer to your appeal. In that
way you will continue in your office a sort of *Revue
Fédéraliste,* in which you will print complaints
from the districts, in which, without taking sides
in their village squabbles, you can keep yourself
in touch with those quarrels.

"While you are talking of the trade and industries of this place and the other, of agriculture and
the harvest, of 'waters and forests,' thanks to your
activity and constantly continued effort, you may
perhaps succeed in re-establishing the communi-
cations so unfortunately cut between the hurried
minds of Parisians and the slower and often more
serious intelligences of the provinces; in our
France, you know, when a single spark glimmers,
very soon there is fire everywhere."

On the spot Mme. Adam organized a series of

clever inspectors, who were sent to provincial functionaries and others of greater note, and at this day an important section of the *Nouvelle Revue* acts as a rally-point and editorial chair for utterances which one never heard before. At that very moment I was commissioned to write the opening article, " Paris and the Provinces," which in a certain sense I wrote under paternal dictation.

There is no doubt that as my father grew older he would have carried out his project of the *Champrosay Review.*

He was not like a great many of his contemporaries who revile the press and are ever ready to ask services from it. By as much as he disdained advertisement, self-advertisement, by so much would he interest himself in those different kinds of information which in a few years have changed the whole physiognomy of the big dailies; and though among his friends he had polemical writers like Rochefort and Drumont, he admired the spirit of order and organization in Mme. Adam, that universal knowledge, that power of action which stupefy every one who approaches the great woman patriot. He was never happier than when those "cursed politics" permitted his old comrade Adrien Hébrard to come and chat with him.

What contests of laughter did not these two Provençals indulge in, completely informed as they were as to many men and many events, and having acquired in their long lives such experience! And nevertheless, without any bitterness!

Those who are now on the summit as well as the most ordinary reporters, whom he received with his usual courtesy and friendly ease, can be called in as witnesses to his sagacity and his delicate " scent."

No one better than he might divine the taste and whims and changing humor of the public. No one had better studied the changes in the " reading crowd " which is by no means the same thing as the active and noisy crowd. He was a partisan for the complete liberty of the press — "that wonderful safety valve for secrets." He used to say: " In France there can be no government capable of suppressing the written word; every effort made in this direction, just as we saw during the Empire, will only end by strengthening irony, putting allusions in fetters and doubling and tripling the wonderful power of the ' iron nib.' "

" We could hardly believe nowadays what a universal stupor was occasioned by the terrible article from Rochefort on the death of Victor Noir — that thunderclap framed in mourning, which transformed and petrified the whole capital into a multitude of motionless figures, reading and weighing the virulence of each sentence."

He took no part in Boulangism because he never got enthusiastic until he had made for himself a clear and independent opinion; but he felt some interest in that movement, as a " combination of a suppressed anti-parliamentary disorder with a patriotic impulse." He was indignant at

8

the judgment delivered by the High Court of Justice which condemned Rochefort to exile for articles in the newspapers: " It is the low revenge of men without cleverness, of vulgar politicians, directed against a writer of infinite brilliancy. They pretend to disdain that pamphleteer who was nevertheless one of the first originators of the actual government under which they are waxing fat; but they fear him quite enough to order him into banishment. They will pay dearly for that infamous deed!" The Panama scandal undertook to realize this prediction.

At home he and I used to joke at the eagerness with which each of us tried to get the newspapers away from each other early in the morning. He read the papers with remarkable quickness; nothing that was important escaped him. He could not resist the pleasure of writing at once a word of congratulation to the author of some article which pleased him. He remembered new names. In the papers as in books he warmed toward every appearance of talent. He wanted to see the writer, make him talk, aid him from his earliest beginnings. It sometimes happened that he reversed the rôles and a reporter sent to receive his own confession was put by him in the confessional.

Many who are famous to-day will recall his encouragements and the genial way in which he reassured timidity: "It is part of the *rôle* of the vendor of happiness to give good counsel to smaller comrades. When I receive one of these

young men who with difficulty gain their bread at
so much a line, I recall my own beginning and
reflect that perhaps I have before me a man of
the future, a real talent." He gave similar counsel to all: "This trade which you are at, and which
disgusts you, will be of service to you later; by
its aid you will have penetrated into many homes
and learned to understand characters not a few
and played a part in various comedies. Information for the public such as exists to-day did
not have its origin in New York or Chicago. It
sprang from the realistic novel. It corresponds
to that need of sincerity which fills men's minds
more and more."

When his words had been dictated or reported
amiss, he would say indulgently: "Historians, the
most severe of them and those surest of themselves,
often make mistakes! Why should not this young
man have made a mistake? Truth is a terrible,
fleeing goddess. Everything that is in the narrator's inside, everything that is subjective in him,
from his passions to his vision, down to a boot that
is too tight, wars against his desire to be a faithful
witness. Consider the smallest fact, the slenderest
episode and observe how in one single second it
changes its form! Note how it takes an entirely
different air in the mouth of one person or another!
Remember that symbolical story by Edgar Poe of
the double assassination and the multiform interpretations made by the spectators."

It was one of his whims to distribute beforehand
the various lines of work on the *Revue de Champ-*

rosay : "It shall be called the *Champrosay Review* because I shall not subject myself to the pressure of Paris, nor the optical angle of Paris. I shall endeavor to classify events according to their real importance. I shall confide reports from the law courts to such a one as possesses good eyes and judgment and style in his writing; and the Chamber of Deputies to such another who has the faculty of the humorist.

"Many writers lose their force in imaginative fiction and stories who would acquire an unexpected vigor if they were supported by reality. Particularly I would wish that my *Review* should be alive and impress the reader with the feeling of an active organism. I would like to pay my fellow workers generously in order to relieve them from anxiety as to money and be able to demand great things of them. I would give an opening to the utterance of every eloquent opinion."

He then passed in review the unexploited riches and treasures of information and anecdotes which exist in the industries and various branches of trade — the features of the different quarters of the city, the confessions of humble folk and what the chestnut vendor has to say. "I would see to it that in each number there should be a well-founded inquiry into some injustice, some great wrong and abuse of power, and in order to have my hands free I should pay my railway and theatre tickets out of my own pocket."

He was prevented from realizing his project, at first through his illness, and then because of his work itself, which entirely exhausted his power for labor and rendered impossible any farther care which made oversight and direction necessary. He was compelled to be content with following the efforts of others. Jean Finot was quite aware of the interest he took in the *Revue des Revues* and in those singular explorations and generous campaigns of his in favor of the Armenians.

In the obituary notices accounts have been given how my father at the suggestion of Finot had the joy of saving the life of an illustrious author in the Orient who was a prisoner to the Turks and was just about to be executed. On that occasion he did not get up a manifesto with a great amount of advertisement, all of which would have been noisy and vain. He preferred direct and discreet action, for which the compatriots of the unhappy man, who is now alive, entertain in memory of him the greatest gratitude. It must be said, certainly, that Europe has not spoiled them !

My father had promised the *Revue de Paris* a study of human customs entitled *Fifteen Years of Marriage*, which would have been the summing up of his experience as a husband and father. The little group which forms the family had particularly enlisted his attention : " The ordinary circumstances of life, the humblest and oftenest performed, are also those that are the least studied. Aside from Montaigne, Diderot and Rousseau, I have always been struck by the disdain which superior intellects have exhibited toward that which I will call the ' small change of existence.' An admirable subject,

if there ever was one! Balzac has written *Le
Contrat de Mariage* and *L'Interdiction.* The
drama of inheritance is complete in his works.

He had in mind to write a *pathology of social
bodies.* Why should the philosopher elude in
that way familiar problems which perhaps are the
most difficult of all? He said to my brother
and me:

"I have never gone contrary to your wishes or
interfered with your somersaults or those changes
of mind in young people which are sometimes very
difficult to follow — changes which make grave
men indignant. You must know that I have
pondered over the rights and duties of a father of a
family. At what line does his power end? Within
what limits can he exercise that power?"

Every day we had reason to feel the benefit of
the largeness of his ideas. We gave ourselves up
to him completely without any drawback and without false modesty. We threw ourselves on his indulgence; no confession was too dearly bought
for us. Reprimand he used very little. Upon
hearing of one of my follies he still preserved his
tenderest smile, and then, going back in memory
over his past life, recited for my edification this
circumstance and that similar error, which he had
paid for in this or that way.

Above all things he had a horror of a lie:
"Don't try to deceive me; your eyes and tone of
voice betray you. How do you expect me to
counsel you, if you send me off on a false trail?"
Then he added: "As to you, my little fellows,

I live again in your youth; this prolongation of life is delightful. When you rush up and kiss me in a hurry, wishing to elude my sagacity, I might enumerate all the tricks, one after the other, wherewith you are sure that you can escape from your old father. Punish yourselves! Give yourselves the necessary training! But explain to me your scruples and state your regrets and tell me of those bitter embarrassments of youth which cause one to bite one's pillow in the darkness of the night with a groan."

He thought that the first duty of a father was to be morally the comrade of his son. He recalled with terror a moving incident in Montaigne wherein old Marshal de Montluc, I think, is in a state of desperation because he lost his son, and never gave the poor fellow a chance to divine what a passion he really had for him.

He listened patiently to all our theories, however extravagant, leaving the care of calming us to circumstances. He seemed to be particularly desirous of seeing us think for ourselves, out of reach of all influences. For in the domain of intelligence he had a perfect horror of imitation: "One of the most terrible statements is that made by Lucretius, namely, 'that the human race exists for very few persons.'

"I can remember a multitude of faces and of hours spent in gossip. I could very easily draw the reckoning of the new individualities and new ideas; some of them who are too easily impressed repeat the lessons they have learned in books and newspapers; others are the idols of a party or of a doctrine — what followers they have! And what a delight also when one hears a sincere accent! Surprises are not lacking; that man there whom nobody has noted, who is lost among his neighbors, suddenly enters into a ray of light, starts out against the background and detaches himself.

"On the evening of a first night the lobbies of a theatre present the image of life. Each one puts his neighbor to the question and fears to express himself without support: 'Don't you think so? . . . What is your opinion, dear master?' . . . Is it not a strange thing, that notwithstanding the herd, the works are classified nevertheless, and a division is made into the handsome and the ugly, and well founded reputations emerge?"

How many times have we not stirred up this difficult problem of the artist's personality! A given man will enlist great hopes, begin with a vigorous and novel work and suddenly, as though he had stopped because worn out and at the end of his inventiveness, write no more. The intensity of the wheels that revolve in the brain escapes criticism. Very often reflection acts as a poison, because reflection elaborates a work in secret; that is why my father counselled the study of nature, its forms and its shades as beyond everything else.

He was nervous at thought which devours its own substance: "That admirable writer has a surprising power for destruction," said he, talking of the philosopher Nietsche. The constantly bitter and sarcastic form of his aphorisms also repulsed him. But especially he reproached him for "having never sufficiently taken the air," *i. e.* gone to Nature for instruction.

It is only a few years now that I have learned to understand the depth of that doctrine which forces the writer to go outside himself and not lose contact with the life around one. The first condition requisite to intellectual joy is the organization of sensations and sentiments. Weariness comes quickly, if one or the other does not renew itself, but allows itself to be worn to the bone. That is the pitfall of analysis.

Now my father was analyzing all the time, but he stopped before he became tired. He had pushed his thinking machine to the highest possible tension. He extracted a most surprising use from the smallest circumstances. That explains why, in spite of his fits of illness and his sufferings, in spite of the attacks of an implacable malady, he preserved to the very end that second sight and that freshness of impression which caused every one who approached him to marvel.

It is quite certain that knowledge and observation when carried to such a degree are two grand springs of happiness. The deep-lying reason for this consists of the fact that one's personality becomes complete and bold. One feels oneself all the more *oneself*, the greater the number of problems one has tackled, and the more of those solutions which the mathematicians call "elegant" have been found for them. In that sense "elegance" was one of the remarkable qualities of Alphonse Daudet. Moral hygiene was his preoccupation. Wounded in his body and condemned to a restricted existence, he might apply all those cares to the nobler part of his spirit.

One day I complimented him on having trained his imagination: "Of a certainty," answered he, "I have always imposed as limits upon my imagination verisimilitude and virtue. I know well its misty domain, those strange countries where fancy is able to carry the heaviest load. But a novelist should not permit himself to employ the mental debauches of a lyrical writer. Besides, before everything else I demand emotion and when the human proportions have been overdone emotion loses itself."

He was forever praising to me tact: "If you wish, it is a minor quality, yet nothing is complete without it. Tact alone causes that little shudder which runs through the reader from head to foot and, winning his confidence, hands him over to the author. Literary tact! Many a time it insists upon hard sacrifices. I have been forced to slash pitilessly this fine speech and that brilliant episode in order to remain in measure. . . .

"But what is far better than the application of any principle, no matter how good, is a gift, a feeling of what is superfluous and what is necessary, the taste for harmony and for proportion. Owing to the complexity of our impressions, we moderns have lost, it appears, that clear and limpid observation of the ancients, that immediate realization of a sober and perfect art. In Rabelais and Montaigne, in whom humanism is mixed with an intoxication that is genius, a delicate flower with a Latin or Greek perfume suddenly unfolds itself in the wildwood of maxims and descriptions — as it were a miracle of revival. With what delight does one not inhale it! How one admires it! How it lights up the page!"

One can see how generalized were the counsels which he gave to beginners in literature. That was because he believed a spontaneous and individual effort was the indispensable condition to success: "The preachments of elderly persons only serve to make people yawn with weariness. Every one must win his brevet at his own expense."

A particular line in which the "vendor of happiness" made his appearance was, for example, the exposition of principles by the aid of which we may avoid envy, tartness and bitterness, which are parasitical plants of the literary profession.

"It is certain that in my time people did not devour their ancestors as they do to-day. Money, dirty money, had not begun then to trouble their minds, nor yet the bait of 'big editions.' That is a modern scourge. People did not have any ambition to reach that enormous diffusion and start the rowdy-dow which now seems to be a mark of success. For us success lay far more in the appreciation of five or six great comrades whom we venerated than the invasion of the show-cases."

At every turn he came back again to that "pleasure of admiring," the charm of which is lost. The most brilliant and precious souvenirs for that generation of writers were the afternoons at Flaubert's. "Pshaw, we shall never sell our-selves, shall we?" Émile Zola used to say with a touch of melancholy. But regrets vanished at the sound of the "fine thunder" which rolled about all sorts of discussions—a tumult of ideas and words. Silent and "hard to read," Tour-guéneff sat by himself in a corner, keeping his actual impressions for himself alone, but esteemed by all. Not until after his death were they to know what his impressions were, and then they made men sad.

Maupassant already showed himself timidly and Flaubert was boasting of his first attempts. There were also several scientists, such as the illustrious Pouchet from the museum, who in that society played the *rôle* of Berthelot at the Magny dinner.

I have often heard Goncourt or my father regret these warm-hearted meetings in which the word "confraternity" had a meaning and in which the philosophy of passing events ran the gauntlet of half a dozen powerful brains, which contact with one another and the desire to shine roused to fever heat: "We kept the best of ourselves for those meetings. One would think to himself: I shall tell them this; or else, I shall read that page and take their advice on it. No truckling, no servility! Neither pupils nor masters, but comrades; respectful to the older men, warming themselves in the reflection of their glory and proving by their choice that in our profession there is something else beside money and vanity."

I recalled all this at the cemetery of Père Lachaise on a pallid and sorrowful winter day, the while that Émile Zola said farewell to his old friend in a few sublime words. Let people discuss as much as they will concerning romanticism or naturalism, concerning the usefulness or the defects of schools, that was a fine literary review which united in the same enthusiasms Gustave Flaubert, Ivan Tourguéneff, Émile Zola, Edmond de Goncourt, Alphonse Daudet, Guy de Maupassant, Gustave Toudouze and a few others.

That was no cenaculum where disappointed ambitions meet to dine, that was no scandal shop where absentees are torn to pieces. And when Flaubert died I can still see the sorrow they all felt; a few days before there had been a reunion of the faithful at Croisset, a little literary picnic, from which they returned delighted. Similarly I recall the week that preceded the death of my father and the dinner in memory of Balzac, organized to renew the fine traditions of old. There were Zola, Barras, Anatole France, Bourget and my father; it was a cordial and charming meeting. Among many subjects that of death was spoken of. Bourget recalled the fact that in his last moments Taine had asked to have a page of Sainte-Beuve read to him " in order to hear something that was clear."

There was a unanimous admiration to be noted
among them for the great critic of Port-Royal, the
writer of the *Lundis*. As we were returning in the
carriage, happy and excited, my father said to me:
"Such love-feasts are indispensable. They whip
the spirit up, they beautify things. By exchanging
ideas we penetrate each other's brains. We see
the same fact and same episode appreciated in all
kinds of ways in accordance with the characters
and habits of the different men. Poor little dinner!
I thought of my Goncourt! *He will soon make
himself clear.*"

During the dinner a eulogy was uttered over
Cherbuliez, whom one of us had made a resolve
regularly to imitate in the future. All of us venerated the modesty of that great writer, who has
prosecuted his labors consistently and written so
many remarkable pages without ranging himself
under any banner: "Thus you see," murmured
my father, "that no effort is lost. Those who represent our humanity as an unrest like the swarming
of an ant-heap tell a lie. This evening we spoke
with one voice in attestation of the power and authority of him to whom we owe *Ladislas Bolski*,
Comte Kostia and twenty magnificent novels."

According to Alphonse Daudet, in order to reach
happiness there was but one path only, that of
justice.

I am here closest yet to the heart which I have
endeavored to unveil to you. I can affirm that the
sense of justice was the most certain and most
vivid stimulus for the talent of my father — if

indeed genius is made up of excessive sentiments which come into accord with each other through the privilege of a harmonious nature, and if the art of writing comes from the fact that these sentiments set in motion vigorous and picturesque words and put to work a corresponding verbal force, and if moreover, between the convictions which the brain sets in order and those movements of the hand that fix their formulas on paper, there are direct and profound paths of connection.

If moral qualities affect even the form itself, I may add without fear of mistake that my father had the literary style of justice.

The very smallest episodes of life show him passionately interested in what is true, an irreconcilable adversary of what is false. No one recognized his own errors better than he and no one acknowledged more readily that he made mistakes. He was constantly repeating: "It would be a martyrdom to me to insist upon holding an iniquitous opinion." In the many questions that arise in a family he was taken as the judge. He seated himself "beneath the oak," that is to say, he listened and weighed the complaints with extreme patience, turning and twisting his pen or his eyeglass, his face gently inclined, sometimes with a sudden smile in his look.

Once being completely informed, he pondered a few seconds, and then, without solemnity, but with a grave gentleness which impressed one, he gave his advice and explained his reasons. It was very rarely that he did not convince. I have tried

to give some account to myself for his instant
action on the mind of a young man as violent as I
was, one so often blinded by self-interest.

I discovered two reasons, one instinctive and the
other moral; the first is the sound of his enchant-
ing voice, which was such as one could hardly
imagine; and I was not the only one to submit to
its charm. It had so many inflections and such
gentle ones that it seemed as if several persons, all
of whom were dear to you, were addressing you,
each one with a particular accent.

The second reason is a suppleness of mind which
allowed him to enter into the views of the man
whom he wished to persuade, merge himself in
his nature and so lead him to the wisest results by
pathways on which they gradually met. That is
the quality which produces the great romancer,
the creator of types. At the bottom of every
genius there is seductiveness.

That is the way I explained to myself the dislike my father had for the platform. His energy
was one the farthest possible removed from the
orator's art. No artifice, no hypocrisy! He could
win over a single mind; he could not persuade a
crowd. For a crowd some such speech is necessary as that by Antony in Shakespeare's *Julius
Cæsar*, which we many a time perused without
exhausting our admiration.

Another speech is more fitting to the individual
— for instance, that which Agrippa d'Aubigné reports in such a splendid way as uttered by Admiral
Coligny, the speech he made at night to his trem-

bling wife, both of them in bed, whilst the tocsin of the massacres was sounding.

There again I find the Christian mark in my father. The religion that inculcates pardon and sacrifice substituted through the confessional another form of action for the eloquence of the ancients, a form better adapted to that individualism which may be discovered in its germs in the sermons of Jesus. Without a public or the prestige of distinction to aid one, the problem is to influence people person to person and convince their minds. The more numerous the auditors whom the words address, the vaguer must those words be.

By addressing a small number, speech becomes particularized and increases its chance of being more exact than it would be otherwise.

Alphonse Daudet had made a profound study of vanity.

"Although pride is a lever which lifts the entire individual and stops at nothing, vanity diminishes conscientiousness. Pride, which is a tension of living forces, may exasperate justice or brutally tear it from the heart; but vanity destroys it underhand. Insinuating and not to be grappled with, vanity glides into the secret folds of our nature and affects the least visible causes of our action. Very often we ask ourselves why a certain man has acted contrary to his character and with such extraordinary bad tact. It is because he has yielded to the power of vanity, the most experienced and crafty of masters."

9

Not seldom did it happen that some fact was observed in current life to corroborate his conversations on ethics, offering him a demonstration as in a picture. Among his acquaintances my father possessed one type of the Vain Man.

"He is coming to-day; try to be present. We will make him *trot*. It's one of his happy days, we may hope to get some remarkable phrases — some of the phrases which spring involuntarily from the ruling passion, like those which Balzac used to find to suit his dramatic moments."

The bell rang. It was the Vain Man. Even before he sat down he began at once to entertain us with his "success," boast of his family and himself, bring out the differences in the situations of himself and his friend and suggest the presence of a malady which "compels the most active to remain in their arm-chair and deprives them of that exercise of the body which the brain needs." My father has often made the remark that vanity and excessive pride end in cruelty; the *moitrinaires*, as he called them, lose all social and moral sense and no longer sympathize with any one but themselves; whatever in the whole universe stands in the light of their overwhelming personality seems to them to merit the worst of disasters.

Meanwhile the Vain Man continued. He had reached the point of tears, thinking of his own particular health while looking upon his sick friend. Then my father interrupted him. He assured him that he had never felt better than at that moment: "My gay spirits have come back;

I am smoking my pipe again, which is a happy symptom, and I am working splendidly. Very soon I shall go out to Champrosay. There in the green foliage and in the sunlight it is certain that I shall finish my book before two months are up."

The other made a face. All of a sudden and without transition and in the most natural way in the world his malicious interlocutor related to him the following fable:

"A rat full of self-sufficiency and therefore envious in his nature went to make a visit to his friend, another rat, who had just happened to have poisoned himself. The wretched creature was turning and twisting with pain in his magnificent domain, but the visitor seated in front of him suffered more frightful agonies yet, which were caused by his despair at the sight of such splendors.

"'You seem to me rather yellow?'

"'Why no, nothing is the matter. It is so comfortable here! But how is it with you?'

"'Oh, as for me, I am very well indeed, I assure you.'

"And they both of them died seated there, one opposite the other; but the envious one died first."

During the recital of this fable I was very much amused at the hesitating expression of the visitor, who only understood about half the meaning. When he was gone my father laughed heartily.

"The dear boy is longing for my death. His usual exclamation is: 'What, you are at work!'

Do you not feel that in him the 'I' amounts to
a regular hump? Oh, what a delightful study,
what a gay and thoroughly French one it would
be, to write about men like him and all the
envious ones! One of those damned souls confessed to me one day with a contraction of his
whole face: *You don't know how much it hurts!*
That man absolutely enjoyed the details of my
pain when I related them to him. I perceived
this and deprived him of the pleasure and from
that time on he took a hatred to me. He was at
the head of a very important administrative department and was a sort of autocrat. Knowing
his mania, his employees and those in places
below him never appeared before him unless
groaning and lamenting, pretending to pains they
did not feel, or with a bandage round their heads."

Numberless are the accounts in the little note-
books bearing on envy and vanity, but I do not
want to take the flowers away that grace those
marvellous pages which will soon appear in print:
"When I read my notes over again, I am aware
of the difficulty of drawing a character containing
that combination of follies which vanity provokes,
nourishes and increases. It is all gas, emptiness,
meat without nutriment!"

He observed with attention the action of vanity
on children and women. The simplicity of this
vice in the latter delighted him: "They are just
like negresses with their glass beads!" He has
even noted the vanity of sick people which causes
them to exaggerate their sufferings. A little sick

man at Lamalou confessed to him his content at
the sympathy provoked by the fine appearance
of his carriage which made him " different from
the others."

" Wretched comedians that we are, and dupes
of our own comedies ! " He remarked how rare
are men who are simple and sure of themselves,
and especially those who, when in public places,
are not in the least troubled by the fact that they
know they are observed and watched. " How can
we, writing men, escape from self-consciousness
when our least gestures are spied out by a gossipy
press, and when people seem to ask our opinion
upon all sorts of subjects as far as possible distant
from those about which we do know something ! "

Actors have been a precious mine of information for him (remember Delobelle) in respect to
vanity: " In those enlarging mirrors that actors
are, one sees the movements of body, turn of eyes
and the attitudes common to all men — but deformed and enlarged by the optics of the stage
and by the effect of the foot-lights."

I hasten to add, in order that I may not anger
the most susceptible of all corporations, that
Alphonse Daudet had the most affectionate sympathy for a great many actors. He often made
the remark, how few among them were mean, dis-
honest or tricky and how actors help each other.
" These creatures have a factitious existence, reality has almost no hold on them at all. When
could they find time to rediscover themselves and
to become like other people between the repeti-

tions and representations of plays? An actor who had returned to private life confessed to me the deep pain which that change caused him, like the blindness of an owl in the noonday sun, and the envy he felt for his comrades who remained the other side of the foot-lights, that mysterious and enchanted side, where human illusions are turned to flesh and blood."

He had an actual affection for certain comedians. Amongst others I would note Coquelin, Porel and La Fontaine. The latter astonished him by his vast memory and his numberless souvenirs of the grand period, particularly his reminiscences of Frédéric Lemaître, who was the king of that sort of man and type of his profession, a person in whom the fine qualities and defects of his class were pushed to extremes.

As to actresses, my father always showed himself amiable and respectful to them. But this very respect was one way of avoiding that familiarity of the green-room, that vulgar use of thee and thou which he hated, just as he did everything which was not sincere. He always counselled me, with respect to them, to avoid mixing dreams with life and to fly from the disillusionment of the reality. It was his opinion that those of them whose business it is to change souls as they change costumes, however frank and charming they may be, offer very few guarantees to a faithful heart. I was never able to make him admit that that very suppleness itself was their charm. He considered it was monstrous that the desire of

a single person should be excited by sympathy
with the desires of all, and that one should admire
in a woman the admiration that other men felt for
her. That was one of our quarrels. I persist in
believing that, well informed as he was concerning
the theatrical world, he ought to have written a
sort of modern *Wilhelm Meister* for our enjoyment, in which his familiar philosophy would have
been increased by various episodes in the eternal
novel of comedy.

So it was that if Alphonse Daudet loved justice,
no less did he hold exactness high, and that which
infringed on the natural pleased him not at all.
Ways of looking at things form as it were a chain.
Vanity and affectation are perpetual causes for
wickedness. What a skilful enemy of lies and
hypocrisy! How little was he moved by false
tears! How difficult it was to make him believe
in them! A change of the voice, the slightest
trembling of a face, the least embarrassment
in a gesture, were enough to warn him. There-
upon he himself took on a change at once and
became harsh and severe. It was insupportable
to him to know that people were discounting
his kindliness.

He made a special point of what he called
" reversed injustice," namely that which people
use with regard to rich and happy people; it
seemed to him a sentimental monstrosity like
" Russian pity," which is limited to criminals and
low women. This kind of affectation, which is so
often found to-day, was odious to him; it consists

in showing sympathy for those unfortunates only
who have less than 3,000 francs a year and considering a catastrophe that befalls millionaires and
those in power well merited: " I myself," said he,
" have often to combat feelings of this kind in my
own breast. They are detestable feelings, just as
everything is which produces castes before the
face of destiny. Bad is everything which adds to
injustice, though it be an exaggeration of justice
and an ill-conceived need of social revenge."

He had a chance of noting very illustrious
examples of that " reversed justice " at the time of
the disaster when the Bazar de la Charité burned
down. Many " friends of the people " pretended
not to mourn over the " roasts " at " ten millions
apiece," as I heard them savagely called. My
father was very angry: " *Cabotinage* — electioneer-
ing views meant for the bars in corner grog-shops!
Those who showed pity and courage in all the horror
of those cries and flames were the humble ones
and, at one and the same time, the brave ones of
this world. The people are worthier than their
representatives ! "

Among our recent notorious hypocrites the
demagogue and false Jacobin were the object of
his disdain. He had seen the pothouse politician
close by — one trembling hand upon his heart,
the other firmly fixed in the pocket of his neighbor! He kept an indestructible recollection of
such men; in his *Soutien de Famille* will be
found such a character in a masterly full-length
portrait, just the sort of man he knew how to paint.

What nausea political life gave to such an enemy of poses and attitudes! Perpetually shocked by the spectacle of the parliament men, his sense of justice was turned into anger. What exasperated him more than anything else was the placarding of big sentiments: " These fellows have an idea that elevated sentiments are nothing more than booby-catchers, and it is only necessary to make motions to suit them. I often ask myself, how it is possible that a man of real worth like Clémenceau was able to pass several years in such surroundings? "

Some years ago, at the time of the election of the existing president, I went to the Congress at Versailles. On my return I gave an account of what I had seen. That frightful witch's caldron, those livid, grinning, hypocritical faces, those personages all in black, wandering, spying, watching, begging, prowling and baying through the galleries filled with pale statues! What airs of importance, what arms uplifted, what whisperings in each other's ears! The greater part of them seemed to be worm-eaten and twisted magistrates, mumbling words like " constitutional, anti-constitutional in the first place "—others, in the midst of a group of grinning idiots, relating terrible secrets to each other in a low voice. Throughout all this rabble there appeared, clearly visible upon those tricky and composite masks, the vanity that befalls people in possession, the vanity at being able to dispose of the future of poor France.

As I was finishing this picture my father, who

had been listening to me with brilliant eyes,
exclaimed: "Oh, our poor France! Whenever
I came near a man like that, I was always stunned
by the fact of his worthlessness, of his prodigious
foolishness. Except in the rarest cases, we see in
parliament the dregs of the country, the doctor
who has no patients, the lawyer without briefs,
the veterinary surgeon whom the animals are
afraid of — but the electors do not seem to be
afraid. According to the vulgar expression it is
just so much " cat-lap," and our mouths are full of
this cat-lap.

The dislocations of these wretched jumping-jacks
are reproduced by the press and carried round
about the world. Ah! it would be a bad outlook,
if we had nothing else but our national representation to represent us!

There is a certain kind of man one often meets
who put my father quite beside himself. It is
he who "for lack of a label I shall call the leveller
of opinions and events."

While there are some who inflate everything
and see an army in five soldiers and a mutiny in a
little meeting, etc., there are others who voluntarily
diminish, annihilate and take from people and
things their importance and vigor. The Protestant temperament, for instance, levels everything
to a sort of negative condition, to a vague neutral
idea and a perpetual condition of "not quite that."
This is one of the forms of Philistinism. In this
category may be placed the man who is so dis-
proportionately proud that everything which turns

his attention away from his own deeds and actions
exasperates him and seems to him of no importance: " Really my dear fellow, as far as that now?
Do you really think so? " or " Are you quite sure
of it?" or "Are you not letting yourself yield to
an excitement, which certainly is legitimate,
but . . . " and so forth.

On hearing such arguments my father would
murmur: " Tartarin from the other side." But as
soon as the other, having reached some personal
adventure, forgot all his prudence and grew excited and feverish, he would dish him up his own
statements again: " Be calm, my dear fellow. . . .
Are you not exaggerating? Where are your
proofs?" And all this, with an eye glittering
with fun through the short puffs of smoke from his
little pipe.

I enter into these details in order to sketch as
well as I can a truthful portrait of a man who was
remarkable in the little as well as in the great
circumstances of life, one gifted with a superior
sense of the ludicrous.

He considered that the sense of the ridiculous
was indispensable to happiness: " Irony is the
salt of existence. It allows us to tolerate beautiful sentiments, which without it might be *too
beautiful.* I love familiar virtue which works behind the scenes without tunic or buskins and
without phrases; I love a kindness of heart so
discreet that it does not even look upon itself.
For pride is so subtle that it satisfies itself with
monologues delivered before the looking-glass;

they are just as destructive of simplicity as a
speech delivered from the platform. I love charity which is so hidden that one can never distinguish the face of the donor, and so no gratitude
can be exacted, which alas, is the vestibule to
hatred. I like a shamefaced pity without pity's
mask, without the delight of the hand which is
stretched forth and without that secret thought
which so often exists, that you are *happy not to be
in his shoes.*

"The person who thinks about a wretched one
who lacks a home during the night or in the
storm, whilst he is warm and in shelter between his
blankets, that man is not far from that Sadism
which increases personal enjoyment by the spectacle of the sorrows of others. I know well the
false look of virtue, the alibi-virtue, the gentleman
just getting gray who from two to five in the afternoon distributes a great many tracts and some few
soup tickets to little working girls, and, along
about six o'clock, goes to see whether they really
are in good condition or not; and the society lady
who mends a pair of trousers for an old man for
effect, with her eyes fixed upon the clock, dreaming about some wealthy young man.

"Oh, charity's mark, charity's grimace ! Behold
a modish 'visit to the poor.' 'The Revolutionary
goat': — The dear, good lady, her dear, good
children and faithful Bridget — the voice from
the throat — the slice of corned beef — grand-
mamma who is coughing in her alcove — the new-
born child pressed to a cold bosom — 'Be of good

cheer, my friends! Here is a pasty which is not made of cardboard and here is some Bordeaux wine. . . . Pluck up your spirits. . . . You there shall be a forester. . . . And you shall take a part in a play of four acts; you will solve the whole social question. . . . . Farewell, my friends, emotion strangles me. . . . How delightful it is here in your house. . . . Come my children. . . . Yes, I am your dear little mother. . . . Who gave you that nasty, filthy thing? That disgusting little girl? Throw it away at once. It smells badly ! '

"Meantime, the benefactors having left the house, the grandmother scuttles out of her alcove, they drink the Bordeaux wine, dance about and stuff themselves with the corned beef. Ha, ha, ha ! what a lark! What a mug she had, that old Bridget ! Wretched little dwarfs ! shoot the pasty. . . ." and so forth.

After this scene of comedy my father became serious again: " Irony preserves us from such follies as these. It teaches the benefactor that he must not put his title on his visiting cards and the virtuous man that he must hide himself away from virtue even more than from vice, and the pitiful soul that pity, if it is not discreet, is the greatest raiser of violences in the world. Consider during the Revolutionary epoch that glittering show of fine sentiments, that fashion of sympathetic attitudes, that zeal for sonorous charity, for alms in metaphors, for equality and fraternity in Latin ! Victims are careful of their words. But executioners

are drunk with a tearful philosophy. Well, in
such mixtures as that one may seek in vain for
irony. It has disappeared along with 'mansue-
tude,' which is its comrade.

" Has it not a tendency to evolve itself from every
extreme opinion? Women do not like it, nor do
children, nor savages, nor the common folk, nor
heroes." He smiled with eyes wide upon the past,
stirring up old extinct flames; and in that smile
there was a multitude of continuations; then he
continued :

" During the war of 1870, which was my great
period of schooling, I was able to take stock of
the anger which irony provoked in the common
people. In my company there was a question of
replacing the captain by way of election. They
begged me in my position as a decorated soldier
and former member of the army, to make a
speech ! Imagine, former member of the army at
thirty years of age ! I yield and ascend the platform which is odious to me and simply paralyzes
me. I begin my speech, then stumble, get all
twisted up and end by calling out: ' Oh, get out !
I don't know anything about this captain, any
more than you do !' Then I climb down from
the platform in a glacial silence."

He stated that he was able because of his long
experience to bring aid and comfort to the most
touchy people, without leaving a single hateful
recollection in them.

" One summer afternoon on a marvellously calm,
warm and golden day, while seated at the cross-

roads of the Greak Oak in the Sénart woods with your mother and the children, I saw at a little distance a wretched van full of gypsies — the children all in rags, a single woman with harsh features and a gloomy man who was peeling potatoes. I took Lucien by the arm and moved toward them. (I had my alms all ready.) They saw us coming. The woman grew very red. The man looked gloomier than ever. I seized hold of a brat with eyes like a torch and I glued my piece of money into his little moist hand.

"He dashed away like a regular wild cat. 'Thanks,' murmured the woman. The man had never budged. But I shall long remember this walk of the *benefactor* to the obliged ones. The obliged ones — what a frightful word, one which justifies ingratitude!"

This chapter would not have a fit ending if I did not sum up now Alphonse Daudet's opinion in regard to that great human problem, the search after happiness.

1. There are as many forms of happiness as there are kinds of individuals. In order to get at them and teach them, therefore, it is necessary to *see and see clearly.*

2. There is no happiness without a strong notion of right and justice. One of the moral levers of the world consists in this axiom: — *Everything pays.*

3. Seeming deviations from justice, even excessive and prolonged ones, are merely a defect in our own observation. In this case it is a matter

of too narrow a combination of facts; in that, it is a question of some particular point which conceals the rest. Or, again, observation dashes itself upon some coarse obstacle and does not go to the bottom of things.

4. There exists a science of justice which is not the code Napoleon, but the *dynamic* of justice, which is nothing else than a search for a perpetual moral equilibrium. A man is not able to have even a glimmer of this science before his fortieth year.

5. The *instinct* for justice is equivalent to the knowledge of justice. Very coarse natures may contain in themselves a much more vivid and pure gleam of justice than very wonderful thinkers. That was seen by Christianity.

6. *Pain* and *pity* are the precious helpers of *justice*, as long as they do not become excessive, because justice always remains in the middle term. When it is extreme, pain hardens and renders people insensible to the outer world. When it is extreme, pity becomes monstrous and loses sight of its principal objective, which is to solace the sorrows of man. And lastly justice, when it is extreme, brings with it the most extraordinary consequences in the direction of beauty and unhappiness.

7. The search after happiness, and this is a capital point, should always apply itself to *others*, not to oneself. A man should not try to escape from any moral responsibility or any social solidarity.

8. In the family happiness is *traditional.* The love of parents regulates and transmits it. In this sense the greatest and only irreparable misfortune is "the loss of those we love."

9. One should never despair.

10. The man who has the gift and the taste of *observation* or of *imagination*, has a greater capacity in himself than others, whatever appearance there may be to the contrary. The *constant exercising of the mind* which gives suppleness to ideas is one cause for happiness in cases where *work for work's sake* is only a means to escape from life.

11. Egotism is a cause of unhappiness. Egotism which attributes to itself the origin of all sentiments without wishing to benefit by them in other respects is a cause of unhappiness.

12. In the search after happiness a special place ought to be accorded to *pardon* and to *sacrifice.*

It should be well understood that my father did not give this rigid and didactic form to his instruction, but I think it is my duty to his method, which resulted from experiences like those of Socrates, Montaigne and Lamennais, to add some apposite things which often cropped up in his conversations.

The interest of these few axioms and others which I will note lies in the fact that they formed a rule of conduct. I have seen them applied with a consistency which astonished me, and caused me to reach the conclusion that the most generous springs of action in our nature form an integral part of our tissues in the very depths of our personality.

I cannot let the question of pardon and sacrifice go without insisting on them. Life without pardon seemed intolerable to my father: "Down here error and vice grow in the very best fields. It is not sufficient to tear them up. One ought to forget their very former place."

One day he explained to me how the greater number of moral faculties correspond with the intellectual faculties. It is for this reason that pardon is more difficult to those who have excellent memories: "Sometimes it has been necessary for me to make prodigious efforts in order to excuse some little treachery of a friend, or some outrage to gratitude. That is because my confounded memory brings before me phenomena which are past with a frightful air of life, *as if under the bright light of some great sentiment.* I recollect things as well as a jealous person or a criminal."

La Petite Paroisse is a very far developed study in *pardon.* As was always the case, he had taken his models from life: "Imaginary deductions made by the author are quite large enough sacrifices to the unreal. At least let the source be human."

As always he had grouped a multitude of particular examples round the central case — in the book in question as it happens pardon is in combat with *jealousy.* There was that gleam of sentiment which Alphonse Daudet discovered in his memory. How true also is this other sentiment from his lips:

"It is impossible for a sincere author not to put his whole self in his work ; which does not mean that he relates an episode from his own life.   But he *animates his own ways of thinking and feeling :* he dresses them and makes persons of them. That which strikes us in the world and that which we perceive and understand the best *is that which we divine to be similar to ourselves.*"

And since he wished to illuminate everything through examples drawn from reality, and since he refused to follow me in my metaphysical digressions, he added :

" Imagine that you are the victim of some piece of ingratitude.   At first your anger is vivid and you think only of the special case in point.   Having become a little calm, you begin to philosophize. You think of all those ungrateful persons who exist in the world.   There you are, vibrating between that idea and its contradictions, ready to weep from thankfulness, ready to scent out the rancorous and forgetful, the debtors and bad friends in the drawing-rooms and even in the street! That is the *period of coincidence.*   Then it is that you re-mark and discover everywhere circumstances very like your own; and the hallucination continues. Well, with novelists these various associations reach the height of a paroxysm.   The knack is to lend them life, make them step forth from their abstract and purely moral regions and launch them — into the *worldly tumult,* as the Jansenists said.

" From this it results that we only understand

that which environs us according as we experience
it. We live two parallel existences which complete
each other: one an existence of emotion, the
other of observation. To give prominence to one
or the other of these existences is to give oneself
up to unhappiness. Happiness lies in their
equilibrium."

The farther along in my reminiscences I get, the
more it seems hard to me to give to those who
read me an impression of the sincerity and serenity
which one of his conversations left behind it. Consider that my father always chose the best moment
and the finest situation to explain his doctrines.
Thanks to him I have in my soul landscapes which
are connected with marvellous moral dissertations;
with good reason he held that what is the most
profitable in sensibility and poetic creation is just
this harmony between the inner and the outer
world.

"Plato's commotions, those of Socrates and
nearer our time of Lamennais, show a lively desire
not to separate the two natures : human nature and
what is exterior to it. On the one hand the skies
and terrestrial views and their moving shades
become so many vigorous, profound and unforgettable images; on the other hand, noble dreams of
imagination add their own mysterious harmony to
the trees and meadows, to clouds and rivers, and
become so many inscriptions, so many signs and
symbols."

And how this adroit philosopher seized upon
the *fatigue point*, the moment when this same en-

thusiasm no longer exists, however vast and
interesting the subject might be ! Then he suddenly interrupted himself and slipped into one of
his delightful pranks, or one of those joyous stories
which made the hours passed with him so short.

IV.

NORTH AND SOUTH.

THE merit of having placed in a striking light a type which up to his time had been merely a caricature, "the man of the South," belongs to Alphonse Daudet.

Such an attempt required the hand of a Southerner, who knows the strength and weakness of his own race, but one also who is subtle enough to place himself outside of himself, observe himself and seek in his own gestures and springs of action whatever in them there may be indigenous and national and different from others.

Among the many human problems to which my father was attached and to which he devoted himself, it may be there is no other which he has so passionately followed out through its different phases and aspects.

"This question is not interesting to France alone. Every country has its North and South, two poles between which characters and temperaments swing. It would be just as exaggerated to ascribe all the moral variations in man to questions of climate, as it would be silly to take no account of pronounced differences which variations in climate bring about."

It was while making researches on this point that one of his master qualities appeared to me in the most vivid light: "Total absence of pedantry."

Our epoch, which pretends to be liberal, is one of those in which perhaps the principle of *authority* in intellectual matters is the most frequently invoked. The revolutionaries merely aspire to found schools, establish a dogma and organize the faithful. The independents at once erect a banner upon which one may read in giant letters the word "independence," and then they start with denying in their adversaries the least good sense and rightful intention. A new kind of hypocrisy, "scientific hypocrisy," has recently come to be established. A multitude of unfinished and confused ideas hiding behind obscure terms and Greek and Latin compounds have become the weapons in the hands of insupportable jackanapeses, who brandish them on all occasions.

I have never heard my father employ a word which did not belong to common speech. He had an insurmountable and well grounded horror for newly invented words; for most of them are "monsters," disquieting examples of "civilized barbarism," formed outside of every rule. However wide a question was and however involved it might appear, he proposed first of all to *remain clear*, and he applied the rule of Descartes, which is to begin with the smaller difficulties in order to reach the greater.

I have repeated many times that he based his

labors upon reality, which he tested in order to
be sure of support; and that he recognized in
very few *facts* and phenomena that certainty and
limpidity, which allow them to act as bases and
points of departure.

The feeling of his race gave him a double touch
of certainty, an intellectual and a physical one.
A single case of the Southern accent delighted
him forthwith. In the railway coach, toward
morning, the apparition of olive trees and white
turnpikes through the smoky panes made him
" sing." That intoxication which the solution of
a mathematical problem gave to Descartes and
to Pascal, that same intoxication was felt by
Alphonse Daudet, the " imaginative observer,"
when in contact with his art and with his " earth."

He loved all those in literature and art who,
remembering their origins, beautify and sanctify
the corner where they have lived, the places which
they have frequented.

Certain people who think that that which is
not sorrowful cannot be profound have reproached the *Tartarin* volumes for their exaggeration. But that exaggeration is in the blood.
Sometimes it takes on the cold form one finds in
Bompard in *Numa Roumestan.* That makes it
all the funnier. It appears that the tree of jollity
growing along the valley of the Rhône still pushes
two vigorous branches toward Touraine and Normandy, one branch of irony in Champagne and
another toward the Île de France.

My father knew that " good humor " is necessary to every stage and degree of mind. It is a kind of illumination. To this virtue he owed the fact of having escaped the current of pessimism and kept his own character intact. Beside him the young people seemed old men. At any moment of the day and notwithstanding his pain he was always ready to laugh and make fun himself over the vagabondage in which his imagination indulged.

"Hurrah for Latin good sense!" How many a time did not that exclamation burst forth to close a discussion and sum up long theories. I can still hear him saying to a friend at the end of a philosophical dissertation from which he had escaped: "Just look there, my dear fellow, look at that rose-colored line of light away down there along the crests of the trees! is that not beautiful and is that not perfect? We are at a distance, I am short-sighted, and yet I can distinguish every leaf; I could believe I was in my own country."

In his *Quinze Ans de Mariage* which he left unfinished there is the story of a couple very different in nature, a combat between the North and the South. It is certainly a symbolical work, for according to him the life of France itself, in a large degree, has been determined by combat and opposition between these two elements, so different one from the other.

"There is neither the same way of feeling, nor the same way of seeing, nor the same way of expressing oneself. Sometimes the Southerners are as completely closed up as are stones; the

exuberance of their imagination wearies them.
Then they fall into a torpor, not at all unlike that of
drunkards reviving from a bout.

"As to their imagination, it differs from those of
the *Northmans* in these ways : it mixes up neither
the elements of things nor the kind of things and
even in its transports remains lucid. In the most
complex minds you will never notice that confused
interpenetration of aims, descriptions and figures,
which form the characteristic mark of a Carlyle
or a Browning or a Poe. Moreover the man of
the North will always reproach the man of the
South for the absence of shadows and mysterious
recesses.

"If we look at the most violent human passion,
love, we see that the Southerner makes of love the
main occupation of his life, but does not allow
himself to be thrown out of kilter by it. He likes
the gossip in it, the light frills and changing faces.
He detests the servitude it brings. For him it
becomes a pretext for serenades, delicate and
strained dissertations, for indulging in teasing and
caresses. It is with difficulty that he can compre-
hend the connection between love and death which
exists at the bottom of every Northern soul
and throws a mist of melancholy over its brief
delights."

One point there is to which he was constantly
returning : the ease with which the man of the
South deceives himself by the mirages which he
conjures up himself, the half sincere confusion
into which he allows himself to drift with a smile

as a corrective. In his talents one may find the impression of that kind of emotion which feels bashful at its own self and fears to go beyond the proper point. A part of the charm lies there; there is a safeguard for a reader with delicacy of mind in the guarantee that he will not have to blush for his own tears.

He used also to boast of the natural eloquence found among his compatriots. At the smallest rural meeting one might be surprised by a stirring speech given in a strong assured voice: "I did not inherit this kind of gift. My tongue gets twisted if it is necessary for me to express myself before more than ten people. My short-sightedness has something to do with it."

A subject for discussion that never ran dry was the problem of lying: "Is it fair to treat a man as a liar who becomes drunk with his own speech, and without any low purpose, without the instinct of deceiving or of getting the better of his neighbor, or of profit, endeavors to embellish his own life and that of others with stories which he knows are untrue, but which he would like to have true, or at any rate probable? Is Don Quixote a liar? And all those poets who wish to take us away from the actual and compass the globe in their wide-winged flights, are they liars?"

Besides, he was wont to insinuate, among Southerners people are not taken in. Every one in his own mind rearranges the proportions of things as they are. As Roumestan says: "It is a matter of focus."

Alphonse Daudet's compatriots feel no rancor
with regard to his jokes; they understood well
enough what an honor the writer did them, when
through the power of his pen he glorified and
published to the world their twists and turns of
manner: "I love my whole country, even down to
the food. Don't talk to me of heavy dishes, nor of
potatoes and weighty joints. An anchovy spread
on bread, some olives, figs and an aioli leaf — those
are the things I prefer. I envy the lot of shepherds, all alone in the midst of their herds, either
in the wide plains of the lower country, or on the
salted highlands of the Alps, between the marshes
and the stars."

For whomsoever has lived in a "mas" down
South in the same way as the "pacaces" or
herders of horses *L'Arlésienne* is a work very extraordinary in truthfulness. There one finds the principal types, the shepherd, the "baile" and the
"bailesse." "Naturals" are not rare. It is very
curious to see how Alphonse Daudet has grouped
all these elements and from their union has extracted
a moving tragedy in which the vigor, acuteness and
harmony of antique poems have come to life
again.

The story of a young Provençal man who committed suicide because of love, and two women
calling to each other across a vast plain, one with
a high, shrill voice, the other with a deep one —
that is the origin of the drama. My father often
spoke to me of it. He liked to work back in his
memory to the *directing lines*, and he applied to

this process great acuteness: "When I heard those two voices of women at twilight alternating through the blue space, I felt that they had impressed me in a singular way, and the plot of *L'Arlésienne* appeared to me as if in a sudden hallucination. In the same way one evening, just as the day ended, in front of the rose-colored and gilded ruins of the Tuileries, I had a vision of *Rois en Exil* and of that formula which closes my book; 'A mighty thing lies dead.'

This problem of the beginning of a work and of the earliest spark of suggestion occupied us very often. My father thought that Edgar Poe in his explanation of *The Raven* had forced the note and used his imagination after the first imagining:

"I believe that in the case of all creators there are accumulations of sentient force made without their knowledge. Their nerves, in a state of high excitation, register visions, colors, forms and odors in those half realized reservoirs which are the treasuries of poets. All of a sudden, through some influence or emotion, through some accident of thought, these impressions meet each other with the suddenness of a chemical combination. It has generally happened in that way with me. I have passed months and months in arranging a drama or book which emerged in one single second and emerged with all its details complete before my astonished mind. The more ardent the imagination, the more sudden and unexpected are these pictures. The entire work of Balzac pulsates with a fever of discovery and of impromptu."

I called his attention to the fact that this is a
kind of "secondary" dream and that, in the case
of poets, reality and recollection, living persons
and phantoms are constantly crossing and changing each other, and preserve nothing in common
at last except the kind of lyrical power which enlarges the features, the speech and the surroundings and arouses enthusiasm.

My father added: " This lyrical gift, this deep-
seated energy are perhaps nothing more than a
very profound feeling of race and origins. Goethe
is the complete German soul. It seems as if the
blood of Lord Byron carries in its flood the Anglo-
Saxon rage and the exasperated imaginings of an
entire people. Mistral is the exact mirror of the
South. . . ."

After a few moments of reflection he continued
modestly :

"Suppose we look to little persons for great
explanations. When I want to tune up my brain
and give it tone, I have recourse to what I have
seen in my youth. It is a habit my mind has taken
upon itself to give a place where every sentiment
has its stand. Words like "love," "felicity,"
"faith," "desire," do not remain inside of me in a
state of abstraction. They take figures to themselves and take part in events. *Well, the light which
environs them is always the light of my own country.*
It is beneath the sky of Provence that I establish
those traits of heroism, obligation and generosity.
In order that I may reach the point of the state of
trance and inspiration, I must have the sunlight

such as exists down there, and even in the course
of extreme suffering I keep recalling to myself
those turnpikes at white heat charged with a raw
intensity which burns me and is my despair."

He sang the praise of heat: "Heat brings our
temperaments to flowering, to fruit and to burgeon-
ing. It gives to the human being his own particular perfume and to sentiments their vehemence.
When accumulated in an individual and in a race,
it acts like a subtler kind of alcohol, or like some
delicate opium; it transfigures and renders divine.
It does not take from the delicate shades of a
character but renders them finer and more fugitive,
just as it supports the great curtain of creepers in
the forests of the tropics and at the same time the
army of giants; and the enormous serpent sleeps
in peace through excess of happiness, the while
his scales glitter and gleam.

"In the South laziness has invented the 'cagnard,' that little corner built of the stalks of the
cane, in which people lie torpid like boa-con-
strictors and roast themselves in the sun."

Then his face darkened : "These sensations
have to be paid for later. We, the transplanted
ones, are seized upon by this homicidal North
with its mists and rheumatism, its mournful rains
and sleet. Wet outside, we are burning within
and are the prey of a twofold nature. Then our
impressions become more tender. The North is
difficult on the question of the choice of words,
their value and their place in the sentence, much
more so than the lazy, voluptuous South. This

was the cause of Baudelaire's suffering, who
learned to know the exuberant nature and power
of heat in the course of his travels, and when he
returned to his own country, searched the whole
vocabulary for those vanished charms, at the
expense of his own brain :

"' Le monde s'endort dans une chaude lumière.' " [1]

So it was that the "transplanted ones" had the
benefit of his tender consideration : " Such is the
mystery of origin, that sometimes the traveller in a
distant land finds again his unknown stock and
blood and everything else that he has loved and
admired since his cradle, but which he knew only
in his dreams. What delicious intoxication to live
in the midst of a wonder which has turned true,
drink in perfumes and enjoy the savor of a landscape which had seemed forever reserved for the
kingdom of dreams! Sometimes music exalts
me in this way. I penetrate to those states of
the soul from which a thousand closed gates have
separated me, gates through which I only heard
confused and vague murmurs before. And then
when one comes back from that region, it is sorrowful to find oneself again in the ordinary world,
where beauty is rare and transports are fleeting."

I took advantage of his happy frame of mind
to demonstrate to him that metaphysics also were
a kind of intoxication akin to music and are capable of furnishing very similar pleasure.

"But," said he, "if I understand you rightly,

---

[1] " The whole world slumbers in the torrid light."

2

these pleasures of reasoning may end in a state of mind which we find elsewhere celebrated by Buddhism, a colorless state without joy or pain, through which the swift splendors of thought pass like falling stars. Well, the man of the South is antagonistic to a paradise of that sort. The vein of true feeling with us is frankly and forever open — but *open to impressions of life.* The other side which belongs to abstraction and logic, loses itself, so far as we are concerned, in mists."

Then following his usual method he descended from those extreme regions toward comic or touching observations, which are able to make one love reality.

"Violent and timid" — these words return many times in his little note-books. My father had collected a great number of examples of these "feelings made supple," which as he explained, balance themselves in some characters and often give a contradictory air to actions: —

"Timidity slowly accumulates painful impressions of all kinds; for example, he has gone into a shop and has not known how to ask for what he wants, or else, embarrassed by his Southern accent, he has permitted the shop people to foist upon him half the articles on the shelves. Or he has met a friend whose talk has wounded him and he has not been able to say so. Or he has wished to take a cab, but he has not dared to make the necessary gestures or signals.

"Now he has returned to his own house and is at rest with his wife and children. But at the least

11

annoying observation the boiler bursts. He loses
his head and throws the plates about. The sauce
slops over, the children yell, the servants are in
terror. That is the crisis. It stops almost as quickly
as it has begun, with a lot of tears and regrets and
promises and transports of tenderness and love.
Sometimes the man goes to bed and begs for a
cup of beef tea to put himself in condition again.

"If," he continued, "the man and his wife come
from the South, this little drama has very slight
importance. But if the wife comes from the North
or *vice versa*, there appears a phenomenon of
weariness; tenderness gives out; the married couple separates; or in other cases there appears a
phenomenon of contagion. Both of them become
violent and that is the better solution of the two."

In the most exact and gayest way he mimicked
the scenes of fury which quickly vanished and the
alternations of extreme tenderness and of wrath
which in the South constitute the small change
of conjugal life.

In *Numa Roumestan*, Aunt Portal, like a good
many other characters, is a family portrait, whose
reality was of such a powerful sort that it was impossible for him to make the reminiscences of her
imperceptible: "Ah, what a power in the thing
which has been seen and observed! — yes, down
to the color of the hair, shape of the nose, the
favorite habit, or a grimace, which seemed to be
necessary and indeed indispensable to the sketch.
That marvellous artist, Nature, when she accentu-
ates a character, rounds out the physical traits

by moral characteristics in such a way that the
simplest modification of a portrait has an air of
deception. The individual and type carry along
with it their furniture, clothes, follies and, in fact,
their complete framework. And the writer who
is not haunted by the necessity of being exact, by
truth in detail and the actual relief, that man is
not a novelist."

I will add here a remark which frequently returned to his lips : " There is an error often found
among prose writers which consists in believing
that the gift of style brings with it the power to
create types : But the means are absolutely different. In general a talented man can tell a story
with himself in it, and if he is clever he will give
titles and springs of action to the different parts
of his composition. He will divide himself into
different parts, some of which are antagonistic,
and these parts will battle and discuss and act,
sometimes with eloquence ; but never do they
give us the illusion of life.

" I call such writers *essayists* and I greatly prefer their studies of ethics or literature to their
creative attempts, which for the most part are
abortive, or turn aside from the path, or stop
half way."

" As to the writer of romances, that is quite
another matter. Imagination is necessary to him,
because without ceasing he must reconstruct an
animal from a single bone, forge a sentiment from
a look, a word, a gesture ; he must divine from
an attitude some passion or vice and give to his

account that harmony and amplitude which are the generalization of some particular event and trace the signs of fate behind the characters upon the wall.

"*Exactness* is necessary to him because he must not dislocate either his heroes or his heroines, in whom he must preserve their logical and senti- mental tones and must respect the conditions of life and likelihood at peril of driving the reader away, and finally because before everything else he must place a guard over the structure of his work, that inner architecture without which there is nothing but disorder and chaos.

"*Observation* is necessary to him because it is necessary that observation shall make of each character a mirror, in which humanity shall recog- nize itself, and because it will enrich the story, the emotion and even the pathetic parts with singular and direct circumstances.

"But another virtue is necessary which has neither name nor label, more necessary than the *imagination* or *exactness* or *observation*, namely, that power of *hypocrisy* (let us use the word in its Greek sense) which allows the author to *slip into the very skin of his characters*, appropriate their turn of mind, their habits, gestures, and to talk according to their formulas, that same faculty which made Shakespeare exist by turns as Anthony and Cleopatra and as Desdemona and Polonius, and allowed Balzac to be Lucien, or a few seconds afterward, both Marsay and the unforgettable *girl with the golden eyes.*

"The more I ponder upon it," said my father with energy, "the more this gift seems to me primordial, indispensable and irreplaceable. Without that we remain outside our creations, and these retain something borrowed, something factitious, which cannot deceive the simplest of readers. Without that a man may be able to fix a single time some unforgettable type, on condition that this type is the nature of the author himself, or *his contrary*, or a *part of his nature enlarged;* but the miracle will not renew itself and the sequel of his work will consist of nothing more than a succession of outlines and sketches, more and more dim, and less and less moving.

"The man who has the gift of transforming himself may be lacking in style, may hurry and write like a madman. There will still be in his work a special power which will cause it to live and last, whilst others which are more carefully wrought and irreproachable shall have disappeared long ago.

"Alongside of Balzac let us take the greatest lyricist of the century as an example: Victor Hugo — the greatest lyricist, that is to say the biggest *me*, the most encroaching personality. What do we see in his romances and his dramas? Beings without measure or proportion, formed by the creasings and unfoldings of the *me* proper to Victor Hugo, a *me* in a thousand manners, but recognizable beneath its borrowed garments through an identical speech, through his metaphors, his unexpected cæsuras, his antitheses —

in a word, through the whole romantic baggage.
They are wonderful poems, but they do not give
us the illusion of life; Javart is the sureness of
Victor Hugo; Sister Simplice is his feeling for
beauty, or the generosity of Hugo; Jean Valjean
is the whole of Hugo, his revolt, his magnificence
and his egotism, all in one. . . . This personality
of his remains so overflowing and incapable of
transformation, that in that marvellous book of
observation, *Chose Vue*, it impresses its mark upon
all the events of the time, reserves for itself all the
wise words and correct conclusions, all the bold
solutions of questions, and appropriates to itself
history with a gravity and a sureness which
approach the comic."

I remember how one day, at the close of one of
our conversations, I asked him whence came that
power he had, that aptitude to slip into the heart
of another person and clothe himself with the
other's manner. He answered:

"You know I am not a metaphysician, but
across all the systems there appeared to me the
idea that philosophy, which is wise in the problems
of reason and intelligence, is only rudimentary for
that which relates to feeling. The latter has remained mysterious, unexplored and full of abysses.
All the attempts of Descartes and Spinoza were
nothing more than bringing logical and cold solutions to problems of passion and attempting to fit
feeling to reason.

"All I have is my own experience supported by
a few efforts of the imagination. But the ex-

perience of a single person is that of all the world, since we form individuals by narrow and special combinations of general faculties.

" Well, human sensibility seems to me like a sort of electrical circuit, each element of which would be an abbreviated image of the whole. Individual pity, individual pain, individual charity, are merely the reflections of pain, pity and charity in the universal sense. Moreover in this domain everything is a matter of contagion and of quick and wonderful transmission; it happens not seldom that a whole people is filled with an overwhelming feeling for some idea of justice, and that to the very death, but an idea which up to that time had left them quite indifferent.

" We writers of romances ought to do everything to render this communion of feeling more frequent. Our ideal task is to excite generous movements, keep souls in a state of metamorphosis in connivance with other souls.

" Certain duties and rules derive from this. We are culpable if we propagate evil or ugliness, whether from thoughtlessness or lucre. We are culpable if we do not console, but on the contrary render people desperate and augment the sufferings or vileness of the human race."

Then he came back to the question of race: " If there ever was a people in whom this gift of *metamorphosis* exists, this transmission of feelings, it is certainly the people of the South. Among us some one in a group may be telling of a frightful accident. All the faces express disgust. They follow the words of the speaker with a liveliness which is in marked contrast with the close-shut mysterious attitude of a Northern crowd. Among the latter, feelings which are better concealed go on accumulating and under the least pretext may suddenly explode.

"I myself," continued he, "can recollect whilst still very small to have passed a part of the night in recalling the sorrowful intonation my father used when he heard of the death of his eldest son. I adored that elder brother, but the correctness and power of the accent and of the gesture which accompanied the anguished, harsh voice, took possession of my sensitive organism, which as you see was already prepared for the miracle of the transformation.

"For it is a real miracle, which surpasses spiritualism and the turning tables. Balzac puts on the scene a character in whom he supposes certain vices exist, then he finds for every circumstance certain typical phrases such as: 'Then I shall take the little girl with me!' the exclamation of Baron Hulot, which one feels could not have failed to have been said. Those are not recollections. That sort of thing happens in every country. It is the *supreme gift of the romance writer.*

"Well, I have heard peasants among us, *story-tellers*, who possess that gift to the very highest degree and along with it a true genius for mimicry. Nature had been prodigal to them just as it was with my dear Baptiste Bonnet. Not only did they have the emotion itself and the power to

excite, but they had *style* besides, a power half
traditional and half spontaneous over form, which
Bladé has very accurately pointed out in his magnificent collection *Contes de Gascogne* and which
causes little by little their laical and perfunctory
education to disappear.

"The sun, transformed into heat and movement,
furious and irresistible, glides into the veins of the
Southerners. Though it may intoxicate and turn
their heads, it never attacks their intelligence,
which on the contrary it renders stronger, deeper
and more lucid. Since the sun permits them to
meet each other on the public square or during
their labors in the fields at every season of the
year, it favors the humanitarian side, the social
connections which flow from love to municipal
activity, the results of which are strong and lasting races. The sun increases the power of the
gesture when it stands out against a bright background. It gives resonance to the voice. It
seems as if the harmony of the sun, the rhythmical
force of its rays, impregnate people with eloquence and the power of the word. And just as
it stops out colors and shades of color, just as it
reduces everything to the same plane, so it makes
illusions easy.

"It pulls the individual together in the present
and simplifies for him a future which is golden and
warm like it, and filled like it with lively and joyous sensations. It gushes forth feelings before
our astonished consciousness in jets and sheets and
cascades; it deploys them magnificently, increases

their rapidity ten-fold and favors that gentle frenzy of the mind in which bashfulness and heroism, generosity and fear, boldness and timidity mix together in a combination of truth which is often ironical.

"This crowd of qualities is the crowd of the human being itself." (Here my father would take on a special expression and weigh his words as he did when his conversation approached some chief point.) "Of a certainty every human being feels that crowd of sensations living and noisy within his own breast, in his hours of excitement, stupefied by the multitude of them rising in the dark shadows of his consciousness; it seems to him that the forgotten hordes of his ancestors are rising there. A universal shudder and whisper run through him. Then some tendency defines itself and becomes the *leader* of the crowd. Decision is the action of this *leader*. Hesitation is a debate between those hereditary antagonisms.

"Well, among the Southerners *the crowd of the human being* makes its appearance in a lightning flash as swift and burning as a pain. The sudden loosing of the cog of decision causes that disorder of the face and gesture, that ardor in love, which seem so funny if one does not belong to that exaggerating race."

My father brought together with great care — they will be found in his notes — all kinds of proverbs of the South, those in especial which relate to the family and the position of woman in the household. He searched among his recollections for the faded outlines of peculiar relatives, such as formerly grew up in the provinces when an over-centralization had not reduced all characters and brought them down to a single commonplace type.

Whenever he was in Provence he made every peasant he met converse, listening with delight to their picturesque and wild explanations mixed with sententious remarks, such as revealed the Roman churl: "At every turn of the road I discover something of my youth. Is it necessary to accept Dante's word? Is it really a pain, or is it not a solace to recall hours of happiness when one feels unhappiness and regret?"

As he has once written, he believed that "In France everybody has a bit of Tarascon about him." In another form he said that "A Frenchman who gets excited becomes easily a Provençal." So it was that during the war of 1870 he had been able to note the propagation of false news, an excessive enthusiasm in connection with exaggerations at the start, and a prostration during the darkest hours in due proportion — those disorderly ups and downs which form the bad side of the "race of the sun."

He stated also that "the Frenchman has a Keltic father and a Latin mother" and that "the play of those two influences determine the somersaults in our history."

Whilst still young he had seen in his native town the last open battles between Protestants and Catholics: "I know a Huguenot at sight, particularly the Southern species, from his accent, gestures,

look and method of reasoning. He forms a being
apart, much more reserved, cool and master of
himself than the Catholic. There are two portals
for temperaments of this kind, just as there are
two gates to cemeteries in our country — schismatic
and orthodox portals."

As I have already shown, it cannot be doubted
that he himself belonged to the Catholic pole.
He had that pity, that complete pity which the
moment it finds its object cares nothing more for
dialectics. He had a taste for risk and adventure.
In talking this way I do not wish to say that Protestants are lacking in courage either; on the contrary, I believe they have a very living moral
energy where it affects their convictions and their
immediate sense of justice. But they weigh their
actions and their words. My father was spontaneous. When it came to the domain of action
he put calculation aside; his natural generosity
placed him by instinct in the heroic path. Finally, as I have often remarked, there is among the
Protestants an extreme difficulty of making a decision, a kind of paralysis of scrupulousness. My
father accepted responsibilities quietly, but immediately, in a few moments, he took his position.

The creases which religion leaves in characters
were often the subject of our conversations. He
understood wonderfully the features which faith
impresses on souls. The history of the Reformation had excited him, in so far as it involved the
opposition in the North to the expansion of the
Renaissance, which was entirely Southern:

"Oh yes, I understand how, beneath a low sky and among the mists, those voluptuous Popes who, according to that admirable joke of one of them, could not imagine how men could live 'without the carnal affections'—those Popes bedizened with ribbons and lace, surrounded by mistresses and painters and music, must have revolted extremely rigorous souls. That is it, there speaks the influence of climate. . . . To the present day the look of a Protestant village in our rural parts differs entirely from that of a Catholic village. But there can be no doubt that Catholicism has on its side the idea of pardon and sacrifice, and the splendid dogma of substitution and ransom which people have so often deformed and badly interpreted."

The Gospels made the tears come into his eyes. In the practice of religion he loved the pomp and ceremony, he loved processions and the charming whiteness of the girls going to communion, and above all things the bell, whose solemn voice filled him with melancholy. Never did an impious word ever slip from his mouth. Was he entirely unbelieving and skeptical? Those are secrets which the conscience holds to the very last. He was much pleased because my mother used to go and pray at the graves of his relations. He showed a desire to see us baptized and go to communion. My civil marriage was very distasteful to him. He was the son of a devout mother. In his extreme youth he himself had shown an almost excessive piety. Through his feeling for pain and owing

to the rude trials of his life, he remained close to
that religion which has offered the most sublime
ejaculations, the most profound restfulness to the
soul, and the most tragic and subtle renunciations.
I have heard him talk of Christ with an energy
and an unction which any preacher might have
envied, showing something narrow and familiar and
as it were fragrant and balmy, which suited well
the latitude of Palestine, but which he got from
his own Provence. Often his eye lit up at some
word of mystery or of miracle; he expressed himself concerning faith and periods of dryness in
faith and the torments of believers with an eloquence which sprang from the intimate sources of
religious feeling. . . . And nevertheless he venerated Montaigne even more than Pascal; nevertheless when one pushed him hard concerning these
problems, his replies showed acute skepticism or
there were long silences of doubt.

To sum up, I believe that that impress of the
race which was so strong in him had marked him
with the *moral forms* of the Catholic faith. I believe that he would have desired to hold the faith
and that absolute materialism and atheism were
odious to him, but his powerful and yet gentle
love of life for life's sake, of justice without recompense and of pity which does not see its own
good, took in him the place of narrow conceptions of a future and better organized world.

In most cases and especially when there were
more than two present he avoided such conversations " to which each one brings nothing but vague

words which have been heard a hundred times before." I remember that he was even astonished that the grandest subjects known to humanity should be precisely those on which the greatest number of follies are accumulated, as if the spirit became numb at a certain level and lost its clear view and fruitful ideas.

One summer afternoon as we were walking he said to me: " When nature seems to us intentionally bad and homicidal, it presents us indeed with a painful alternative, but what is much more sinister is nature's indifference when it appears to be separated from us by an impassable gulf.

" So the way I explain it is, that believers close their eyes to this world, stop their ears and shut themselves up in the strange palaces of the soul. Outside they would find nothing but perils, deserts and temptation. As for me, in whose blood doubt and the reminiscences of belief are at war, I have a two-fold view of that which lies about me, of this garden for instance, of the sky and the waters. Now all this vibrates and it affects me, it traverses and enthuses me; again, I have remained cold and unapproachable, and familiar places have seemed to me unknown abodes which are almost hostile. . . . Is it not perhaps pain which takes the color out of my little domain? "

My father, at one and the same time nomadic in temperament, a lover of change and a follower of tradition, respectful toward religion, scrupulous and a mocker, detesting officialdom, cliques, the lying honors of society and every kind of convention, seemed to me a finished type, but a purified one, of the man of the South.

Purified — because it is when he is in action that the Southerner degenerates. My father did not ignore this at all and judged very severely certain celebrated politicians, his compatriots:

"A morality as loose as one's belt. Streams of faults, talk as facile as their impulse and their promises, yes, as their *mendacity*. When it comes to those frightful politics, our good qualities change very quickly for the worse: enthusiasm becomes hypocrisy, loquacity and charlatanry; gentle skepticism becomes scoundrelism; love of things that shine becomes rage for money and luxury at any price; sociability and the desire to please turn to cowardice, feebleness and turn-coatism. Alas, for the lofty comedies! What breasts smitten by the hand, what low, moved voices, hoarse but captivating, what easy tears are theirs, what adjurations and calls upon patriotism and the lofty sentiments! You remember the famous phrase by Mirabeau: 'And we shall not leave except through the power of bayonets;' well, a legend which may be true adds this growling, oblique continuation, given in a murmur aside with his eye on the wink: 'And if they do come, we shall skedaddle!'"

The love of solitude and reflection which had gone on developing itself in Alphonse Daudet is rarely a virtue of the Southern people: "Everything outside" is a motto for that race of "brown crickets," so changeable and noisy. That phrase of Roumestan's: "When I am not talking I cannot think" is a profound truth.

I may remark in this connection how many formulas, metaphors, phrases and definitions invented and made popular by my father have made quick fortunes and are currently employed by many people who ignore their origin. That is because those formulas and definitions have "the living virtue" in them, that mysterious attraction arising from picturesqueness and ease of application, which continue them as they are, but sometimes deform their original sense.

However slightly affected by pride he may have been because of his talents and success, still he was delighted with these survivals. Somewhere he tells how his heart swelled in his breast with pride when he heard people say: "That man is a Delobelle, or a d'Argenton, or a Roumestan, or a Tartarin."

Is it not one of the glories of men of letters to make species in this way out of characters and types of men who, before they wrote, were lost in the indistinct crowd of human beings? "It seems," said I to him, "that one of the purposes of art consists in differentiating the vital elements, characters, landscapes and even objects, and rendering beauty in its smallest aspects visible and present."

He answered: "That reflection springs from the letters which you wrote to me from Holland with regard to the great realistic painters: Rembrandt, Frans Hals and van der Meer. I have always thought in that way. A pencil of light upon a face, a feeling which touches one, a gesture, a look, have each its own proper value, immediate and immortal, which separates it from all the luminous rays, feelings, gestures and looks which are possible. We make everything into an individual and we break up classes in nature."

The same kind of work which he undertook with regard to the Southerners he desired that each author should do for the men of his own race. "That is the way in which one becomes representative. Such special studies, far from hurting general views, are useful to them and feed them with examples."

In the little note-books a series of biographical and historical remarks of the highest interest may be read, from Mirabeau to Bonaparte and Thiers and Guizot and Gambetta, all of which tend to find the origins of their acts and words beneath that heap of hypocritical conventions and lies which the contact of other ambitions occasions in men of politics, as well as their natural love of combat and desire to exert their influence.

According to Alphonse Daudet the novel is a prop to history. In some places it may even enlighten and do it justice. Among the works of contemporaries there is a good example in support of this theory in Gustave Geffroy's *Blanqui.* Whilst studying a great character this conscientious artist, this "poet of reality" which Geffroy is, has explained modern processes of investigation and description. The result is a rare and remarkable work which doubtless will serve as type and model to many other essays in the same line.

Let no one imagine, however, that my father pushed this taste for analysis from the point of view of race to the limits of a fad. His "Latin good sense," his love of proportion preserved him from such an excess. He venerated Michelet; he read and reread him; he used new terms of laudation for the sublime author of *L'Histoire de France — de la Femme — de la Mer — de la Bible — de l'Humanité.* He admired Taine, whilst at the same time on his guard against that writer's strained method of systematizing and whilst finding him too hard on heroes and enthusiasts.

Lover of equilibrium and harmony in the domain of thought as he was, he understood and excused fanaticism in the domain of action. And I am ready to believe that he preferred Taine's *Littérature Anglaise* to the *Origines de la France Contemporaine.*

This love of history sometimes brought out dialogues of the sort that follows:

I. — How is it that you have never yet written a grand study on one of your heroes, or on some period of the wars of religion in your country, or some episode of the Renaissance or of the Reformation, which I see you studying with such tremendous energy?

He (with a sigh). — The man of letters does not march in the direction he wishes. A subject carries him along and turns him away from his goal. In my notes you will find a *Napoleon as a man of the South*, which our dear Frédéric Masson has made a reality and more than a reality, also a

Guerre des Albigeois and a *Soulèvement de l'Algérie,*
also a monograph on Raousset-Boulbon and
another on Rossel, etc. Subjects of that sort
exist without end along the borders of history and
romance writing. I wish to sound them and treat
them in accordance with the *documents of life.*

I. — Always concerning Southerners, episodes in
the combats between the North and the South?

He. — Have I not repeated a hundred times that
all one man can add as contribution to truth is
infinitely little and weak? I think it well to accept
with caution a great many singular observations
on my race, its virtues and vices. A man cannot
note down everything. I believe in the future.
Reality possesses an incredible force which is distinct from the force of truth.

I. — Is n't that just the same thing?

He. — By no means. Truth is a moral judgment
made by men or facts upon reality. That judgment
may be obscure and weak and wreck itself. Truth
has a susceptibility far more delicate than any
printed paper of whatsoever kind. The atmosphere and the sunlight, and the breath and everything causes it to degenerate. Reality however
exists and dwells forever. But a poet is necessary to lend to reality the power to revive, the
power of propagation and duration. Michelet was
a " visionary of the real."

" Rarement un esprit ose être ce qu'il est." [1]

That line, which I think is from Boileau, was apt
to be launched suddenly into a conversation by

[1] " And seldom dare a soul be really what it is! "

way of an encouragement or reproach. Very
often he explained how *character* is the result of
a moral courage which causes a man to develop
himself after his own proper nature and bring
into relief the virtues and the vices which come to
him as a heritage.

"In the same way," he added, "there is an inner
timidity which prevents the individual from development and stops the realization of his own type
and produces that quantity of worn and half-
defaced medals devoid of interest which constitute
the mass of men.

"A man of letters who is thinking of the
passions has necessarily to do with that mass and
those indistinct outlines. For it would prove a
wearisome convention if one were to put to work
characters alone. It is in dealing with these half-
tones and these passages in chiaroscuro that our
task becomes most difficult. 'A hero of the non-
heroic,' there is the masterpiece which Flaubert
has realized in *L'Éducation Sentimentale.*

"Well, a man of a different race or a different
epoch becomes typical for that very reason.
Roumestan or Tartarin would not stand out from
a crowd in the South. It is Paris that puts them
in relief. In the same way we still visit certain old
men or old ladies living apart from society, who
have preserved unchanged the prejudices and ways
of looking at things, the generosities and warm
sentiments of 1848. And so for us it is a delight
to find them, as it is a joy to the numismatist to
discover a finely preserved medal."

In some romance by Jean Paul Richter there is a character who has passed his childhood beneath the earth, and the day when on stepping out upon the surface he sees the sky and flowers and waters and forests he thinks he has entered into paradise.

A similar impression awaits any one who, having lived in the North, suddenly discovers the South and the joy of sunlight. Alphonse Daudet had preserved piously that same joy. In his soul it dominated suffering and melancholy. Whatever his observation of the world brought to him which was cruel, whatever his imagination suggested to him that was harsh and vehement and terrible, was softened and tempered by the golden warmth of Provence, made serene again by those pure horizons and harmonized in tune with those lines which have been the directors of human wisdom since the time of classical antiquity.

That marvellous sense for proportion is the safe-guard of the mind. The man who descends into his own soul and does not hold fast to a love of harmony, plunges very soon into the blackest shade. He becomes unintelligible. He loses all power of instruction. This conducting clew is a very little matter. It would have rendered such a work as Ibsen's *Peer Gynt*, for instance, immortal. Of a certainty a multiplicity of interpretations is a sign of weakness. The poem becomes a sort of game or labyrinth in which the cleverness of the reader exercises itself. What brief mental excitement it occasions is not worth one clear recollection.

On that point my father was quite tranquil.
According to him, despite some rare exceptions,
French thought has remained in love with all that
is limpid and true and faithful to its origins. He
admired certain pieces by Ibsen, but not all. For
some there are, the symbolism of which seemed
to him infantile and false. For example he found
once more in Ibsen's northern sarcasm about the
wild duck the "India-rubber laugh, the laugh of
Voltaire congealed by Pomeranian sleet." He
had a warm admiration for Tolstoï, the Tolstoï one
finds in *War and Peace, Anna Karenina,* in
the *Souvenirs de Sébastopol* and in the *Cos-
sacks.* The *Kreutzer Sonata* was revolting to
him in certain places. But the neo-mysticism of
this author and his last evangelical works did not
interest him at all.

"Tolstoï," said he, " has enjoyed in his youth
everything that there is in life which is exquisite,
luxurious and brilliant. He has loved the chase,
masquerades, races in sleighs, pretty women,
friends and the arts. But now he would like to
forbid that others should enjoy pleasures which
his old age prevents him from repeating. In a
conversion effected on a man of seventy I shall
always be on my guard against regrets and that
envy — oh, very distant, underhand and indirect,
but tenacious — which can be read between the
wrinkles."

The reading of *Crime and Punishment* had been
for him a *crisis of his mind.* That book had
prevented him from writing a work which he

had projected on Lebiez and Barré, and the action
of badly understood Darwinian theories on the
youthful poor. That deviation from scientific
formulas, the continuation of theories into practice
disquieted him, and we owe to that disquiet his
books: *La Lutte pour la Vie*, *La Petite Paroisse*
and *Le Soutien de Famille*. To return to Dos-
tojevski, he did not esteem the less *Frères Kara-
mazov* and *Maison des Morts;* but he preferred
the harmonious beauty of *Anna Karenina* and the
sumptuous sonorousness of *Guerre et Paix* to the
rousing fanaticism and actual hallucinations of
the Russian Dickens.

So the reader may see that his love for the
South did not cause him to disdain northern
literature. As to the climate itself, that is another
matter, and very often I would joke with him upon
the contradiction which existed between his horror for fogs and frosts and his taste for Arctic
expeditions.

V.

AS A MAN OF FAMILY.

MARCEL SCHWOB, the author of *Roi au Masque d'Or* and of *Livre de Monelle* and other striking works, insists with very great justice at the beginning of his admirable work *Vies Imaginaires,* that when it comes to the biography of great persons, family details are of the highest importance. Very often a preference or custom or some habit of the person will reveal more to the reader than a long theory, or a whole body of dogmas. Whatever is individual and specific in a person can often be defined with greater exactness by means of one of those remarks which the *academical spirit* is always ready to look upon as something that may be ignored.

That is one of the reasons why solemn eulogies and discourses beside the grave almost always reduce themselves to the same theme, colorless and ecstatic, in which according to a ritual and a formula, virtues without saliency and monotonous circumstances are raised to the seventh heaven.

In his dress Alphonse Daudet showed an exemplary modesty. It was not always so with him. At the first representation of *Henriette Maréchal* a young man with long, dark hair, whose

frantic applause caused a shimmering silver waistcoat to scintillate was noticed among the enthusiastic defenders of the play. The future Mme.
Alphonse Daudet, then Mdlle. Allard, was
present on that memorable first night: " Young
girls can be taken; there will be such a row that
they can't hear anything," those were the very
words used by the friend who brought the tickets
of invitation. During the latter years when he
dined in town with his friends, or at his own house
on Thursdays, my father wore a jacket of black
velvet. He himself speaks in some part of his
works of objects that had been dear to the de-
ceased — " little figures, little effigies," which cause
irresistible tears to flow. My brother and I used
to be glad to give him our arm and were proud of
his good looks, which on certain days were really
extraordinary. But with what reserve did he not
conceal his suffering! It contracted his features
for a moment, but so quickly that we alone could
divine it: then he would reassure us with a smile
and at once relate some jocose, brave story which
was accompanied by a little quivering of the eye
that put us in touch with his heroism.

Very often, and we used to repeat it to each
other, what he did not say, what he gave us to
understand with his look, was just as penetrating
and prophetic as his speech. And what kindliness!
" In order to hold well what one has in hand,
always leave the cord a little loose. If children
have souls which are well-fashioned to start with,
such tenderness as one shows them will never do

them hurt. It will bolster them up later during their hours of wretchedness. There is always that much captured from our foe — life ! "

As a matter of fact, and I say this for those who have not not known him, he was not at all the hollow-cheeked and pallid Christ which some people have represented him to be. When his sufferings gave him respite he gave one the impression of complete health. The table was decked with flowers and shining glass. There were the most diverse kinds of comrades : Drumont, de Banville, Hébrard, Gambetta, Leconte de Lisle, Zola, Rochefort and how many others! At the very soup my father had already put everybody at ease, delighting his guests with a brief and brilliant story, one of those winged improvisations which were habitual with him, or else by some observation irresistible in its fun. Then with wonderful cleverness he would launch the conversation in some direction favorable to the lively spirit of one or other of those present, he would direct, protect and breathe new life into it, he would raise its quality and keep it human.

Now he would attack the whole company and fly into an excitement, when the sound of his voice, so warm and subtle, so ardent and engrossing, together with his brilliant eyes and gestures made a most extraordinary picture and combination. Again he would yield the floor, make himself scarce and hide away, in order to allow some champion in conversation to carry off an easy triumph. He knows the value of opinions, the rush of dispute and the intoxication that comes from contradictions. On one point he is severe. He holds to a decent tone in pleasantries and woe to him who shall permit himself some risky allusion, some word which might shock feminine ears! Then his looks grow black and his voice changes; dexterously and swiftly he recalls to the mind of the clumsy fellow what the forms of politeness are: "those pleasing frontiers, standing on which one may say everything so long as no disgraceful image appears, nothing that would soil or degrade."

Gifted with an extreme sharpness of hearing, my father heard what people were whispering ten seats away from him; he often took a hand in an "apart" when he was not expected, and nothing amused him more than to put to the rout some slight mystery, a beginning of a flirtation or a timid advance.

But it would not do to be the dupe of so much kindliness and take this sweetness of his for weakness and, as he says himself, "pull the chair from under him." I have known two men who had the finished gift of repartee. One was Alphonse Daudet, the other was our dear and admired friend Paul Hervieu. Such is the craft of the fencer, who when unexpectedly attacked avoids the blade of his antagonist and strikes for the breast with a disconcerting swiftness.

There was the same sharp look, suddenly black and implacable. There was the same choice of unforgettable phrases, poisoned and barbed words, which flew from his lips. A precious gift was his, the abuse of which need not be feared in men of that sort. A gift which has taken on enduring form in works like *L'Immortel* or *Peints par Eux-mêmes*, a gift that masters and keeps in subjection the fools, hateful ones and cowards, and one which, if it were wider spread, would improve the health of society by renewing the air of rude worldly assemblies which is often filled with it as with a pest.

"Naturalness" that was the present which my father made to every assembly in which he found himself. He delivered people from the thousand different bonds which hypocritical conventions fasten on them, from the prejudices and folly of snobs. Though a revolutionist and foe of abuses, he preserved all the forms of politeness. And while it appeared soft outside his satire was really a terrible dissolvent. Very often grave, reserved and cold men to whom all familiarity is repellent seemed to change their character and gave themselves up to the author as if delighted to throw aside their pose.

At dinner on a certain evening an elderly lady, a much envied woman who occupied a brilliant position, one whom he saw for the very first time and who drank nothing but water, confided to him the actual disaster in her life with a candor and simplicity and naïveté which fairly took his breath away. Yet such confessions were by no means rare. The attraction that certain people have, which causes others to give themselves up to them and consult them and take them for guides, despite all distances and social fictions — that attraction is and ever will be mysterious. Oftener than people think there is a desire to *strip the soul nude*, cast off the robes of ceremony and pull one's wig out of curl.

"There is," said he, "in life a critical moment, a *vif de la vie*, into which two people, who did not know each other the moment before, all of a sudden cast themselves with a singular lack of prudence and with that thirst for truth which torments scrupulous people and believers."

As to good food, he preferred very simple and well-done dishes; for a hatred of artificiality may reach to the most different kinds of feeling. Coarse, dark or red dishes repulsed him. A regular Provençal, he loved olives, well-done dishes and salads — all the salads. We happened to be at a counter in l'Hérault.

"Madam, is this piece of cold meat disengaged?"

"Certainly sir. . . . Are you taking it with you?"

"Of course I am taking it away."

"And the pickled peppers with it?"

"Of course!"

In our gastronomical reminiscences that slice of cold veal will always hold a famous place.

He spiced his meals with various discussions of Southern cookery, designed for restless and burned-out stomachs. "In order to eat well down South, you ought to eat with a Southerner.

You may as well believe me that Bonnet's *saquette* contained marvellous titbits. It is the same with eating as with everything else. It is no good except with national surroundings. Then the golden wine of our vineyards has its own merit. And the game larded with little leaves of the vine has its proper value, as it turns and bastes before the crackling of the vine wood in the tavern.

"This dish is a landscape in itself!" Such was his greatest compliment. He preferred Burgundy to Bordeaux. "One vulgar delight is drinking the little wine of the people, whatever kind it may be, the ginguet as it is called, so long as it bites the tongue and is drunk along with a hunch of pretty high cheese, a 'horror' as ladies will exclaim when one brings it home all terrible and smelly."

When in Paris my father's day was divided between work, visits from friends and an occasional walk.

As early as eight o'clock, placed at his own writing-table, he began by dictating his copious correspondence to his secretary, the same that he had had for thirty years. As he has many a time related, it was one morning in 1870 on the firing-line that Alphonse Daudet made the acquaintance of Jules Ebner, who was quietly reading an ode from Horace in the face of snow and foe. Since that time the two men have never left each other until the death of one of them, the "master" namely, for whom the other possessed an admiration and devotion the like of which I have never seen.

For thirty years, without missing a single day, notwithstanding often fatiguing work as secretary in the editorial office of a great newspaper, Ebner has sat there before my father with his pen in his hand. He had to answer comrades and editors and translators and beggars, and sift the good from what was useless or piteous, or mere knavery. . . . There's a ring at the bell. . . . It is necessary to stop. . . . My father's welcome is always pleasant; his kindly air is in no sense a mask, for according to the visitor, he passes from the liveliest tenderness to mere ordinary cordiality.

Often a comrade passing through our quarter of the town would come to "warm himself" in the presence of the master, demanding advice or counsel. He was so indulgent to young men! One of the last careers to open, in which he took an interest, was that of Georges Hugo, whom he loved and whose new and precocious talent he admired. The cry of revolt in the latter's *Souvenirs d'un Matelot* went to his heart, just as every vibrating and sincere word overcame him. For my part I have sometimes written violent and even bloodthirsty pages, but he never imposed the slightest restriction upon me. Besides, he knew that anger is only another face of pity. From my earliest age he counselled me to use moderation when in doubt and boldness when sure of my ground.

I was hardly ten years of age when he caused me to take my first lessons with the sword and pistol "in order to give me the chance to be as patient as possible, but when the right moment comes to astonish an adversary." Until it began to fatigue him too much, fencing was his chief exercise. He gave himself up to it with enthusiasm, holding the floor for an hour at a time; in the game his whole nature came to the surface; a mixture of strength and delicacy, a prudent method broken by sudden fits of audacity and violence, made him a very difficult adversary.

He has written some excellent notes on the game of sword and foil and on the revelation of a character through feints as well as on irresistible rushes, the truth of which will surprise professional swordsmen. At the same time he used to take long walks at a rapid gait through Paris, turning over in his mind projects of books and characters and associating the outer world with them at any moment:

"The moment that an idea excites and makes us quiver, at that moment through a singular paradox we become most frightened and most impressionable. The state of half consciousness is the treasure-house of accessories, the store-house of the romance-writer."

When his declining powers no longer allowed him to take his long walks, as often as not he made the house of his father-in-law Jules Allard, "his best friend," the goal of his saunterings. At the time my grandparents inhabited a handsome house with a garden at the top of Cherche Midi Street; a description often recurs in the little note-books. There are reports of long conversa-

tions held by my grandfather, who was a connoisseur of men and a poet as well as a republican
belonging to the great epoch, with my grandmother Léonide Allard, a woman of broad and
mystic mind, who was wont to defend the rights of
the supernatural against the railleries of realism.

For my father was always rebellious against the
manifestations of the world beyond and held to
the opinion of his friend Montaigne concerning the "unknowable." "My dear Mama!" that
was the way he called her, "I have remarked that
superstition and skepticism form an equilibrium
in the same family, just as virtue and vice remain
equal, prodigality and avarice — and in general all
such oppositions in character."

Since the increase of his malady, he went out
very little in the evening. It had to be a very
exceptional occasion to decide him to break the
rule. Nevertheless he loved the world and society;
the presence of strangers was good for him and
took him away from his suffering. The general
rehearsal of *Sappho* at the Opéra Comique was
one of his very last pleasures. He took the very
liveliest interest in the staging of his pieces, in the
performance of the actors and in such a "preparation" as dramatic authors understand, a preparation which is one of the pleasures of the craft. He
generously distributed on the stage that mass of
observations "from the life" which he never
ceased to heap up, and he insisted that each detail
should be scrupulously regulated in consonance
with the actual.

It is hard to imagine greater interest than that in a rehearsal of a play directed by Porel, who has the very genius of the stage and a limitless invention, when aided by my father, who was life itself. What art, what care is necessary to reach the point of illusion! How difficult it is to cause a character to move and to fix the entrances and exits!

At the beginning of winter the year before, Massenet had come to the house to rehearse his opera on the piano for the benefit of his chief interpreter Emma Calvé, the authors of the libretto Henri Cain and Bernède, and his friend Daudet. When the touching overture of the last act was reached, that long lamentation broken by sobs, my father was not able to withhold his tears. What did he imagine, what did he perceive through the waves of those sonorous agonies? He left us to imagine, but we shall never hear that piece of music again without trembling.

Portraits of Alphonse Daudet are numerous and some of them are very close to life. But what they are not able to render and what is forever lost is that voice of his with inflections as delicate and numerous as the sentiments it expressed. Devoid of the race accent but not of melody, it was as if filled with sunshine when the soul was gay, or again it trembled when the mood was melancholy. That voice has remained so completely in my ears with all its shades of sound, that when I open a book by *him* or when I quote some of his sentences, I seem to hear him talk. Irony was

revealed by a brief hesitation, a sort of stoppage
in the midst of phrases which the listener himself
sometimes had to finish.

His laugh was frank and splendid, full of an irresistible contagion. Some slight discontent, such
as the small tiresome facts of paternity, used to
be expressed now by silence, without pouting but
very embarrassing, and again by side remarks,
made "without seeming to mean it."

"Hello, you seem to be going out a great deal
this week. . . . It seems to me, that work is n't
getting on very well. . . ." and other innocent
stratagems.

"If people attack my own, I turn into a savage
beast." In his case that sentiment was not exaggerated. By the exercise of generosity, kindness,
gentleness and humanity, he overcame his own
nature, but at bottom that nature was violent and
ardent in the extreme. A wound given to his
affections was provocative of anger which was all
the more dangerous because he knew how to control himself and await the hour for punishment,
which, according to him, could not fail to arrive :
"Just let destiny work itself out." he said to me
when I was hot to avenge an affront, "she will
shoulder the burden of your hatred." But in such
things as affected himself alone he was always incapable of rancor: "Bah, life is too short!"

Nevertheless I ought to remark that he very
rarely went back on his judgments and that
people were not apt to escape from his scorn.
Like those who love in good sooth, in friendship

he was very susceptible. Treachery struck him to
the heart. And when he thought that he himself
was in the wrong he would do everything in order
to repair his fault and would confess it without a
single drawback.

No man was ever less hypocritical; none detested so sincerely a lie: "That parasitical plant
which grows in people's looks, voice, gestures and
gait . . . which one has so much trouble in completely driving out."

So far as belongs to the comfortable things of
life, my father did not care for them at all; he was
attached only to some few very simple things and
these always the same, his pipes, pen-stand, his
ink-pot, little souvenirs we gave him which were
strewed about his table. If we presented him with
cigars he distributed them to everybody who
came in during the day: "I have the greatest difficulty in the world," he used to say, "to make
myself believe that anything whatever belongs to
me."

Here is the end of those "moral" souvenirs
which I wanted to bring together, lest along with
Alphonse Daudet the atmosphere of his charm and
tenderness should disappear entirely. And now,
having come to the end of my task, I perceive how
difficult it has been. Some will reproach me for
having been too chary of "stories." I did that on
purpose, believing that it is better to display the
heart and soul of a man like my father than to
fritter them away in episodes and anecdotes. What

more have I to add? In accordance with my soul
and memory I have sketched the portrait of a
human, simple yet complex, sensitive yet prophetic
in mind, in the strength of his age and his works.

If it has happened that I have grown weak by
the way, his great shade will pardon me for it, for
that shade knows that I was sincere; hereafter
it shall precede me on the short or long pathway
of my life, even as formerly *he* guided the steps
of his child.

LÉON DAUDET.

This 28th of March
1898.

APPENDIX.

APPENDIX.

APPENDIX.

CONCERNING THE IMAGINATION.

A DIALOGUE BETWEEN MY FATHER AND ME.

To MME. ALPHONSE DAUDET:

Conversation is my greatest delight. To stroll through the field of ideas, to play the vagabond with words and points of view, to loaf about, regarding human beings and things — that seems to me the highest of all pleasures and the moment in life when a person is the least distant from the joys of imagination.

But one must have a good partner. Lovers of this lofty game prefer that all good qualities and all defects should show themselves in their full boldness and color; for instance, that the violent man should be violent, that the close reasoner should reason, the sensitive man should nervously lay bare his sensitiveness, the philosopher should coldly develop his theories. Every character is a good one which does not try to dissemble, because then fear of humbug makes the conversation heavy and deprives it of that flowing, unexpected and golden ease which makes it like the natural forces in their quick and lively beauty.

I have known feverish and fanatical talkers whose vigor was a thing to admire. A troop of reminiscences and impromptus poured forth helter-skelter, as if through a portal of life, across the magnificent fields of their minds; and these memories were fragile, unforgettable winged things, and their impromptus rolled out with the thunder of a torrent, enriched by every surrounding object or whatsoever the heavens and aspect round about, whatsoever waters and gestures, whatsoever the fields or the streets might provide for the clever conversationalist —what time the prophetic tripod of his eloquence shudders hard and his opponent, contradicting him, shall start the flame of his imagination!

I have seen heavy wains which were difficult to start, but at last shook the very earth like the phenomena of nature; and I have known expert bowmen whose arrows reached the empyrean, like swallows in good weather. I have known subtle intellects who talked by means of symbols and of signs that expressed signs, just as the Japanese work in jade or ivory, and lovers of clearness who with their flamboyant metaphors pierced holes in the darkest shadows.

I have known scientific men supported by the "actual fact" and conscientious to the verge of craziness, and also poets whom nothing can stop, who are wildly excited by the absurd; and all those voices, heavy or sombre, shrill or light, feverish or calm, biting or whining, have in my recollection such an intensity that at times they return to vex my dreams.

I conversed best and most with my father. I shall permit myself to state this one only from amongst the crowd of truthful eulogies which my rôle as a son prevents me from declaring — that he, my father, is inexhaustible and always ready to engage, two wonderful qualities which every good talker will appreciate. In addition to this, in order that the flame shall always be big and bright, he throws fresh wood all the time to that hearth where ideas and words are smoking. And to conclude, he listens to his partner and does not, like certain egoistical bores, drag him over upon his own ground. Any field is good for him, and, because of an inconceivably brilliant imagination, he makes it fertile at once.

Now it is just exactly the imagination which is our commonest subject — a rich and fertile matter without end that never wearies one. Through man's will imagination embraces the whole world, and in man's mind imagination causes the whole world to find its place. It is the grand treasury of poets, heroes and of all beauties. Imagination alone renders life possible, which without it is flat, monotonous and dark. It alone gives value to love, even to death and annihilation.

So, then, let us suppose that my father and I are walking arm-in-arm about the garden at Champrosay on one of those clear and golden mornings in summer when a bird seems to hide behind every leaf. I am hardly well awake after twelve hours of a dreamless sleep. But my father's voice puts life into me and little by little thaws me out.

MY FATHER somewhat ironical, as one can see in that corner of his eye which I know so well). — Oh, oh, so you have a theory concerning the imagination! Beware of that; a theory is a hard load to carry, it is fearsome! Once you are in it you can never get out. One finds it necessary to fold and crease facts and deform them in order to make them fit that strange and uncomfortable trunk.

I. — But, my dear father, one has no clear ideas

without theory. Otherwise facts lie side by side like children's toys and the mind does not progress. Without general ideas our most acute sensations and most delicate sentiments remain in the domain of the animal kingdom.

MY FATHER (*getting excited*).—But let me tell you that oftenest these general ideas completely fool us and that one good fact which has been carefully observed by undimmed eyes is as vast and troublesome and as fruitful as any hypothesis you may mention. Of course I do not ask people to plant themselves on a note or a commentary; I do not ask a man to be a mere observer, a fellow with a pair of spectacles or an eye-glass or any other kind of diminishing-glass; but just look at Darwin, look at Claude Bernard—there are solid and true friends of reality; I admire their way of doing; their method is the one that delights me!

I.—They also built hypotheses.

MY FATHER.—Quite true; but not in the way the metaphysicians do. They have observed this, and then that, and then the next thing. They tell you that ingenuously, like the poets they are, with a strong bias toward the picturesque. And they allow the obscure work of generalization to go on in the mind of the reader. . . . But I don't want to discourage you. So, then, you're going to unfold to me a theory concerning the imagination. . . . How did it come to you?

I. — While reading Shakespeare and Balzac. As soon as we can get to the country, where, as you know, they compose along with Sainte-Beuve the library, I seize upon them with a lover's madness. There be the mistresses who never deceive you! I know them by heart, the way you do, and still every time that I plunge into them again my brain is the richer for it and I feel myself more energetic and alive.

My Father. — 'T is the wine of life. . . . Magnificently does it circulate in man. They made a deep impression on me at an early age as they have upon you, and to such a degree that I can recall having made some character in Shakespeare, Polonius I think, the hero of one of my first stories. The names of Balzac and Shakespeare, Shakespeare and Balzac, are mingled in my mind; I hardly separate one from the other. It has often happened that, confronted with a new person, or a new sensation, I have had recourse to them in order to label the said person or sensation with the name of one of their characters or with one of their stunning formulas. You have, of course, noticed the subterranean analogies between those two geniuses?

I. — Most striking analogies! They have treated the very same subjects. Père Goriot and King Lear, Père Grandet and Shylock. *Les Chouans*, that admirable romance, has the same story as *Romeo and Juliet*, namely, love between two people which has been held in check by family or race hatreds. On this side are the Montagues, who are the same as the men of the White Cockades; on that are the Capulets, who are the Blues. Montauran is Romeo. Mademoiselle de Verneuil is Juliet. And that odor of voluptuousness and death which sheds its perfume around the lovers in Verona renders the lovers of Fougères fragrant during their tragical wedding-night.

My Father. — *Les Chouans* is one of my favorite books. It is amusing that you should have inherited that taste. What I perhaps admire the most in Balzac is his power of dialogue, the way he puts in the mouth of each of his creations the exact word, what I call the dominant word, that phrase which displays and opens up a whole temperament.

I. — And yet Balzac was always a failure on the boards.

MY FATHER. — It almost seems as if his imagination was too powerful and representative for the footlights, the painted cheeks, the monologues and all the rest of the hypocritical cant of the stage. That monster carries everything along with him, both scenery and characters. And how well he knows how to place his footlights; how he understands the way of throwing light into a town or a ward or a room! And what an art he has for the gradations! To-night, after dinner, if nobody comes to bother us, let us read in *Les Chouans* to the children the assassination of Galope-Chopine by March-à-Terre and l'Ille-Miche. You remember it, don't you? . . . The mist-hung morning, the tragical approach of the two Chouans, their silence and their hats? And that drop of cider which falls rhythmically from the pitcher! There is a detail which would be ridiculous on the stage, and yet which, in the book, is sublime. And then those globules of milk which their knives crush against the surface of their thick hunches of bread! Ah, what a man, what a man!

I (*insidiously and with an eye on my theory*). — Yes, he contained all the rest within himself!

MY FATHER. —That's it — or at any rate he made them live again "according to the swing of his imagination" as old Montaigne would have said. When you have asked me in what talent consists, I have answered you, talent is an *intensity of life*. That is not a mere conventional explanation. I am firmly persuaded that

Balzac and Shakespeare had within themselves a number of violently excited lives, and that they had distributed them through their works.

I. — There you are right into my theory! I shall try to be clear and not to jostle your *Latin* spirit, as you call it. There is one sublime faculty which the philosophers have neglected too much, and it is in my humble opinion one of the keys to nature : the faculty of *Imitation* or in the etymological sense *Hypocrisy;* the desire to slip into the skin of another person, pull on his mask and submit oneself to the passions which torment him.

MY FATHER. — The desire of approaching other human beings and assimilating their habits of mind and opinions is just as violent as the contrary desire to resist them.

I. — Well then, that faculty of *hypocrisy* is common among human beings, but when pushed to the point of paroxysm in men of genius it constitutes their greatest beauty and their highest gift. By means of it Shakespeare is Shylock and Balzac is Grandet or Gobsek ; by means of it one is Rosalind, Desdemona, Miranda and then again Caliban, Richard III., Macbeth, and the other is in turn Madame de Maufrigneuse, Madame d'Esparre, the Princesse de Cadigan, and then Hulot, Philippe Brideau and de Marsay. It is perfectly certain that Shakespeare and Balzac did much more than observe the men about them and reconstruct life in accordance with their observation. They *metamorphosed* themselves into a multitude of characters and temperaments, whose mere outlines they possessed within them. Their works are the result of *two series of metempsychoses.* That is why they astonish us to such a degree. That is why their dialogues are lit with a glare of truth so intense that the meanest characters show the reflection from it on their faces.

My Father. — I just recall a speech by Balzac to a mystic writer nowadays little known, but a very eloquent one — to Raymond Brucker, author of *Chas de l'Aiguille :* " My dear Balzac, where do you make your observations of your heroines and heroes? " — " Ho, my friend, how do you suppose I can find time to observe? I hardly have time enough to write." That proves that the mechanism which you indicate was known to Balzac himself.

I. — Balzac knew everything. An imagination like his has perceived everything and co-ordinated everything. He even had the gift of prophecy, since they say that he molded his own period on the model of the " Comédie Humaine." In order to be a sibyl it was necessary only to reason rightly and to arrange the events in their right series. But do you not find that venturesome idea seductive — that a spirit should include within itself all the passionate or sentimental characteristics — in a state of germs, of course? Then observation would merely play the *rôle* of the resurrector. That idea would give meaning to those moral crystallizations which are called virtues and vices — those deeply-founded structures of avarice, pride, luxury, timidity, heroism, etc.

My Father (*laughing*). — When the *association of ideas*, as the pedants say, is rich, it is called imagination. Such an hypothesis concerning the imagination would not displease me at all. In the morning when I get to my work-table and find in my portfolio all my characters standing about, waiting for the life which I am to blow into them, I certainly seem to myself like that magician, or, if you prefer the word, that "hypocrite," who is so clever at slipping into temperaments and characters and at rousing sentiments and sensations by the light of the sparkles of memory.

I. — Are there not moments when your illusion is absolutely complete, and when, like the actor whom his *rôle* carries away and transfigures, you enter so deeply into the flesh and blood of one of your children of romance that you almost forget your own personality?

My FATHER. — That happens seldom, but it does happen. It is very possible that with certain privileged writers the phenomenon may be habitual. I think it was Balzac who answered some one who reproached him for melancholy: "I am sad . . . I am sad, because I have just killed Vautrin!"

I. — This essay on the metamorphoses of the author into his different characters would be narrow if there were no continuations. I am astonished that our period has not produced a grand philosophy of sensibility, creating its own object according to Hegel's formula. All the philosophies which we have had up to the present day, all without exception, have been philosophies of the intelligence, grand systems very cleverly arranged by induction and deduction to tell how our brain acts when it studies itself. Pascal, that clever and nervous mind, that martyr with a singing soul, Pascal has conceived of the universe within us as a series in slight disaccord with the series of the universe without us, and has reconciled the two by means of Grace. By a prodigious effort Spinoza has united sensibility with intelligence, and by studying the woof of our impressions he made the discovery that it was identical with that of our judg-

14

ments. There cannot be two tapestries in the loom of destiny. We might have doubted it, had it not been for that great man, but we ought to be thankful to him for having painted an original picture of the human sentiments in so far as they are subject to reason.

All those monuments are admirable : *Le Discours sur la Méthode* and the *Pensées* by Pascal, and the *Ethics* and the *Monadology* and the *Foundation of the Metaphysic of Habits*, will rightfully remain the object of respect for future generations ; but in a certain way they are the dwellings of the past. As little as we possess a truly modern architecture do we possess a modern philosophy which satisfies our existing culture.

My Father. — Now you explain why philosophy has so little interest for me. It is all very well to apply and force myself, I yawn over the *Pure Reason* and the formulas of Spinoza have always given me the impression of a set of prepared skeletons.

I. — Because you are a complete " sensitive," conscious and sincere. What you would like to find in a philosophical work is an attempt at explanation of those mysterious flashes of sensibility, those fugitive appearances which cause us to see a contrary emotion even in an emotion itself. Carlyle, Emerson, Novalis, Maeterlinck — there are marvellous dreamers for you ; and very often the will-o'-the-wisps of the swamps leap and dance on their dreams, so intense and charged with intellectual fever are they. But although they have approached contemporary sensibility they have by no means taken possession of it yet. A book difficult to write would be an essay on the *sentient states of consciousness.*

It is certain that it will be written. It will spring

from a general desire for it, as all great and necessary works which are the offsprings of the times and of enervation do spring. Just as round our *over-refined states of sensation* (new words are surely necessary for new ideas) there rises a sort of vapor which excites and makes us lucid in mind, so in the same way certain signs announce a great epoch-making work about those periods which are fertile in intellectual work.

MY FATHER. — Here is one of my liveliest sensations. One day during a terrible heat I was crossing the Place de la Concorde which was shining and vibrating like a copper saucepan. A watering-cart passed by. A little butterfly was playing and dancing about the thin rain of drops which the cart was emitting and turning into vapor along a narrow luminous spray. That butterfly played and danced with a fever and an agility in following the jet of water and a sense of pleasure which seemed to enter into my spirit to an unaccustomed depth, and troubled me like the sensitive gradation-marker for every kind of intoxication and vivid enjoyment, it troubled me with the subtlety and ephemeral wisdom of such joys. Under that implacable hot sky, in a flash which was almost painful through its intensity, I had a glimpse of a multitude of impressions, some of them melancholy, some of them joyous, the exact sequence of which I should have great difficulty in recollecting, but they trouble me still, and too hot a sun recalls to my memory the *tumbril and the butterfly*.

I. — The philosopher of whom I speak and whom I would like to see would take account of observations like those; your anecdote is an admirable step in my argument. For every theory having to do with sensibility, every study applied to those miraculous regions whence our power, our joys and pains derive, all philosophy at such heights, presuppose a thorough study of the imagination. For if reason and judgment govern ordinary acts and all movements which tend to struggle for life and preserve that life notwithstanding obstacles, the imagination and the faculty of receiving images regulate sensibility. Sensibility and imagination are two connecting terms. That is what is not sufficiently understood. When I see a very joyous or very melancholy child who knows how to amuse himself alone and do without his little comrades, thus affording the proof of a lively and a personal sensibility, I say to myself: there is a future "imaginative." It is a rule that never fails. The philosopher whom we are clamoring for should write it at the head of his essay.

MY FATHER. — Is it not sensibility which allows those metamorphoses to take place of which we were speaking just now? You know my love for vagabonds, for all those poor devils just the same color as the turnpike, who stop at the well to take a drink, and whose slightest movements I used to watch when we dwelt in that house by the side of the high-road? Well, you must not laugh, but I assure you that sometimes I have left my room and house and my own skin and have entered underhand into those organisms, penetrating those wretched longings and terrible thirsts, those frightful feelings of contentment in bread, wine and shade. There lies a chapter on sensibility! Was it pity, that great moral spring which led me on, or was it a central and basic curiosity which sharpened my sight and wits? I do not know. All that I know is that I have lived the life of those wanderers and nomads, of those unconscious poets. What delightful things might be written about them ! Did you ever ponder — it is that *butterfly* which rouses me still — did you ever ponder on their long and deep melancholics, on all the beauties of nature which penetrate them without their knowing it, those grain-fields, that rustling and moving yellow sea of wheat-heads, the rose-colored swales and solitary woods where the rabbits hold their congregations, the fringes of the forest, so fresh and beautiful and impressive? One day whilst you were still a child I was taking you the other side of the Sénart forest and we saw two white pigeons that were winging their way side by side beneath a thunderstorm, skirting the opaque and copper-edged clouds. Well, all that poetry of nature circulates through the vagabond along with his blood and his wretchedness, and so, in that philosophy which you talk of, it ought to form a chapter apart, because there lies an assemblage of true and primordial sensations.

(*After a moment's reflection*).—Now, you see, abstract ideas do not constitute healthy nourishment. Very soon they degenerate into a juggling trick and the mind that gives itself up to them loses in relief and color. The man who desires to talk about the imagination splits up his subject into chapters and for each chapter he devises a series of cold arguments. Why does he not proceed by examples? Contemporary novels, the historical romance, such as we make it to-day, have taught me one thing: Everything hangs together in the moral world. All the while that certain given personages are in combination to form a given situation, beneath or above them a comedy or little drama plays itself along which is the "fresco" or caricature of that very situation and defines it; very often a miser has in his dining-room a common print representing the *grasshopper's visit to the ant.* Hamlet, preoccupied by a crime it is necessary to perform, receives the actors at Elsinore instigated by a marvellously just intuition, and orders them to play a scene which will give everybody a foretaste of murder and that terror which is felt when the torches are carried out. We are Hamlets for ever and ever. We never accomplish an act which is not accompanied by additional phenomena in which that act is reflected and made ready; alongside of the masterpiece nature accumulates conscientiously the preliminary sketches.

All this I say in order to explain to you why the philosopher, while he shall be tracing the similar laws of imagination and sensibility, ought to describe on a parallel line various examples and episodes to illustrate his text, just as we do for little children. I do not know a finer book than the work on English literature by Taine. Every moment the writer turns to the picture and shows us an example of his theory. His formulas are enriched by admirable verses from Shakespeare, Byron or Keats, or by some incisive tirade from Swift or Fielding. Literature is so abstract an art, so separated from actual things, that one cannot bind it to the earth by too solid and powerful chains. And I would make the same statement concerning philosophy, if indeed it cares to really touch us and make an impression upon our period.

I. — A convenient method is to describe human beings as types in order to make them carry that faculty of mind which one is studying. According to me, Balzac's works ought to be considered a phenomenon of the highest cerebrality, as a series of examples for just such a philosophy of feeling. Alive within himself the incomparable author of the *Comédie Humaine* had a power which permitted him to place outside himself those human characteristics with which his soul was filled. That power is Desire, " the essence of man " as Spinoza said, that desire which we all feel but which we understand so badly and of which *need* is nothing but a reduced image.

'Tis a singular result of modern civilization that *desire* increases while realization diminishes. The more society sets men in frames and fixes them into immovable ruts which are generally degrading and embruting, the more does it place them in contact with a number of luxuries and pleasures they cannot help longing for which become so many nightmares for them. Most of our fellow-men of the present day are in the condition of peasants after a visit to a Universal Exposition, whom the commonplace of their condition disgusts, who dream of dancing girls and houris, and kill their old parents in order to enjoy a single night of riot. This rise of desire has for corollary the rise in the number of suicides.

" Je sortirai, quant à moi, satisfait
       D'un monde où l'action n'est pas la sœur du rêve." [1]

Now in the case of Balzac, as with Shakespeare and Racine and Dante, action is the sister of imagination. For *desire* kills the man who lacks imagination, or sets him crazy; but it forces the imaginative man to find means to escape from a world which resembles him and has the imprint of his own exasperation and frenzy; but he is the grand creator of ideas and characters.

My FATHER. — And then, through a strange concatena-

[1] " For me — with satisfaction would I spurn
       A world where action is not fancy's twin."

tion, beauty is the mainspring of *desire*, or if you prefer, the illusion of beauty. As a matter of fact there is where poetry delivers or rescues us. A spectacle too beautiful, an impression too vivid, incline our souls at once to melancholy. And if we are not able to cast our emotion into song, then that melancholy turns into sadness, and behold! through the force of desire beauty becomes the spring and cause of pain. Beauty, Desire, Pain, are three stimulants of sensibility which the imagination softens, extinguishes and takes with it into its own depths.

There are hours in life when the reasons for the existence of things seem to be on the very point of appearing to us, when, leaning over to watch ourselves, we perceive the deep wheels going and the glittering sheen of our machine.

You remember seven or eight years ago a certain visit we made to Mistral in Provence? We passed a charming day filled with light and poetry, and Mistral, that great creator of dreams, had fairly intoxicated us, as much with his talk as with a marvellous wine. Toward the close of twilight we took our way towards Tarascon. It was the time of the wine harvest. Slow carts brushed past our quicker carriage, they were filled by laborers with faces proud in their lines and girls showing a pagan grace. How pale all those faces were above the long pale highway, underneath a sky, rosy to exasperation, where warm mists were floating! The vine-dressers had hung bunches of grapes upon the wayside crossings, their offerings from remote antiquity. In that light air happiness, power and delight in work harmonized with each other to such an extent that the spectacle became a glorious one and our eyes became wet with tears, as happens when all of a sudden Beauty raises her veil from her face. . . . (*a silence, then after reflection*) . . . . Yes, that is it, that is it exactly : Beauty, Desire, Pain.

I. — Such phases of excited feeling must have been the normal state of a Shakespeare or a Balzac. They only saw the outer world through the medium of the world which they carried in their own breasts, or the opera-glass of their imagination. And in fact all their characters, no matter how close they approach reality, share the mark of the Master, that is to say, something gaunt and excessive which from time to time seems to shock our good sense and ceases to move us. King Lear and Père Goriot degenerate into monsters of paternal love by the mere exercise of that love.

Do you not feel that those exaggerations are yet one proof more for the origin of those colossal works *within*. The greater number of human beings do not possess complete sentiments, or feelings that are pure, as when they leave the forge in heroic minds. They do not drink without much adulteration the wines of Love, Hatred, Pity, Anger and so forth. . . . They are willing to content themselves with vague mixtures, and so the hatred of this man is partly supported by fear, and the pity of that man is limited by his own egotism, and the remorse of yonder third is quenched by his rage.

In a word, passions for the majority of human beings become lessened in consequence of contact and mixture. They lose their sharpness, their edge and color. They become weak and without interest, because they cease to have anything in them which works toward splendid deeds.

Now it is among the "imaginatives," among those who are not afraid of surpassing reality, that we would

find the model and typical passions if they quitted the
ordinary world. They subject them to the movements
of their own soul, its fever and ups and downs. They
lend them that beauty which consists in marching
straight toward an end and to the extreme limit of reality, notwithstanding events or obstacles. Every one of
their characters accomplishes his destiny impetuously
and with an imperious air and drives life before him as
if it were some great cloud of dust. There is a miser,
Grandet. He will be miserly to the very verge of the
mania of avarice. His hands and feet, his whole body
will take the form of his own vice, his looks will take on
the sheen of metal, each one of his words will be
timorous, gloomy, but at the same time bearing the impress of a hard, implacable egotism. Here is a knave,
Philippe Brideau. No one has gone so far and with
such ferocity in the direction of knavery. One may take
them all and stamp upon the brows of all some vice or
some virtue. And that vice or virtue will be without mixture of attenuation such as existed in the first man.

Such works as those move us to such a degree because
they spring from *Truth enlarged.*

MY FATHER. — Are we not close upon the old debate
between the Real and the Imaginary? Although you do
not belong to that period, you have heard of the howls
which greeted Flaubert and his continuators, Zola, the
Goncourts and me. People could not pardon us for
introducing the ordinary facts of life into novels. Yet it
is true that since then realism has lost ground and turned
aside into vulgarity, and it is true that people have tried
to find a doctrine where there was nothing but an emancipation. We demanded the right to talk about everything, treat every subject, select our characters and

pictures from any class we chose. It cannot be denied that *L'Assommoir* is a masterpiece, nor that *Germanie Lacerteux* is another. Good or bad, our opinions have given a lively jump to the national literature and certainly no one has a right to complain of that.

But the old reproach is different : " You wish to paint reality ? Then you will be mere photographers, passive mirrors, phonographs, mere machines which reproduce what falls into their mouths or their pipes and moreover reproduce everything without choice or discrimination. You wish to paint reality ; but we already know too much about reality. Reality is here about us every day ; it besieges and throttles us. What we ask of art is precisely to take us away from the real and show us other faces, other skies, other lands than those about us which weary us by the monotony of their constant presence."

That is a specious reproach. It troubles one because it does include a certain modicum of truth. Absolutely unjust when it applies to writers like Flaubert, Zola, Goncourt, it does have grounds when it comes to wretched copyists and scribblers who apply without any talent formulas they have badly understood.

And the knot of the problem — that is why I am attacking it just now — the knot of the problem lies entirely in the *imagination*.

I. — I must confess to you that the adventures of magnificent characters, such as heroes, will always interest me more than those of little ordinary citizens ; and I call magnificent characters not only kings and captains, but likewise philosophers, authors and artists. The bursts of rage which that which has been so coarsely entitled " naturalism " has provoked have nearly caused us to turn to literature of exceptional characters. From this point of view *Symbolism* was an inevitable reaction.

MY FATHER. — It is not a question here of symbolism or naturalism. You know how little importance I have always given to schools and classifications. I hate them all. I belong to none of them.

We have to do here with reality and truth. Now there is nothing outside of the real. There is nothing outside of the true. And those two terms meet again in a certain virtue : Sincerity. Note that my formula is broad. A sincere lyrical writer is in the way of truth when he gives himself up to lyricism, and though he may change the lines of reality in accordance with the laws and build of his brain, remains true so far as his conscience is concerned. *He does not seek knowingly the false.* A sincere mystic is in the way of truth when he constructs his castles of clouds and mists according to his own consciousness and in accord with those changes in line or shape which that same consciousness of his produces in the real.

In other terms, reality is subject to the metamorphoses of the imagination, but without it, lacking such nourishment, the imagination would be grinding upon emptiness, it would break down and fall to ruins, turning into craziness or imbecility. And whatever may be the form and degree of the imagination, the owner of that imagination is sincere in regard to it, so long as he shows his products just as they come from his factory.

There are no forms of art, there are merely temperaments. Well, these temperaments are so numerous and varied that they never exhaust the real. An original spirit when it comes into this world may have the plan of reconstructing the world. As long as this world lasts he will never use up all the innumerable resources which life, and the harms which life is subject to, present forever to the imagination.

Innumerable resources! I have lived a good deal; when still quite young I had the faculty of observing; and, so far as the imagination goes, I have known during my childhood all the terrors felt by corsairs, explorers and the abandoned ones. Well, every day I get a surprise and have some new observation to make; *and particularly I realize that I have made mistakes.* To recognize one's mistake and to confess it is the beginning of that science which has not yet received a name, and nevertheless 't is one that seems to me the highest and most important of all sciences, since it consists of extracting from life all the instruction which that life contains, since it includes morals, psychology and physiology, since moreover it does not destroy pity and does not excite pride, since it has neither professorial chair, nor pedants, nor institutes, and since it carries its recompense in itself.

I. — Is not that science in which imagination finds its resources precisely the school of sensibility?

MY FATHER. — It is that and something beside. You are right in saying that it enriches the imagination. The great " imaginatives," the great observers of the human heart, have carried that science with them as though it were some new organ in their breast and have used it as easily as they breathed or digested. It exists in every page of Montaigne, showing itself in that good-humored and fragmentary form which alone suits it, because it is a science which must fear axioms, deductions, formulas and other fribbles. It ought to wear its belt very loose. Pascal, who has enriched it with many admirable discoveries, nevertheless had an imagination too mathematical for it, and since it is the science of life, what is necessary to it, beyond everything else, is a lively imagination.

I. — Do you believe that this science is destined to have a great future?

MY FATHER. — Greater than any other. Since Auguste Comte and the *Philosophie Positive* the scientists in all the exact sciences have been imagining that their progress was continuous and without limit. And they regard artists with disdain, because, as they say, they do not progress. Now in the first place, do we not progress, are we stationary? Down the long history of letters and arts, is it not possible to observe certain modifications of this *Sensibility* and this *Imagination*, concerning which we were talking just now? There is an entirely new problem and one which will not be wanting in interest !

But apart from all that, it does not seem to me it is at all demonstrated that the progress of science is continuous and without limit. In science as in art every original mind tends to quit the paths trodden hard by his predecessors in order to make a path for himself. It results from this that very rarely does a field of study in which some man of genius has accomplished tremendous progress continue to attract the attention of superior minds ; the domain of science seems to me thus filled with regions of great importance which have not been thoroughly explored.

I. — If one were to study the movements and march of the scientific imagination in this century, one would find a striking confirmation of what you say in the list of discoveries. Since the time of Bichat, who has taken up

again the microscopic study of tissues and of their relations? a study which was entirely different from those
histological labors which are so much the fashion nowadays. Since the time of Claude Bernard, who has taken
up again the thorough study of the vaso-motor nerves
and the source of animal heat? The school of La Salpê-
trière has popularized the works of Duchenne of Bou-
logne, but it has completely abandoned the study of the
relations between the muscular groups and manifestations
of feeling, that is to say, the portion of the work of that
great and misunderstood man which contains the most
genius. What can be said of medical science in France
during the last twenty years? The spirit of competition
and of clique has destroyed all initiative among us. But
the field has remained clear for men of intrigue and
fools; a good many more stages are necessary before a
reaction can be produced. Moreover it appears that
the marvellous labors of Pasteur, which in the beginning
were so bold and broad, are about to be wrecked in officialdom, and scarcely will be likely to have continuers.
You are not wrong in believing that the lines of demarka-
tion are more apparent than real and that in the one, as
in the other, progress is occasioned by independent
minds which are innovators and breakers of formulas.

My Father. — All very true; but the *science of life*
of which we were speaking might march on with giant
strides, thanks to the multiplicity of its points of view.

The work might be divided up. As to that which
belongs to the imagination, those who are earnest in
considering abstract ideas might look upon the science
under that aspect. In that way they might inaugurate
that Philosophy of Sensibility from which you expect
marvellous things, and which in any case would lift us

out of the problems of the Pure Reason to some
extent.

Those who like myself are zealous servants of the
"concrete" would occupy themselves less with imagination in itself than with the human beings who show it.
Some of us would take the scientific man. Others would
study poets. But examples, many examples! It is
through examples that one gets lasting results. Consider Plutarch and Saint-Simon. Those who are fond
of monsters will study the changes wrought in that sublime faculty which constitutes criminals and madmen.

I. — When it comes to intellectual enterprises, have
you any confidence in co-operative labors? I would
expect that more should result from the efforts of a
single mind; a book for instance which would be for
Imagination what Taine's book was for *Intelligence* — a
clear and a correct summary.

MY FATHER. — I think the task would be very heavy
for one person. If you wish we will search out some of
the principal objects of such a work and trace a sort of
general summary in big lines.

I. — Very well; nothing could be better for clearing
up one's own ideas than to see how one should go to
work to explain them to another person.

Let us begin by defining Imagination, and, as one
describes a continent, mark off its boundaries, its relations as to neighborhood to or dependence upon other
faculties.

MY FATHER. — I am no lover of definitions at the
start. Besides, the framework of gender and species is
very narrow for that voluminous faculty; it would burst.

I think it might be well at the start to lay down this
chief principle : that *Imagination* and *Sensibility* are two

connected faculties, or else that *Sensibility* is the reservoir used by *Imagination*. Just now we sufficiently laid stress upon that point. But it is basic and it will at once assure originality to our work.

I. — That having been done and with examples in support (Balzac and Shakespeare will do admirably for our demonstration) we can establish the necessity of considering *Imagination* from two points of view . . .

MY FATHER. — The concrete and the abstract : 1st — Study of *Imagination* among individuals ; 2d — Study of *Imagination* in itself.

After this rapid preamble we will enter at once into the heart of the subject by giving a few portraits of famous representatives of *Imagination*. Faithful to our method of using examples, we will take a poet, a scientist, a philosopher, an artist and a man of action. Our chief care shall be to demonstrate that this faculty changes with the innumerable forms of life, just so soon as it is a question of a living faculty. We are seeking laws and truths, but we shall insist on the *differences* and the *exceptions*. That method will reduce error to a minimum and stifle all pedantry.

It shows us what we really are, poor observers in a blind way and by no means arrogant men of theory hidebound within their formulas even when their formulas are false.

For the poet we could not have a better example than Hugo ; and for sub-title thereto " or sensitiveness to the word ; " as a sub-title for Lamartine preferably " or sensitiveness to the rhythmic period," and that for Baudelaire " or sensitiveness to nicety." Poor Baudelaire ! It was that long research for the exact word which killed him.

15

As to Victor Hugo, if we compare his verbal sensitiveness to sensitiveness to cold and heat for example, we perceive that his most admirable poems are veritable "shudders"—and prophetic shudders besides. In the wear and tear of life, through rubbing and degeneration, most words have become vulgarized, and so we employ words without force and lacking blood; they are mere anæmics. Thanks to his verbal sensitiveness Hugo has given all their energy, all their reflected gleams back to words. This kind of miracle takes place with him particularly through the placing of the word in the phrase. Just as jewellers present certain jewels at the most luminous point and after such a fashion that they shine with an unexpected and burning brilliance, so does he present a word. In his hands a word follows its unconventional *rôle* just as the butterfly before mentioned followed the stream from the watering-cart; here in the midst of the 19th century he gave back to the vocabulary all the burning power of the 16th century, whilst the terms used in a new way shone and flamed in the sunlight of the idea.

I.—But that verbal sensitiveness is a precipice. When Hugo makes an error he errs magnificently. He takes sonorous sounds for arguments and alliterations for proofs, and then he contents himself with puns pure and simple. This happens to him particularly when he assails ideas or those appearances of ideas with which lyrical minds proudly play, such as the briefness of existence, the probability that there is a superior justice, the difficulty of curing oneself of love, the cruel stress of remorse, the delights of liberty and so forth. In such commonplaces as these Hugo's mill grinds away at nothing. He always displaces the same amount of air, whether his subject be beautiful or vulgar, so that his come-downs are simply colossal.

MY FATHER.—The results are peculiar enough if one compares the imagination of Hugo with that of Chateaubriand. In the latter there is a combination of verbal sensitiveness and sensitiveness to the period. Particularly does he excel in the promptness and lightning-like brilliancy of his descriptive wholes: here a happy and new epithet and there a fine noun, dull and abstract, or gleaming with a low color-note. So does Chateaubriand enchant us. This method is so characteristic of him that any two lines from his works are at once recognizable.

It seems that the phrase as Chateaubriand uses it has preserved the rhythm and movement of the sea; the rush of his crises comes from the farthest line of the horizon; their return is broad, quiet and majestic. Another example of sensitiveness to the period in writing, Gustave Flaubert, is the only one presenting in the same degree as Chateaubriand that verbal wealth which gives a sensuous satisfaction to one's mind when reading. But it is Normandy over against Brittany.

I.— One morning, after a wearisome night in the train, how well did I feel that relationship between Chateaubriand and his sublime source of inspiration, the ocean! I was making a pilgrimage to the crag of the Grand Bé. All the horizon of Saint-Malo was powdered with a fine and penetrating rain. Gulls were wailing through the damp air, and along the suburbs of the city, those crooked, green suburbs, the drums of the military school were beating. I seated myself near the balustrade which guards the splendid sepulchre; of a certainty that glorious horizon excited me no more than did

the name etched in the stone. But it caused me to
understand him who lay beneath. The author of *René*,
the bold poet perched at the portal of the 19th century
like an eagle on his crag, he at least had the *rhythm of
the high sea.* As in the big sea-shells that were about
his bedroom as a child, so in every one of his phrases
that humid expanse was condensed, that expanse where
the wailing gulls turned and twisted. What I perceive
hovering above his literary work is the sky of the ocean,
heavy, impenetrable and without limits, that breeder of
fogs and misery, that risk-filled sky and melancholy,
which is ever mustered by glances of disquiet. Thus did
the lighthouse of the French tongue cast its rays over
our wretched epoch, as if in the midst of the waves
where they tumble in a majestic tumult underneath the
vast gray expanse. One's sensations experience an unexpected grandeur whilst traversing the works of that
man. Rain, wind, forests and ocean, or by way of contrast the grandeurs and miseries of human beings, unroll
themselves from the depths of his brain and carve pictures grandly upon the live rock of the written word.
The imagination of that great nomadic bird was ever
turned toward his black sun, Death ; it was the thought
of death which filled him with melancholy and a disdain
so magnificent that the world was darkened thereby, and
with a bold and haughty irony which dared to attack yet
another glory, the glory of that other eagle there before
him : Napoleon.

My Father. — Oh magnificent imagination of Brittany, imagination opposed to that of my race, but one
that I passionately admire — the ocean, the North and
its fogs !   At the dawn of light I drank my glass of
brandy in the little yellowish house and then I embarked

on the pilot boat which left the port of Quiberon, and
there lay the soul of Brittany all about me . . . (*after a
moment's thought*) Chateaubriand, Lamennais, Renan
are the most splendid revolutionists of the century, tremendous figures carved in granite upon which the flying
scud of glory ever beats! And those severe images
which haunt them are the images that rose from their
old, black, heroic country where ocean and mankind
forever war upon each other.

I. — Should we not note here, in those powerful
minds, the extraordinary impression which was made by
the images which they perceived all about them during
their childhood? Entering into their brains at the time
when brains are most impressionable, those images
became an integral part of them and developed as they
developed. The ocean, sky, forests and mountains,
those were their natural outlooks, those the horizons
which were destined never to be forgotten. They must
have been insinuated into them through the slow attention given them in childhood, or else during those
moments of excited feeling which constitute the deeper
life of a person. This cloud or that shade in the water,
or yonder shape of tree, river or plain, were the phantoms which haunted them and gave to their work that
majesty, that sombre glory which belong only to nature
and to them. Guardians of the sublime secrets which
the natural world whispers to the child, when they
became men they preserved in themselves the eternal
majesty of space.

Thus the words of Chateaubriand give us glimpses of
horizons which move us deeply. Thus Victor Hugo has
a part in the rose-colored morning, feels the heavy heats
of noonday and falls asleep in the golden edge of twi-

light. That which their little eyes looked upon during the fevers and transports of their years of growth, grew grander with increasing age. Images conjure up images. At first appeared athwart the vague whirlwinds of memory that rose-tinged shore where shadows fall. Thereafter came the melancholy of that moment, and the sensation which is grafted upon it, as when at the barking of the shepherd's dog the staggering sheep creep close together in a flock. And the sensations of early manhood made those pictures only more vivid. When love appeared in the burning heart of the famous one, it called at first upon all the living forces of early youth, the gladsome awakenings and the days burning with unconscious desires. Since love renders everything more beautiful and rich, it causes the memory to pour forth a multitude of keen and brilliant sensations, which furnish food to prose or poetry.

A young girl singing as she turns her spinning-wheel — that to the mind of Goethe is the most lively image of chastity and grace. It is an image which returns many a time in his works. If it is Clara waiting for Egmont, or Margaret waiting for Faust, that purring of the spinning-wheel gives the cadence for the amorous attempt. I have always imagined that when he was a child Goethe had that spectacle before him. If one should make a selection in their literary work from the early years of the greatest poets of those parts which relate to imagination, I am sure that the part such things play would astonish people. It would astonish them because we forget the extreme vividness of first sensations; but although they are benumbed they remain living even in the most ordinary men. And some-times they come of a sudden, returning to inspire old age with joy or sorrow at the sight of long-forgotten faces indistinct of feature.

MY FATHER. — In the case of those whom genius has touched with its wing, such sensations afford a constant happiness. Look at any one of them — Goethe, Hugo, Chateaubriand, Renan — how they turn their heads backward with a melancholy smile! See them bending over their own cradle. But in the most secret part of their souls there are regions which have never been explored, whence their singular dreams mount up. Whatever their little hands have touched, whatever their young eyes have seen, haunts them thereafter, and haunts us. Their finest pages are gemmed with the dews of youth.

Besides, imagination likes to explore the regions of the unconscious. It plunges into the black depths of our soul and brings forth those miraculous dreams, that which touched and tempted us, and especially that which troubled us when we were making trial of our own senses and were acquainted with but few of the forms of the vast world.

I. — The first time that I turned the leaves of Hokusaï's *Mangoua*, those extraordinary albums where the genius of the most impressionable of all draftsmen has tried its flight, I felt an intuition of the meaning of such wandering forms. Goethe said that our imagination was not able to trace a single line or appearance which did not previously exist in a real and possible state of existence. It might really seem as if Hokusaï had found in his own soul quite as much as in the enormous reservoir furnished by nature that sensational crowd of trees, unknown animals, attitudes, movements and objects of which he *delivered* himself by means of his drawings. Exactly as Balzac and Shakespeare did, so this powerful artist traced on paper, not mere copies of the external world, but a series of figures projected from his own brain. When he talks to us about his dreams, and when he puts his wits to work tracing them — and doing it with what vigor and relief! — we must understand by that that he *dreamed Nature*.

MY FATHER. — But isn't that exactly what children do? All the time that the world is blooming about them and offers itself to the delicate tentacles of their senses, a parallel world is boiling within them, a world over which they have in no sense the mastery. The meeting of these two circuits, their combination or *mulatière* creates their originality as geniuses.

And then whatever the imagination of the child has taken hold of, just as it is with the imagination of the artist, is in a state of constant movement. The child and the man of genius *see things that have no motion move about*. They are struck by accordances and analogies, they perceive that closely woven web in nature where everything has its place and each thing accords one with the other and where the reverse of the weft itself has no deception in it. Because the reverse consists of the science and order with which the threads cross each other, whensoever the face of the tapestry itself consists of art and beauty. When Albert Dürer places side by side a mass of hair and a falling stream of water, he knits the world together like a child by the employment of such exterior resemblances.

Such reflections have carried us aside from the poets, but it is right to vagabondize a bit when one is occupied with a wandering faculty. Particularly in our century have there been poetic and literary imaginations of a very strange sort which would fit well in our museum;

among the Anglo-Saxons and the Germans still more than among us, I think, because the images in the North, troubled and numberless as they are, growing one from the other, are very different from the images in the South, among which lucidness is never wanting. This is demanded by the Latin law.

I. — The inheritance of the Aryans has been divided between two great captains. I acknowledge that heretofore I have accused you of exaggeration when I saw you giving so much importance to questions of race; but to-day, since my education has broadened, I see very well that you are right. As it always happens, great causes determine great effects, and a theory of little causes — the theory of Cleopatra's nose — is a mystification, for many other motives would have been necessary beside the paradox Pascal has offered, before the whole face of history could have been changed.

It is by studying the writers, poets and artists in general that one understands best the influence upon the imagination of latitude. In the North images are tumultuous, heavy and filled with germs of fermentation. Of course one should avoid too easy analogies, but the Valkyrs of god Woden who fill every point of the compass with their furious galloping are in good sooth the daughters of the mists. Just to quote a poet haphazard — the distance between the poems of Robert Browning and those of Frédéric Mistral, that is pretty much the difference.

My FATHER. — Beyond everything else the Southern imagination is violent and rapid; but in its greatest frenzy it keeps in touch with reason and holds solidly thereto. Its lucidness is sometimes more apparent than real. There are cool springs whose limpid waters

mask their depth. In any case it never becomes intoxicated with itself. There is nothing of the somnam-
bulist, nothing of the artificial in it. It remains always
sticking close to life. Sometimes writers of a Southern
race have attempted to tear themselves away from their
natural temperament in order to be misty, abstruse and
symbolical. But there comes their Latin clarity to
bridle them, envelop and restrain them, forcing them
to remain within the limits of the comprehensible, no
matter what they may desire! These contortions amuse
me. Unquestionably the hypothesis of limpid horizons
which oblige the imagination to stay ever transparent
and direct seems commonplace. But is it not a right
hypothesis and one not to be gainsaid?

But apart from questions of race, and on parallel lines
with them, what is more amusing and side-splitting than
the case of Népomucène Lemercier, the author of the
Panhypocrisiade? Certainly he was a man of imagination, but of Latin imagination. And the more the
wretched fellow tried to escape from clearness and the
basic qualities of his own intelligence, the more did
the tapes of commonsense bind him down and make him
impossible for any artistic diversions. He was strange,
it is true, but his strangeness was classic, obedient
to rules and regulations, forced into an extraordinary
mold.

The imagination of the North, and I beg you to
understand that there is no fault-finding in my words,
is on the contrary in its essential nature complex.
Without question it would have been impossible for
Carlyle, as well as Browning, or Jean-Paul Richter, or
Walt Whitman, to express himself in a transparent
fashion. Those subterranean analogies of which we

spoke just now, that obscure network of the universe possessed them to the point of madness. The beauties in
their works are like torches waved with tremendous
power in the blackest shade.

Carlyle's explanations, like those made by Jean-Paul,
only make the blackness blacker. These men move
with ease in a mysterious land. Similar sounds, words
and formulas that seem to clash, analogies and alliera-
tions take on a sibylline aspect in their style and are the
source of perpetual dreams.

I. — But, as a Latin, do you not feel a sort of repul-
sion or compulsory shrinking from such masses of symbols and from those precious stones in which truths and
enigmas of color are as it were in suspension?

MY FATHER. — I have moments when those troublous
images seduce me too. I understand marvellously well
how a certain class of minds should delight in them and
refuse every other nourishment. They render one's
palate *blasé*, and everything else seems tasteless. I
only find fault with the fact that obscurity often only
covers some matter of very little importance which
would not attract attention if it were transposed into
simple terms. When a whirlwind of ideas and impressions falls upon poets, it is allowable in them to translate
those ideas and impressions in that sequence under
which they present themselves, lucky enough to be able
to fix the mystery thus forever. What is to be objected
to very strongly is the habit of intentionally obscuring
one's language.

But for a Northern imagination there are plenty of
ways of being cloudy and yet sincere. Now it is an
analogy, or all the glittering following of some word or
some thought, which carries away pen and mind. Again

it is a poet like Swinburne for example, who digs down until he arrives at black and unexplored regions where his own little smoky lamp alone can guide him. In one case lyrical impressions present themselves to the mind with a tremendous tumult and a rising of the mists which he who translates them respects. In another case extreme brevity and a praiseworthy attempt to make a formula precise and rare bring together words of a narrow and hard meaning, which one finds great difficulty in breaking up.

Lovers of the shadowy are right in alleging that we are surrounded with mystery, or, to use the charming excuse made by Stéphane Mallarmé, that one has to *write with black on a white ground.* But is there not a primordial convention without which a work of art would become impossible, according to which one must believe oneself in possession of a certain stability and light, certain laws in whose shelter the book, drama or painting flourish, before one attempts to tell the story, paint the picture, or make oneself manifest in any manner whatsoever? That which causes obscurity in some people is the fact that they make everything uncertain in their first sentence; after that they move along in an artificial and terribly complex world, in which words have an unexpected meaning and sonorous sounds attract or repel each other and everything happens just as it does in dreams where no will acts as guide to appearances and acts and everything floats in a sea of the inexplicable.

I. — By way of the names of Hokusaï and Albert Dürer we have reached the question of Imagination among draftsmen and painters. There are two fields of feeling here quite distinct one from the other, that of *line* and that of *color* — Leonardo da Vinci and Rembrandt for example.

MY FATHER. — One primary and important observation — the duel between light and color, to which in his *Italian Painting* as well as in his *Flemish Painting* Taine seems to me to have failed to give enough attention. The antagonism there is a real one. The most vivid image of this question, so far as I am concerned, consisted of a flower from Spain which happened to be placed in the yard of that little house formerly occupied by Eugène Delacroix, which we were then occupying. When evening came and the sun gradually died out that flower and shrub flamed like the host above the altar.

J. — That remark receives confirmation through a visit I made to a certain great museum in the North, that of Amsterdam. The Rembrandts, the Halses, the Terburgs, the Vermeers of Delft have been the real kings of color. A low and gray sky, or else some snow-filled heaven corresponds especially well with the delightful shades of color in houses and canals in their country. In such circumstances colors spring forth with a most extraordinary violence. One can believe that in a certain way they have forced the eyes of painters and aided in the formation of the earliest pioneers among the realists.

As to the imagination, it exists there in details, exactitude and intensity. Rembrandt imagined a special world of his own, containing a warm and sumptuous atmosphere in which a shadow has the soft heaviness of velvet; with him faces and bodies are always placed just at the intersection of this light and this shade, in such case that they offer an alternation of gold and dark red and shadows.

However dangerous and deceiving parallels may be, it does not seem to me that those were wrong who compared the imagination of Rembrandt to the imagination of Shakespeare. Just like the Dutch painter, the English playwright has an atmosphere entirely his own, which is like some emanation from his genius; and his characters play alternately from a golden richness to a deep black, which causes them to approach those unforgettable captains of the " Ronde de Nuit " and those stupefying " Drapiers." Virtues and vices, kindnesses and brutality, dreams and acts, perform in his case the duties of light and shade.

Another series of reflections came to me, but always with regard to Rembrandt, when I made a visit to the museum at Madrid and mentally compared the marvels there with the marvels in the Amsterdam Museum. It seemed to me that the imagination of Velasquez and Rembrandt differed radically and completely from each other. That shows itself in the different way each had of arranging their masterpiece. Just go up to the portrait of his mother by the Dutch master and see if you can find any traces of work or excitement or vibration of the brush. No effort, no suggestion of *subjectivity*, if one may use pedantic language, is to be seen. The painter has reproduced life in its full relief and warmth, but he has remained impersonal, and that life which he has depicted is covered with a glaze under which the traces of labor are no longer visible.

On the contrary, walk up to the " Fileuses " by Velasquez; whatever of carefully directed brutality, subtle vehemence and restrained audacity show themselves to the observer through the furious play of the brush, the frenzied spread of the impasto, the sudden jets of gray,

rose and black — those burning and dead colors the secret
of which he carried off with him — whatever of such
things the brain of a man of genius can contain, spring
to the sight. In the presence of that magnificent " go "
a kind of hallucination befalls one. The artist seems
to be caught at work. One seems to see him painting
a hand which moves, painting it in five strokes of the
brush, or bringing out an embroidery by a few scratches
of his palette knife, or inclosing in a pearl the reflection
of some figure, or in some figure the reflection of a race.

Are there not two distinct forms there clearly and de-
cisively apart — are there not two opposing inspirations
there? When Rembrandt had finished that portrait of
his mother, Rembrandt had disappeared. But in the
canvas of the " Fileuses " Velasquez is always there.
He shows the secrets of his method and seems to defy
those who are to follow him.

My Father. — According to that, his imagination
would be nearer of a kind to Frans Hals, whose tremendous " go " is equally plain. I recall a dining room
entirely hung with panels by this master. It was life
itself.

I. — Ah that little museum of Haarlem opposite the
church on the little provincial square! Seated about a
table at some excuse for a meeting of an archery club
are all the varieties of human sensuality, bold and manifest in their several types. There's representative imagination pushed to the point of paroxysm! The timid
man, the arrogant, the savage, and the man who is
conciliatory, and the man who hates his neighbor in
secret!

The old regents of the club near by with their wrinkled
faces and trembling hands signify the decay of the

human body, the slow usage and decline of life. One of them exceptionally has an unctuous and waxen face with a veritable patina on it which makes it look like old ivory. Frans Hals more than any other artist has proved that it is possible to be symbolical by giving an exact representation of reality.

My Father. — I am thinking of another painter, this time a Spaniard, but one who had an extraordinary sensitiveness for cruelty and pain, and was possessed with an overwhelming imagination . . . Goya. All the while that he spends his wit on bull fights and fills the black shadows with figures of enthusiastic spectators, whilst the principal actor, squat and black, while the *beast* hurls itself ahead, while the fatal trumpets blow — all the time that he carves with his pitiless and savage burin the " Horrors of War," bloody scenes from the Inquisition, monks with mouths distended by a holy ferocity — all the while that he trifles with the elegancies, caprices and perverted smiles of little rosy faces, he remains anguished and cruel through the force of reality, and even through the force of color, which runs through all the shades of blood whether dry or fluid, in jets or sheets or blotches. He represents a barbarous epoch.

I. — If we leave to one side the technical imagination of painters in so far as it touches drawing and color, the other portion of their minds seems for the most part to be somewhat akin to the dramatic art. But according to my idea Rembrandt and Velasquez are not in their moved and decorative pictures at the best of their genius. Marvellously do they render the perpetual *static* drama of existence, that namely which lurks in a smile, a finely twisted mouth, a gesture, or even for example some window through which we see an interior, a garden, a knot of people assembled, or else a single person, a clown, a court jester, a philosopher, or in a princess or in a horse. There is a general theory spread among men of the profession that *painting should not express ideas.* Rather does it seem that painting should express ideas after its own fashion; the imagination of great painters can be just as rich and excited as those of great playwrights. Painting has the advantage of restoring for us the speechless, motionless and intervening part of the drama or irony of life, that part, namely, which the drama can legitimately make real because it is always in movement and sounding. But at certain moments the arts approach each other and merge one into the other. That is why the plays of Ibsen, with their characters who keep silence for long moments and are so preoccupied with looks and the fleeting aspect of things and with their own changelessness, are not entirely without connection with the pictures of the great Holland epoch, for the latter are an apotheosis of intimate and interior life — among which some lives indeed include so large a proportion of the tragical !

The imagination excites itself most vividly when it receives very little material, but that material sincere and arranged in proper order. In all the modern theatre is there a single scene more impressive than that assemblage of merchants, than that council of regents about a table? What are they at? We do not know what it is that these men with heads like cats, these old men with weasel heads are discussing. What moves us is the expression of their faces. Notwithstanding their speechlessness, a flood of profound utterance, a dialogue in Shakespeare's manner seems to us to flow from those mouths with thin and yet ruddy lips.

16

MY FATHER. — Ambulatory life shows us a similar
dramatic side in the swiftly passing spectacles of the
street or the fields. An old man reading at a window
or a balcony, an old woman grafting her rose bushes, a
young man and young girl seated at twilight on a terrace, a peasant in his field — all these human beings
bowed down by the monotony of their life are so many
interior images whose leaves we turn in our reveries.
Without willing it we create concerning and about them
little stories. We fabricate the circumstances; and I
believe that artists can never be too rich in visions of this
sort. These guide artists toward truth of rendering,
right slant of the light, the expression of faces, characteristic attitudes, calm gestures and looks; the bringing
together of all these elements brings beauty into life.
For my part I have never ceased feeding my imagination with such spectacles. Many of them have remained so vivid in my memory that I no longer know
whether they belong to art or life.

I. — Dutch painting makes me think of one of the most
singular phenomena of the history of art and therefore of
imagination. There are epochs in which minds are exercised in favor of painting, as in the seventeenth century in
Holland, or for the dramatic art, as in the sixteenth century
in England and in Spain, and in the seventeenth century
in France. All of a sudden we are face to face with a
simultaneous blossoming out of very dissimilar geniuses,
but all of them abounding in power, all marked by love
of life and forms, *all observers of windows.* That may
last twenty, thirty or forty years, and one masterpiece
follows another; art passes on with giant strides, refines
itself here and excites itself there and shines with incomparable splendor. Then all of a sudden an unknown

hand takes away the torches. Queen Mab flies with her little laugh. The shadows darken down. Feeling for life is lost. Behold the reign of flat works, of allegories and imitations! After Rembrandt comes Lairesse. After Racine, behold Voltaire! How explain such changes as these?

My Father. — Enough to state them. In the most gifted man sensitiveness is not forever. In an artist those wretched hours "without grace" as I call them, are very frequent, and to be compared to that dryness of soul feared by theologians. Do not the physiologists demonstrate that there exists a *periodic insensibility of the heart?* It is to be noted that such phases follow periods of excitement, periods of those intoxicated moments when nature gives up her secrets. What takes place in the individual is doubtless repeated by the race. Imaginations have need of periods of silence and rest. Then it is that the torch of Lucretius falls by the way.

I. — There is one art which has been silent a long while, yet is the most impressive of all, since it consists of history fixed in place, I mean architecture. You know the saying : *stones no longer speak.* Who will ever explain to us why at a certain given period the soil of Europe began to bristle with a harvest of churches which raised the voice of faith toward the sky? Outside the pale of religion there were always palaces and magnificent buildings and even most curious dwellings of citizens. All that is gone. In some unknown city a haphazard stroll by twilight, which mercifully softens the actual ugliness of the scene, permits us to divine the old lyrical beauties of architecture like gray, antique lace ; but, for our contemporaries, there's a sense dead and gone !

MY FATHER. — That is not true for music at least. . . . Wagner was a phenomenon in this century just as he will be one in the time to come, and no one is more fruitful than he in remarks of every sort.

He was a man belonging to another age. Nevertheless he found a way to our nerves and our brains far more easily than one would have thought. If imagination has representatives he was one of the giants. A Northern imagination, it is true, on which all the beauties and faults of the North have left their impress. He insists, he insists with violence and tenacity, he insists so pitilessly! He is afraid that we have n't understood. That language of motives which he has imagined and of which he makes such a magnificent use has the fault of leaving us very often with an impression of weariness and satiety. It becomes a veritable cause for suffering in the case of his many and odious imitators, because nothing is so terrible as ideas imposed by another, nothing is worse than routine.

Still, it was absolutely necessary for him to invent that system of motives in order to utter that connection between the drama and music realized by him, a connection so perfect that his characters seem to us clothed in sound. Besides, these motives ally them in an irresistible way, sometimes a happy way, with the grand circumstances of life and their destiny. And finally they express those mysterious things which remain unexpressed but understood in the libretto.

In Richard Wagner the imagination is so representative and violent that it saturates his work to overflowing with all the sounds of nature and leaves a limited space for the episodes. The passion between Tristan and Isolde plunges into the tumult of the ocean which overwhelms it, then it appears on the surface, then it plunges under again. One invincible power raises the waves and the souls by a single movement. In the poem of Wagner, water, fire, the woods, the blossoming and mystic meadow, the holy spot become the more powerful characters. In this paganism of to-day all nature has become divine.

Your generation is accustomed to these splendors, this torrent of heroism and life, but you cannot present to your fancy the impression which that music exercised on men of my age. In cold truth it transformed us. It renovated the atmosphere of art. Then it was that I understood the vanity of all those discussions concerning realism, lyricism and symbolism. There is everything in Wagner, and in everything he is admirable, because there is nothing in him which is pedantic or intentionally low. Turning his face toward Gayety he wrote the *Meistersinger*, turning toward Pain, Love, Death, the *Mütter* of Goethe, he wrote *Tristan und Isolde*. He made use of the entire human piano-forte, and the entire superhuman piano-forte. Cries, tears, the distortion of despair, the trickling of water over rocks, the sough of the wind in the trees, the frightful remorse for incest, the song of the shepherd and the trumpets of war — his tremendous imagination is always at white heat, and always ready.

That imagination of his, excessive and feverish, has not only renovated music but has also overwhelmed poetry and philosophy. Although theories disquiet me, still I feel them trembling in Wagner behind each one of his heroes. The gods talk of their destiny and of the conflict of that destiny with the destiny of men, they talk of ancient Fate in a way that is sometimes obscure,

but with a rush and go that make one forget to question
them. It is the famous wall of the *Légende des
Siècles*, crowded with tubas and the trumpets of Sachs,
tumultuous and glittering in their mass.

I. — Do you think it would be possible to analyze the
imagination of a man of that sort?

MY FATHER. — Everything can be analyzed, but it
would be a pity to take the divinity down from a
pedestal. Let his methods remain in the dark like his
orchestra ; his sensitiveness, which was one of a special
kind, seems to me before everything else *legendary*. It
is quite possible that he desired to have characters of a
size suitable to their surroundings, and that one would
feel uncomfortable while considering ordinary men who
should be victims to the Ocean of Tristan, or to the
Forest of Siegfried. What difference does it make?
He succeeds in moving us with these superterrestrial
passions. In *Tristan* humanity has a larger part.
Those are our own wounds which are bleeding in the
flesh of the lovers, wounds that the sacred spear, which
the hero brings back with him, shall never heal.

I. — I have heard amateurs of music uphold the following thesis — that the musical imagination has no need
of the dramatic element in so far as it is manifested by
the characters and passions : " The drama " say they
" lies in music itself and the architectural development
of the different parts of a symphony in which everything
holds its place, binds and helps the one the other, and
produces a veritable construction of sounds. The
classic phases of the symphony are modelled with a
truly Platonic sagacity upon the movements of the soul
whensoever a vivid emotion powerfully shakes that soul
and the latter sings its agony after the wound has been

received. *Andante, Adagio, Allegro, Scherzo, Finale* — those are the stages of sensibility which philosophers did not invent and which correspond to the sublimest reality, an intuition for which only belongs from age to age to a few privileged persons."

I am ready to adhere to that opinion whenever I hear a symphony of Beethoven. It even seems to me that at that moment my emotion includes a deeper and rarer quality than it does when listening to a fragment of the *Tetralogy.*

MY FATHER. — It were better to say that the masterpiece by Beethoven being more concentrated and closely woven makes a total impression upon you in a much shorter time than does a drama with its necessary stops and changes of scenery and delays for explanation. Now it is necessary in our study to give a large measure of consideration to the element of *duration.*

There are some people cast in a lighter metal who immediately begin to vibrate and emit a sound of enthusiasm which quickly stops even as it was produced. There are others of a thick and resisting bronze who retain the transmitted vibrations. There are minds which are slow to put themselves in motion, lazy imaginations which, when they have once been persuaded and captivated, will not easily abandon that object which has been given them for food. They transform it in a thousand ways. It has entered so deeply into their being that there is no longer a fear that it will escape. It has become part of themselves and of their individual structure. With people of that sort, apparently massive in their make, the phenomena of the outer world assist a genius powerfully, since they slip into the flesh and blood of the artist and undergo there his own vicissitudes.

It thus happens that many creators have a tremendous but restricted originality. With them everything turns to intensity. Everything that reaches them from the outside suffers at once the changes of their individual rules and impressions ; whilst others have a far broader field of humanity which can be ploughed and sowed throughout its entire extent. It seems to me that Beethoven belongs to the former category.

In relation to him you spoke of " Platonic sagacity." The state of soul to which Plato has given his name might well merit a place to itself in our little work. Platonism would mean that the imagination submits itself to laws which would give it more energy whilst moderating and guiding it.

A person who feels a powerful impression and who is gifted with extreme sensibility is naturally inclined to restore that immediate impression to the world in the shape of some work of art, some picture, poem or symphony. The method is entirely instinctive and it causes our brain to be a veritable vat in which fermentation goes on. It captures the quick admiration of those who require violent emotions, and that is the greater number of men. But there is a great class of artists, painters and philosophers who will not admit that the mind is not influenced by a rhythm and does not obey a certain harmony, which represent a higher condition and the beauty of human intelligence. What Plato taught to his disciples was measure, that is to say a mental equilibrium which has a perfect horror of monsters and will not be satisfied with a hasty and confused improvisation.

The state of mind which has been named for Plato and of which he was certainly the finest example is

brought forth by that same self-control, by those deep
ponderings which are destined to purify images and by
that intimate and rich arrangement which puts the
bridle upon lyricism; this moral state is found again in
literature at all ages and throughout the entire field of
art. It is found in Beethoven. It furnishes the artist
with a mysterious and well-contained beauty and a wider
action upon the human soul, because that which it
creates is subjected to deep-going movements, to the
rhythmical motion of the human soul at the time that it
is filled with noble thoughts.

Happy are those beings of imagination compact who
have known how to control their own mental images
and have not allowed the tumultuous products of their
brain to escape from them like a torrent that often rolls
down mud! Such concentration and self-mastery make
a long duration of admiration certain, one hardly knows
why. It is will knit to intelligence, it includes also the
power of order and equilibrium.

To return to music; with respect to that, I own to the
infirmity or the virtue that I love it so much, I find it
difficult to make a selection. I love military music passing down the road, the thunder of the sea, the gale
through the pines. What puts me into an enthusiastic
condition with Richard Wagner is just that impressionability of his for every sound in nature; how that same
nature does saturate and overwhelm his work, as it were
with the force of a hurricane! His orchestral parts
cradle and swing me to and fro. His gentleness and
his power cause me to pass within a few hours through
the most powerful emotions, emotions in fact for
which no one can fail to be grateful forever to the man
who has excited them, because they reveal our inner

depths to ourselves. I love and admire Beethoven also for the wide and peaceful landscapes which he knows how to open up in the soul of sound, in what I am in the habit of calling "the other planet." Italian music enchants me and in Rossini I experience that extraordinary impression of melancholy anguish which an excess of life gives us. There is too much frenzy, too much movement; it is as if one were trying to escape from death. I adore Mendelssohn and his delicious pictures of nature, such as the *Symphonie Romaine* and the *Symphonie Écossaise.* There are certain hours toward nightfall when the soul of Schumann torments me. . . . But to number them all would be never to end. I have lived through the power of music; I am a dweller upon its planet.

I. — It seems to me that we have brought back some useful observations from our rapid incursion into the arts. But the arts are not all alike. There are men in whom imagination is forever bridled by their will. They are interesting for us to observe, because in such cases we see that same faculty warring with another faculty which constrains and limits it.

Happy are they who are able to manifest clearly those sentiments which move them and cause the world to partake of their transports! As you have remarked in a celebrated phrase, the imagination of the orator has like everything else its license, its broad play-space, its free development. It increases its power through that special kind of intoxication which comes to the orator from the listeners and fills him constantly with new energy. The length of time is of special importance when it comes to this. For rapidity is its first necessity, since the man who uses his imagination in public must before everything else imagine quickly and truly. Truly, that is to say, in the way and with the aid of formulas capable of impressing those who listen to him. Moreover the art of oratory is unfortunately too often nothing but an avalanche of commonplaces, because the remnants of the mind generally present themselves first to one's memory.

But what is of greater importance to our study of the phenomena of oratory is the imagination in the man of action. If he is tormented by this great faculty, the man of action will surely suffer deceptions and dissatisfactions incomparable, since he is forced to be *realistic*. The result is that with him the imaginative act has less importance than the means to arrive at a result. And it is the equilibrium of these two endeavors that constitutes the fate of the hero, just as Carlyle says.

We know well enough what the poet or the orator or the writer sees during his spectral revelations of imagination — words and sounds that his spirit can grasp, and, higher up, strange ideas which are in constant change of form because they are about to enter into very varied bodies, — splendid costumes — a traversing of seasons and climes — merging and mixing with others — carrying crowds with them — rousing up memories of the past! And in good sooth there is nothing more delightful for the mind than to follow up the life of an image, its longer or shorter existence, its origin from the moment it forms itself in the brain of its master to the time when, having moved about the world and having realized its power, it falls into the common reservoir of *show-case beauties*, beauties which have no longer any effective action.

We know also how the painter sees when he paints

and the musician when he composes. At any rate we have in regard to such creative states of mind certain notions and testimony which we enlarge into theories and which satisfy our intellectual laziness.

But on the other hand that of which we completely lack knowledge is the manner in which mental images comport themselves in the man of action. Certain recent philosophical hypotheses concerning which we must soon vex ourselves attribute an effective power to mental images. It is certain that when alive and active they *tend constantly to become real.* According to Fouillée's phrase, they are "*motrices.*" A beautiful picture, a lovely symphony, a magnificent bit of literature do not only infuse power into us ; such things drag us along in their wake and put us into a mental condition as close as possible to themselves. It is thus that war-like songs and the rolling of drums pour heroism into the hearts of citizens.

If you would only accept the characterizations and definitions of metaphysics I would gladly say that the *man of action is he in whom mental images have the strongest tendency to become real.*

MY FATHER. — My fear of philosophy does not go to the length of causing me to reject a formula without examination which is at least convenient. What I object to in your definition is the fact that it eludes the difficulty and gets out of the scrape by the use of words.

Let us look at an example, the grandest and most striking of this century, Napoleon. And then at another, Bismarck. And again at a third, Stanley. Our modern epoch which is reproached for the poorness of its blood seems to me nevertheless a privileged period so far as the existence of heroes is concerned, for these three are characteristic.

The closest to me is Napoleon. His Southern race is the reason why I can class him best, because his formulas touch me better and his means are a little clearer to me.

It seems that his imagination, like his will, was excessive, ceaseless and I might say frightful. Above all things it was tenacious, and in spite of his celebrated phrase it did not altogether die at Saint-Jean-d'Acre. What kept him in motion and roused him always was his *sensibility with regard to glory and authority.* The example of the grand captains and leaders of peoples were forever present in his thoughts. He quotes and invokes them, never will he admit discussion about them. He is a Latin to the very marrow, through his mental uprightness, through his lucidity, through his judgment. There are even moments when he shows himself a Philistine, and he the enthusiast appears timid in the name of enthusiasm and fears the results of first impulses. It very seldom happens that passion and imagination are not connected and up to a certain point parallel. Now this "imaginative" was a grand creature of passion. We might have doubted it a little, but the researches made by Frédéric Masson have made the light upon this point absolutely clear.

Well, in a brain like that, the most insensate and grandiose, the most unlimited projects wing their way in flaming line. I do not in the least believe that he confined his desires to that which he believed he could realize. His desire and his mental images march far before him and his will follows them far behind — enraged against himself and others about him whenever he

did not reach its aim, and yet at the same time calcu-
lating chances of success with an energy and a hare-
brained audacity and a tenacity in application which
have never had their equal in this world. Whenever he
secured a triumph, whenever he satisfied his own ambition on any point, triumph and ambition had already
been discounted a long while. And, as we have positive
witness, they no longer gave him any pleasure. Alas,
that is the fault of the imagination in activity! It
devours the crop when in the green shoot and the
result always seems piteously inferior to the desire.

I once had a friend who, notwithstanding that he was
always lucky in whatever he attempted, was always constantly morose. He adored travels. When he was
about to undertake one he talked without end about it
and for a long while before he left. He surrounded
himself with guide books and information. He asked
questions of every one he could. You would find him
seated in the midst of charts, plans and photographs.
But at the very moment of starting he had already
enjoyed all his pleasure. His imagination was a lively
one and in that way became a constant scourge. If he
undertook anything, he represented to himself alternately success or failure with such a power that neither
the one nor the other could give him the slightest sensation when they came. On this little side of his my
friend recalled to me the Great Emperor, the Unamusa-
ble. " I have yawned my way through life ! " cried
Chateaubriand, who was another powerful imaginative.

What strikes and moves us, moreover, in the mental
conceptions of Bonaparte was his rapidity and universality. Roederer shows us the Emperor at the State
Council occupying himself with everything, a man of

detail to an excessive degree, following out every question in all particulars, calling for replies, making notes, classifying and asking the advice of inventive minds. And it is the same everywhere and always, whether in his armchair or on the battlefield — what disconcerts us is the going to work of an imagination of admirable suppleness, one which facts could never repulse.

Which facts could never repulse. That imagination of Bonaparte differed in this particular from any others which have been perhaps more surprising than his own but have engaged with other objects or projects that lie beyond and outside of reality. After all, clever turns of thought are easy enough when they are compared with that long patience which is able to make something actual.

And in fact Napoleon was very much incensed with those persons whose grindstones turn on nothing, with those useless windmills! If he had a detestation of ideologues, it was because such people represent lost strength, and nothing irritated that great man like bungled work and failure. One is sometimes ready to ask whether he was wrong after all, considering the abuse which people make nowadays of words and formulas. For my part I feel a certain displeasure when I see human thought flying wide of humanity and spending so much power in hollow speculations.

I. — Do you not think that the imagination of metaphysicians has its own distant utility? It seems to me that in that mist where they move great events prepare themselves. There is no doubt that it represents the disquiet which attends an epoch. Deprived of immediate objects on which to work, or disdaining them, thought takes itself for its own study. There is a revolutionary virtue in the constant questioning which she causes all problems to undergo ; let us avoid dissimulation ; a perpetual state of revolution is the best state for the brain. Ideas which congeal and fix themselves solidly become authoritative and odious. The Church has not been alone in offering an example of a philosophy of liberty which supplies weapons to despotism. All principles have a tendency to become immovable and play the tyrant to their victims. Metaphysics have this thing in their favor that they engage with the radical principles themselves and at the very moment when the latter think that they are victorious, destroy them and give place to others.

Let us not separate, if so you please, the imagination of ideas from the imagination of acts. The hatred of Napoleon for Ideology must not make us forget that he himself fought in honor of an Ideology, namely his own, and that he wished to impose it upon the universe.

My Father. — That man was a veritable element himself and the elements alone were able to draw bounds and limits for him ; heat in Spain and cold in Russia said to him : " Farther than this thou shalt not go." The man who reaches such summits of power is intoxicated by his sudden ascension ; his outlook does not extend in accordance with the heights to which he rises ; it is only his desire which increases.

After everything has been considered, if it were necessary to give a sub-title to the history of Napoleon, that sub-title might perhaps be " Or the Man of Imagination." What he actually realized in his short and frantic life is a warrant for us concerning what he dreamed. How many dreams must have gone to produce a single act !

Note in passing the extraordinary attraction which imaginatives exercise one upon the other. They trail each other by the scent. They divine each other and understand each other with half a word; they are all ready to help each other.

Up to now we have been considering as the representatives of that *faculty which delivers* only the artists, philosophers and men of action, in a word the great men who are the representatives of the *lofty imagination*. Our reckoning would not be complete if we took no account of types of the *lower imagination*.

Such types are numberless; we rub elbows with them every day. I thought it was my duty to give them an important place in my work. In his dramas like *The Wild Duck* Ibsen has also interested himself in them. Some are found in the novels of Dickens and those of Tourguénieff; and I certainly forget others.

Many who are imprisoned by the realities of life do not for that reason lose their illusions. Like people plunged in hallucinations they march on in their wretchedness, seeing nothing, feeling nothing, always expecting the inheritance or the extraordinary chance in the lottery, or the kind gentleman who comes their way and adopts them, or the lady who calls to her coachman: " Halt ! " and turning to the foot passenger, " Get in, this is your own carriage ! " Admirable hopes are these which help to make all evils bearable. Those who carry about with them in their feeble brains that transforming virtue have no need of alcohol, nor opium, nor any kind of exciting things. If they have no fire they can make a hearth; if they lack bread, they form a mental image of a feast.

Don Quixote is an admirable book because it consists

17

of a monograph of one of these inferior imaginations, and another example is *Madame Bovary.* That is why I call the faculty of evoking images *that faculty which delivers.* Just as those children are sheltered from sorrow and melancholy whom we see amusing themselves all alone and inventing games without the help of comrades, exactly so the wretched to whom Providence has intrusted the magic wand support their burdens with ease.

Such " stories " and " legends " as the little as well as the great call for have only one aim : To supply what is lacking to imaginations which are weak, introduce into an often hard and implacable life another life which does not belong to it, where things come at the right moment, watchful fairies combat evil geniuses and pain and suffering roll away, permitting Gladness to be seen smiling upon her pedestal. We have just been judging art from a bird's-eye view with regard to its intrinsic qualities in the Chinese fashion, but not according to its results ; now art has the sublime destiny of creating about and above our souls enough consoling or amusing images to prevent existence from crushing the souls — whether because these images become an enlarged looking-glass reflecting their condition which permits them to look upon themselves in beauty, or because they represent a condition far superior whither illusion will drag them. Pascal has celebrated dreams in a memorable phrase which puts shepherds and kings on the same level. The *rôle* that our faculty must play is to create a perpetual dream. The world would soon come to an end if it were not for the imaginatives and the story-tellers. Compassionate reality takes care to put on her programme from time to time the realization of some beautiful

dream in order that illusion shall not be altogether lost.
So it is that we see treasures discovered, a shepherd who
wins a princess to wife, and reparation for great injustices.
Such short respites from evil and baseness are sufficient
to perpetuate hope. In proportion as the religious
imagination which offered wretched men pictures all
ready and painted has disappeared, it would seem that the
other imagination of which I am speaking has augmented.
Mankind has more than ever need of those dreams
which uncompromising realists would like to suppress.

I. — The chances of conversation have caused us to
follow a singular path; we certainly might be allowed to
return upon our steps to examine the road we have
traversed.

We began by *recognizing* the importance of Imagination and rather than define it we have mentioned its
powers in detail. Then we established the closeness
of connection which it entertains with the faculty of
feeling, and to such effect that it appeared to us finally
as an *extended sensibility.* Every man carries about in
himself a faculty for being an architect which pushes
him to complete any active feeling, but he is not satisfied
with that, his life has impressed him strongly. He looks
for something more and that prolongation of effort constitutes the faculty of receiving images.

After these premisses we then entered into the heart
of the subject and we resolved to proceed by examples.
We have traversed with long steps the arts and sciences
and their method, and on our way have examined all
the imaginary trails and have followed them whenever
they seemed to us worth while.

In this way we have arrived through the representatives of humanity to the very frontiers of life itself; and

it is very easy to see that I have undergone your influence, since, having taken our departure from an abstract
point, we have arrived at the place where we are examining absolutely concrete points of view.

Once or twice we almost deviated into metaphysics,
but with a little energy we have kept that method in
reserve for the moment when we might wish to endeavor
to make a synthesis instead of an analysis.

MY FATHER. — That word " method " makes me
smile, not that I have not the greatest respect for
Descartes, but it seems to me that his *Discours* has now
reached to a certain extent the state of dogma. Descartes understood the mathematical sciences very well
and his entire work is based on them. To-day while
biological sciences are ruling the roost, it seems as if
method itself had undergone certain modifications.

It is intentionally that up to the present moment I
have kept our conversation within the limits of live
things. I know only too well that one rambles whenever
one goes aside from humanity. The faculties or passions,
considered outside of those who possess or suffer them,
appear to me to be false entities : " the straw of words
for the clear grain of things " — that is a reproach from
a metaphysician, Leibnitz, I think.

The position of a romance writer therefore in modern
times would be at one and the same time historical and
philosophical ; historical, because he lives in a certain
epoch and saturates himself with the turn of mind of that
epoch and its characteristics and leaves a picture of it
which moves the reader ; philosophical, because he seizes
upon the passions in their activity within the human
tissue where they dwell, and endeavors to elevate them
from the *particular* to the *general.*

I. — Since we have reached the question of persons affected by their passions, do you not think that they introduce important modifications into the phenomena of imagination? We see, ourselves, how much our intelligence is upset by various episodes in our existence.

Thus *love* is a very powerful and very mysterious source of images. Like a poison it transforms the entire look of nature and opens in the soul novel regions. Then it is that one perceives to what dire extent one ignores one's own character.

There are human beings in whom the imagination has, so to speak, nothing to say, or is reduced to its simplest expression. They are content with such natural phenomena as life presents to them, or more exactly according to that routine which the habit of the senses traces for them. They never leave their exact limits. They consider any one who raises himself a little bit above the ordinary level, seeks to interpret that which moves him and make more important that which surrounds him, as crazy or diseased.

Well, when love touches human beings of that sort they change completely, so that their surroundings can hardly recognize them. Owing to the new sentiment strange forces agitate themselves for the first time within their breasts, forces which disquiet and upset them. They attribute virtues to inanimate things. They hear the birds sing. They perceive that stars exist. In short it is the education of Caliban. Nothing more moving than this metamorphosis ; it causes us to imagine some secret education conducted by nature.

MY FATHER, — There is nothing like *love* to rouse the sleeping powers of a man. Every violent movement of consciousness has the same result. Undoubtedly *jeal-*

ousy may be able to make a poet out of a very commonplace individual. As we have known since Spinoza, this
vice particularly favors the imagination. It excites
pictures of exuberant richness in the most burning
regions of the soul, forming the worst of tortures, which
renew and transform themselves, or else, increasing in
depth, become a veritable obsession.

But apart from jealousy let us look for instance at
avarice. That passion wonderfully sharpens the wits of
him who carries it about him. It makes him aware of
a multitude of small details which he would never have
remarked without its presence. When his favorite topic
excites him, it causes him to utter sublime phrases, remarkable utterances which we are not surprised to discover in the mouth of a Père Grandet, and which of a
certainty Balzac actually collected from misers whom he
knew.

And there 's the *egoist*, of whom George Meredith has
traced so wonderful a portrait — what stratagems does
he not employ and through what persevering rounds
does he not gradually bring back the entire world to
his own personality !

The *scrupulous* man is less studious and less favored
by literature, although he is nevertheless a character that
occurs very often ; the scrupulous man may be considered a victim of his own imagination. It is imagination
which swells up the slightest acts in his mind, such acts
as an ordinary man never considers as of more than
secondary importance, and with excellent reason, because
otherwise they would clog and destroy his life after the
fashion of parasitic plants. *Scrupulosity* is a very wide-
spread malady of the soul. Theologians understand it
and have made excellent descriptions of it. But they

have noticed only one of its forms, the religious variant, although it takes on the most varied aspects and torments the most dissimilar souls. What characterizes it especially is an anomalous condition of the moral vision caused by imagination which excites and turns it aside.

And by that step we reach *remorse,* in which imagination plays a leading part. That person who is able by an effort of his mind to reconstruct a scene from life, hear the sounds and see the colors and gestures of it, and recall the odors, that man would do well to abstain from any wrong act.

I. — Don't you think that one might make an interesting study of remorse showing itself in an undeveloped character, which has been hitherto rebellious to feelings and even to all sensations apart from hunger, thirst and weariness? Little by little one might see him enlightening himself from the flame of the torches of the Eumenides. His torture would be a revelation to him.

MY FATHER. — That is a miracle which often occurs. Whether undeveloped or over-refined, the greater number of mankind are delivered through suffering of the forces which are contained within. A telling moment in our study would be the connection of suffering with imagination. The person who groans understands the groaning of others. The man who has a sore readily sympathizes with the sores of another. That is it, *pity* . . . that is the great intermediary. That penetrates not only hearts, it penetrates brains also and makes the nerves sensitive. Nature opens wide her portals for the person invaded thereby and he believes that the world has been revealed to him all of a sudden, so much

does he become aware of the lamentations round about
him, so much does he interest himself in a new and profound way in trees, animals and his own fellow-beings.
Artists who are especially marked by pity have in that
respect a very particular mark which distinguishes them
profoundly from others.

Pity it is which excites inspiration in Dickens and
Dostoiewski. It is by the way of pity that they glide
into the souls of children, debauchees, martyrs and
criminals with a truth that amazes us. For if Dante
appeared to his contemporaries like a revenant from the
infernal regions, from what accursed countries did not
that Englishman and that Russian return, bearing such
pallor on their faces and showing such a trembling in
their hands?

It is pity which conducted them down into the sombre
trench where human suffering moans. It was that which
raised the trap-door. They leant over the abyss without
disgust and they have brought back to their fellows new
cries of anguish and new subjects for indignation.

For after the pity which widens the imagination
comes that anger which fixes its features and gives it
the necessary warmth. The two feelings are connected.

I. — In your last remarks there is the germ of a
theory which I believe is true with respect to the origin
of satire.

Satirical writers are *reversed lyrical minds*. Gifted
with nerves of prodigious sensitiveness and a marvellous
imagination, they have been placed by their lives in
such conditions that their pride was broken, their pity
exasperated, and their anger perpetually roused by the
spectacle of oppression and pain so far as men apply
oppression and pain to their fellows. A new sense is

then born in them which renders existence a pain, and leaves them no repose, the sense of injustice. In Aristophanes, Swift, Fielding, Rabelais, Cervantes and Voltaire, in fact in all the great men filled with indignation, it is possible to perceive the lyrical power, but drawn aside and transformed by a feeling of universal iniquity.

Whilst on the one side human beings, steeped in lethargy by their laziness, their cowardice or simply habit, support the spectacle of oppression without complaining, these liberators of the human spirit, who are enemies of all power and control, I almost said of every law, insist upon seeing nothing in mankind except an animal which is in pain and which when it is in pain is no longer responsible for its movements of reaction against suffering.

Still, in their hands literature rises out of the rule of the mandarin and issues from the ivory tower. It assumes a social importance and thus we see that the part played by imagination may be not only that of the liberator but the avenger.

MY FATHER. — The sad doctrine of the fatalists states that one can do nothing to nothing. Despite all efforts the sum of injustice will ever remain the same upon earth and the cries of the satirists shall be in vain.

Of a certainty the spectacle that history presents fills us with deep melancholy. For men like Michelet or Carlyle it furnished the stimulus to their imaginations; bent over that spectacle as over a deep abyss, they heard the distant enormous tumult of battle and perceived shapes flying in rout, combats and metamorphoses. The vanity of all laws which cannot maintain men within the limits of the good and right struck them, laws which are often the daughters of tyranny, laws which one day brings forth and the next destroys, laws which ever present themselves with a harsh, immovable and savage face.

In the minds of those great *poets of fact* pity and anger must have been carried to the point of paroxysm by the spectacle of horrors for which they could not furnish any remedy whatsoever. History is like the bottom of the sea with its races between voracious foes, its ambuscades, its perpetual struggle for life, its implacability.

But there is another painful aspect of history which is very well calculated to strike violent imaginations and that is its automatism. I had all of a sudden, whilst listening one day in the garden to the singing of a bird, a vision of nature regulated in its manifestation, nature without the unexpected, without joy and without mystery, somewhat like a series of scenery in an opera succeeding the one the other according to hours and seasons, through which a certain number of changeless characters ever marched clothed in their usual costumes and placed in their conventional poses. What a horrible nightmare! Liberty issuing from the world and leaving behind only the automaton . . . never before did fatalism seem to me so living and terrible!

Well, the spectacle of history is somewhat differently powerful than the song of a bird, that it should make us believe in certain periods, certain laws, a necessary rhythm, a long-foreseen succession of murders, wars and empires. That murmur which rises from history has likewise its predetermined phases, its movements of *piano-forte.* From a great distance communities appear like those ant-heaps, the destiny of which some English scientist, I know not which, profoundly changed by pouring upon certain kinds of ants a spoonful of another kind of ants — so much does such an act furnish an abbreviated picture of the making of races and realms.

Beauty of imagination consisting as it does more especially of belief in that liberty which it gives us, I can foresee a true torture for the historian if he should reach the point of view of modern fatality and determinism.

I. — I hold to that phrase you have just pronounced which delights me : "Beauty of imagination consisting more especially of belief in that liberty which it gives us."

Whether you admit it or not, that is pure metaphysics, and it is certainly strange that we can never approach any question great or little without the Science of Sciences making its appearance at a given moment and forcing the mind to dig deeper yet, down into its own substance.

This torture of determinism, which is very apparent in history and the historians, is in sober fact the scourge of the imagination ; it seems to impose limits upon the imagination, it makes the imagination believe that it is itself a prisoner to formulas and embarrassed by laws and that it is impossible to free itself from that despotic rule to which all things, all beings and thoughts, must submit.

It is a scourge of the imagination and a greater one than we suppose, because it limits it forever ; not only does it tear its heart but it restricts it besides. Unquestionably the melancholy of wise old men sprang from no other reasons and the belief in fatality which came to them through the exact sciences will soon appear among the races of the West in as frightful a form as opium.

Like opium *determinism* has had its phase of elevation,
followed very soon by a phase of depression which carries
a man toward melancholy, dark thoughts and suicide.
And the son of positivism was modern pessimism.   During the flourishing age of that sombre doctrine great was
the boldness of the scientists.   They pretended to control and lead everything, even as far as the most secret
operation, the most mysterious movements of the human
brain.   It coincided exactly with certain researches made
in that same brain, certain hurried and hazardous physi-
ological incursions, which were afterwards called *localizations*. And from the Physiology which the doctors
thought they had mastered, there sprang, with what
pride and boasting ! a new philosophy, a psycho-physiology ! Every week appeared some volume with red
edges, in which some faculty of the soul was analyzed
according to the most recent methods, methods, it may be
said, which recalled the efforts of Bouvard and the illustrious Pécuchet in their finest periods of scientific zeal.

Strange discussions arose in which ideas were dis-
sected and feelings were weighed with a laughable zeal !
Through what strange aberration of mind did men come
to indulge in such childishness who were no more foolish
than others and quite as capable of becoming professors
and assistants, just as well as their comrades? The
moment arrived when they were just about to draw
up a chart *ne varietur* of the human passions, with all
the districts neatly bounded and with a table of exceptions fully drawn up. At that period the "schema"
flourished, that schema which has been termed *the last
concrete vestige of an opinion which has become abstract:*
it soon became a source of errors. They drew on the
board the schema of pride or of avarice side by side

with the schema of the reflex actions in the same. They calculated the variations of sweat and other secretions in a lover, an angry man, an indifferent person, during their crises, apart from crises, during periods of calm, etc. Every assistant professor very soon thought himself an admirable philosopher because philosophy had shrunk to a narrow chapter of medicine. As to metaphysics, that was railed upon, scorned, gibed at, and relegated among old superstitions. It was considered the attribute of degenerates or fools, for it may be noted that this was also the blooming period for the mind doctors.

Filled with zeal, vigor and authority, these mind doctors saw no obstacle before them. Desirous to furnish on a new system their houses thus built, they claimed as their clients not only men of talent but also the men of genius, and in preference artists, whoever had been distinguished through his pen or his pencil. The slightest suggestion of art became suspicious. This conversation upon Imagination would have left no doubt whatever as to our condition of mind. And on their side the mind doctors started a rivalry with the psychophysiologists, for they themselves were likewise seriously occupied in weighing, localizing and analyzing the human faculties, and really nothing was prettier than those little red, blue and green houses which they attributed to them on the surface of the brain.

Suddenly things changed; a new generation of metaphysicians, ardent and vigorous, rose from the earth at the very moment that it was thought that metaphysics were buried. Then was there in the camp of the Diafoiruses and the Purgons of philosophy a rout indeed! They made a sieve of their follies. People began to look askance at the mind doctors. Serious works appeared in which things returned to their former state because so many pretended discoveries were reduced to their real proportions. It was seen that many of the localizations were false and that some of them were even absurd.

To-day treatises on Psycho-physiology are mouldering in a deep shade. To their great regret the mind doctors have been forced to renounce their pretensions concerning art and artists. We sent them back to their douches and dark cells with no little rudeness. And finally as a culmination of mortification, a metaphysic of liberty was installed anew by sharp and perspicuous souls which is thoroughly in the swim of modern ideas.

And since in the moral world everything hangs together, it may be remarked that the theories of determinism, like everything else which gives itself up to fatality, flourished during the epoch of oppression, during defeat and distress, whilst on the other hand the theories of liberty belong to the vigorous and well-constituted generation. For there again it is — fatalism deprives people entirely of energy like opium. Is it not singular that modern Germany should have sprung from Hegelianism and the doctrines of Fichte and Schelling? The man who believes himself the master of his own acts is a thousand times stronger than he who believes that his acts have been ordained. What is the use of attempting to move if movement has pre-established causes, if free will has nothing to do with it?

MY FATHER. — This moral point of view is important, and it is certain that ideas have an active virtue in them even if they appear abstract and detached from all human connection. The moral world exists in the interior of the social world like water in an aquarium, water in a constant state of movement. This world is impressionable to everything which comes from without. A doctrine upsets it which we thought had no danger in it. A bad law works in the same way. Men are so interknit that everything holds together in whatever springs from them.

For my part I have never been a partisan of narrow fatalism; the moment that my conscientiousness seems to me free, I have admitted that it was free, and as to incursions into the domain of art and philosophy, I think they are as misplaced as they are foolish.

I have even been astounded to see to what a degree science leaves me cold. I admire science in its living manifestations, when it solaces or heals, but it seems to me feeble and vacillating in its theoretical part and all the more pretentious because it is peculiarly subject to error.

So far as feelings and their variations are concerned I think that I have brought to this study absolute upright-ness and zeal. After forty years of a constant, and I might almost say, sickly observation — so greatly has my fellow-man always tormented me — I have reached this certainty that I know very few things and possess a very small circle of clear ideas. Those who pretend to explore that delicate realm with measuring instruments, "schemas" or theories, are poor, wretched, lost ones. They, more than any other people, deserve the reproach of craziness. One must be mad to suppose that one could concentrate into a single little book the last word that is to be said upon any question whatever which re-lates to the intelligence or the will.

So far as scientists are concerned they have interested

me, after my whim, to a greater or less degree, according as their science was more or less human, directing itself toward our great virtues or our feeble sides.

I have known admirable physicians who were not geniuses, so far as theories are concerned, and who were nevertheless healers. They went straight for the evil and fought it. In diagnosis should not a faculty for mental images occupy a preponderating part? A good clinical physician ought to represent to himself the complete chart of the human body with its *terrae incognitae*, its lions and its tigers, like those on old geographical maps, which were placed there to show our ignorance. He should also represent sickness, its causes, march and progress, then through heredity — that heredity which he has so deplorably abused — his imagination continues and prolongs itself beyond the individual as far out as to the species and race.

I. — So far as *discovery* and its mechanism is concerned, I think it is Claude Bernard who has shown that it proceeds more especially through *analogy*.

The phenomena of the universe form one vast tapestry in which everything hangs together and knot is interknit with knot. Ordinary eyes are perfectly content with the figures shown upon it and do not search farther into their co-relations the one with the other.

Observers, however, are anxious as to the contour of these figures, their resemblances and differences. It is perfectly clear to them that the tapestry has some meaning and that, beside its immediate significance, it possesses another less obvious one. They notice moreover that there are crossings and defects and missing stitches, that there are pieces overlaid and marks of pauses in the work and returns thereto.

But those who use their *imagination* are interested in the relations and analogies between parts of the tapestry which are far distant from each other — analogies of form and color and direction which seem to them to correspond to mysterious and profound relationships. A group of a number of such dependent relations constitutes the "discovery."

Thus the discovery seems to us, generally speaking, a relationship between distant phenomena. It connects regions that are far apart; between the primordial figures others rise into sight, suggested by the union of corresponding points.

From this it results that the imagination of scientists invents nothing. But it associates and clears up ideas. That is especially visible in the mathematical sciences, whose adepts suck from them such an amount of satisfaction and vanity that they scorn all the rest of human knowledge. And in truth, since their minds move along a series of combinations which the mind itself has created, they are in a state of perpetual joy because the sections of their reasoning adapt themselves exactly to the results of such reasoning. Their imagination only sums up a set of facts, but this gives them the illusion of enlarging its sphere, and they are not troubled with those discordances and discrepancies, those mere approximations to reality, which science has used for its own purposes during recent epochs.

MY FATHER. — Yet we have to grant their own grandeur to scientific imaginations. Men like Darwin and Claude Bernard fill an ignoramus like myself with admiration, because I feel in their words the fever of truth and a marvellous scrupulosity which enchants me. They are not ashamed to acknowledge their own mistakes.

They will not hesitate to upset their *system* itself if that system does not correspond with facts.

The life of that great man Darwin is notably a constant example of sincerity and kindliness; I know few works as precious from our point of view as the account of the voyage of the "Beagle," that voyage which he made when young and when the greater part of his ideas were forming themselves in his powerful brain.

Here we are present at their birth. His imagination is aroused by a constant, assiduous and exhaustive observation. His eyes are not covered by the bandages of routine and convention. He has divested himself of that fog through which habit causes us to see everything. He has preserved untouched the *faculty of astonishment*, that wondrous gift of infancy which educates us in a short while, causing us to acquire more in a few years than in all the rest of our life. Moreover his uprightness is absolute; he freed himself from the common tendency which consists in our persistence in an error whenever that error is convenient to us and has become a habit. "People do not make their ideas over again when sixty years old " — a mournful statement which I have often heard repeated and which fills me every time with indignation. We change our ideas at every age! Are we not only too lucky to free ourselves from a mistake? And if we have shouldered that mistake for a great many years, all the more should we find it necessary to hate it!

Darwin fears misty generalizations and only advances step by step. Nevertheless there never was a man more capable of vast theories and of using those enormous nets with which one can sweep up facts in masses and therewith astonish the ignorant. There is no doubt that he would have suffered much, if he had been present to see the strange distortions of his doctrine and their crude application to the social, moral and political world.

Our minds are so at the mercy of error! If error has not corrupted the originator it assails his imitators and his disciples. It is the fungus that grows a parasite upon every fine act of the imagination. The subtler, more ductile and stronger an idea is, the more people draw absurd or premature conclusions from it, so that sometimes a truth succumbs under the weight of the follies which it drags along in its wake, follies for which it was never responsible.

We have seen Darwin's doctrines put to use as a political catch-word. Anticlericalism has used them, but it has been fatal. People have made the poor great genius say a great many things which had never been thought of by one who was scrupulous to excess, by the man who waked up his friends at two o'clock in the morning after a long conversation on the " Sentiment of the Sublime " in order to warn them that he had made a mistake in some anecdote.

I. — Science has before everything else the craving for proofs. It has need of long patience and lays on the most brilliant imaginations a bridle which must often become painful.

Moreover the scientist when he does make a discovery has the sorrow of having to say that he only makes a statement in corroboration. The artist, however, enjoys the illusion of creating. As a matter of fact this creation itself is for the greater part a mirage, since art consists of a happy choice and an assembling together of beauties that have already existed. The man of letters does not invent a new sentiment or an unpublished character any more than the playwright does. The very rhythm and cadence which he gives to his work, his style itself, proceeds from some one; let him be as personal as he chooses, he must admit an origin and birth for it somewhere. Neither painter nor sculptor represents anything which did not exist before in the world. It is somewhat different in regard to music. But looking at things a little closer, music is the lofty manifestation of a harmony, the models for which exist in nature. Nevertheless the writer, the painter, the sculptor and the musician, whenever their work bears them along, believe honestly that they are adding to the world something which did not exist before their time.

Sublime illusion, and one that makes a man invincible! It is very painful to acknowledge to oneself that one lies in a prison where one can but count the prison bars. It is painful to remember that the human mind has its laws of limitation and that imagination cannot pass beyond a certain point, and that it is impossible to break away from gravitation, whether cosmical, social, or moral.

If one looks at the matter from that point of view, could one not believe that the imagination is a constant counsellor of liberty? The doctrine of Finalities has served its time. We do not admit that a given faculty has to be granted to man for a definite and restricted purpose. But it is certain that the moral universe, exactly like the material world, has a tendency to preserve and continue its equilibrium and harmony. But to preserve this, sometimes marvellous sacrifices are necessary.

What would the world become for us if we could not

continue and modify it through images? It is through the latter even more than through the association of ideas that our power of feeling is perpetually awake and in action.

Do we not know a class of minds in whom the imagination is nothing but the introduction to the divine? After a period of darkness, behold us interesting ourselves again in the mystical writers ! The grand breath that blows through them has once more a meaning in our epoch and the gropings that go on about symbols show the disquiet of human thought which wishes to free itself from its bonds.

When conscience is laid captive it escapes through the imagination. What does the prisoner do? He dreams of the time when he is free, out in the fields, beneath the sky, among the flowers. He thinks of everything which moves and agitates itself outside the walls of his prison. Man is a perpetual prisoner. Such is the law of his desire that he wearies of that which he has obtained, and those who are most completely satisfied are at the same time the most miserable, unless indeed they can escape through the imagination. When you applaud reality, you speak of a certain kind of reality that is neither flat nor low nor vulgar, because your imagination enlarges it. If we examine the world which surrounds us, marking its forms and outlines and the signs that represent its figures, then it suddenly widens out. Whether our tendencies are abstract and inclined to be satisfied by formulas, or concrete and in love with actual examples, the effort of respiration is the same in all of us and we ever march onward toward the heights.

MY FATHER. — I think I have known suffering but I

have never understood *ennui.* It is the imagination to which I owe that; sincerely do I mourn for those who are lacking of it. I am ready to go farther — whoever does not imagine is incapable of observing. For observation always surpasses reality, lending it the sounds and colors of the senses belonging to the observer.

I once returned from a journey with a friend and we were recounting our impressions. When my turn came he did not interrupt me, but I saw from his astonishment that he accused me in his heart of imposture. Yet both of us were absolutely honest. Only, he had not re-marked at all the things which struck me the most and he believed that I was inventing. A similar error is common. We, are always ready to believe that he lies who has seen more than we have. In the eyes of many people poets and visionaries are either children or half idiots. The number of eyes which do not see and of ears which do not hear and of fingers which have never touched and felt is simply immeasurable.

Ever since we have been talking of the imagination we have failed to discuss its morbid frontiers, its deviations and shames. Is that an error? It is my belief that monsters do little in the way of instruction. They are objects of fright, far more than subjects of study, and the disgust which Goethe felt for them had the deepest of reasons.

One of the advantages of this admirable faculty is that little that is exciting is necessary for its existence; a glint, gesture or word are sufficient. A man with imagi-nation does with one look that which Cuvier did with one bone, he reconstructs an entire individual.

I. — Indeed it is extremely curious to see how too many details and over-richness of nourishment harm the faculty for images. And is not that an indication as to its mechanism with which we have not yet occupied ourselves?

Like the greater number of phenomena within and without us the imagination proceeds by *whirlwinds*. Those who possess this faculty to the point of paroxysm find that the slightest cause of exterior action falling upon the brain through the senses arouses at once an excitation of all those impressions of the senses which memory had treasured up heretofore. It has always seemed to me that a window pane affected by frost, upon which beautiful wintry pictures have suddenly formed themselves, presents a picture of what passes at such times in our mind. There, within the mystery of the nervous cells, a quantity of unknown laws set to work — attractions, repulsions and combinations of various kinds which are without doubt just as complicated as those that rule the movement of the stars.

But it is easy to distinguish a *rapid* imagination and a *slow* imagination. The former is in perpetual observation; the second is a mechanism apart. All of a sudden, thoughts and embryonic thoughts, sensations and memories which have remained benumbed within the crypts of our substance are aroused by new impressions. Then slow and tenacious figures form themselves in the spirit, so tenacious that they become in some human beings *fixed ideas*. Is it not in these phenomena of slow imagination that we should look for the key to craziness, concerning which we still possess only very vague indications?

But quite apart from craziness, the artistic life and more especially the life of the man of letters give us daily examples of the rapid and slow imagination, for the two are associated in the work of composition.

My Father. — What a singular study it would be if one were to work at the state of the mind whilst imagination is in action!

It is impossible for me to work when noise goes on. At that moment my brain is in such a state of super-excitement that the slightest sound and the smallest change in light upsets my thought and carries me away from my point. That mechanism of which you speak seizes everything which comes to it through the senses.

There are others on the contrary who are able to abstract themselves completely in the midst of tumult, of the coming and going of people and of children. It seems as if a deadened wall had been lowered between their imagination and external life.

The choice of a word is an exhaustive operation whenever we wish to seize and hold a sensation as closely as possible. We make an exact image of it to ourselves and that alone is a fatigue. Then we compare to it the various words, adjectives or nouns which memory brings to us and we try them by the eye and the ear just as a jeweller tries his precious stones. A close adaptation of a word gives a particular kind of joy which all writers know and the reader will find for himself. This is the most wearisome of work.

For the imagination is a machine which requires special care. The livelier and more easily excitable it is, the more delicate its springs may be, the more dangerous is it to strain it too much. Woe to those who hope to inflame it through poisons! The progress of the latter is fatal — a fraudulent excitement which makes us think the least effort sublime, and then a depression which makes us incapable of realizing the effort. One of the laws of images consists in this, that normal life alone must bring it to the spirit. And that is done without our volition. That is not subject to rules.

The hygiene of the imagination is simple. When it is fatigued it demands repose from its own action and its repose consists in diversion. The moral occupations of life rest and quiet it. How many illustrious writers have there not been, who have paid with their life or their reason for some abuse of that faculty which is our tool, and from which one should not ask too much !

I have talked about *diversion*. That is likewise the greatest remedy for the too great persistence of images. Now that shows us, those are not the most singular scenes of nature, nor the most remarkable episodes of life which seize upon and fill the memory most. Often some word or gesture, some insignificant act remains in our mind to torture it. Is not this a proof that without our own volition our sensibility undergoes plenty of alternatives which offer a chance or destiny to our images? That which finds us in a state of receptivity enters and penetrates us deeply. That which finds us in a state of closedness or of half-closure, carves itself in but shallowly and is quickly effaced.

LÉON A. DAUDET.

THE DAUDET FAMILY.

MY BROTHER AND I.

RECOLLECTIONS OF INFANCY AND YOUTH.

By ERNEST DAUDET.

PREFACE.

ALPHONSE DAUDET, to whom these recollections
are consecrated, is to-day (1881) at the height of
his renown. His works are sought for by pub-
lishers and newspapers and are translated into all
languages; they are popular in London as well
as in Paris, at Vienna as at Berlin, in New York as
in St. Petersburg. If there were any need of justification for these intimate and personal notes which
you are about to read, I would not care to invoke
any other excuse than this very legitimate popularity which is so perfectly adequate to explain
their appearance.

As to the special attraction which they may
offer to readers because of the relationship which
connects the one who writes them with him who is
the object of their appearance, I have but a word
to say. Ever since Alphonse Daudet was born,
life has hardly separated us to any extent. I am
perfectly convinced that no one is in a position
to speak of the man and the writer with greater
exactness than I, unless indeed it were his own
self; and I have besides the advantage of being
able to state what certainly he would never dare
to mention of himself.

For a long time now my mind has been besieged with the temptation to give this account and to render precise and fix various recollections from which Alphonse himself has often drawn inspiration for his novels and studies. I have said to myself that at a time when the novel tends to draw its nourishment more and more from actual facts; at a time when the need for sincerity is imposed imperiously upon whomsoever holds a pen, such true notes as these concerning an already distant past would have hardly less chance to please the public than some work of fiction which only owes its success to the effort its author has made to reproduce mankind and life exactly.

It is under a form of this kind that the mental siege of which I speak has for a long time involved my mind. Perhaps I would have overcome it and would never have got the better of my scruples, had it not been for the endeavors of certain friends who have undertaken to demonstrate to me that I owed these documentary proofs concerning my brother to the history of our literature of to-day, and that I was bound to write my account, even though I should postpone its publication indefinitely.

So then, I began the work as if it were something which was destined never to leave the circle of our intimate friends. But destiny had decided otherwise in the matter; hardly was it done, when an affectionate piece of violence gave it to the public under the title *Alphonse Daudet by Ernest Daudet.*

Perhaps I may be permitted to say that its

success was very great among the readers of the
Nouvelle Revue. On the other hand, my brother,
whom I had not been able to consult, because at
that time we were far apart one from another, he
being in Switzerland and I in Normandy, was
somewhat moved by perceiving that he was being
treated "as people only treat the dead." He
wrote me: "I am alive, and very much alive, and
you are much too quick to make me take my
place in history. I know some people who will
say that I have caused a piece of self-advertisement
to be made by my brother."

Whether well-grounded or not, the objection
came rather late. The book was launched and
there was nothing for it but to let it sail. So that
is what I have done, in perfect agreement with
Alphonse Daudet, after having at his own desire
suppressed many warm eulogies of his talent,
which, from my fraternal pen, carried with them
no authority, and after having changed the original
title which he thought too loud. He advised me
to use that which is seen on the cover of this
volume (*Mon Frère et Moi ; Souvenirs d'Enfance
et de Jeunesse*) and although I have always professed the most profound disgust for the " moi,"
still, I had so many excuses to make for my
audacious undertaking that I felt constrained to
accede to his wish without discussion.

That, in brief, is the story of my book. I owe
the explanation to the public, to whose good will
I confide it. I will only add one word — I must
be forgiven if I place myself on the stage side by

side with my brother. Our lives were so closely
united that I would not be able to speak of him
without also speaking of myself. I have tried to
do it with discretion, because these pages are
before everything else inspired by the greatest
brotherly tenderness and by no less lively an
admiration.

E. D.

MY BROTHER AND I.

CHAPTER I.

THE name Daudet is pretty widely spread in Languedoc. Some of the families which bear it have suppressed the last letter; such are Daudé d'Alzon, Daudé de Lavalette, Daudé de Labarthe. It is often found in the Lozère district at Mende and at Marvejols under both forms of writing. In the seventeenth century it was brought before the public by an engraver, an art critic, an engineer and two Protestant theologians; a certain Chevalier Daudet wrote and caused to be printed an account of a trip made by Louis XV to Strasburg.

Have these Daudés or Daudets, who were all originally from the Cévennes, a common origin? It is to be supposed they have. What is more assured, however, is that the branch from which we, Alphonse and I, issued, flourished in a little village called Concoules a few leagues from Villefort in the Lozère district at the spot where that department joins with the Ardèche and the Gard.

At the beginning of the Revolution our grandfather, who was a peasant with a mind that was rather broad than cultivated, had come down from

19

those wild mountains with his brother to establish
himself at Nîmes, in order to work at the trade
of "taffetassier" or silk weaver. He was called
Jacques and his brother Claude. A royalist of
the most violent kind, Claude was massacred in
1790 during the bloody days of the "bagarre;"
and Jacques himself very nearly met his death in
conditions hardly less tragical.

It was in the midst of the Days of Terror. The
gallows remained permanently standing on the
terrace at Nîmes. In a single day thirty inhabitants of Beaucaire were made to mount the
scaffold, charged with being accomplices of the
royalist conspirators in the Vivarais; they were
artisans for the most part, since it was a curious
fact that in the South the Jacobins seemed to
recruit their victims by preference from the folk.
These wretched people went to their death inton-
ing the *Miserere.* Having only recently come
down from his hill country, Jacques Daudet happened to be on their path and his soul opened out
with pity whilst his eyes filled with tears, —

"*Ah! li paouri gent!*" ("Oh! the poor creatures!") cried he.

At once he was surrounded by the men belonging to the escort of the victims, who maltreated
and hustled him into the melancholy procession
whilst threatening to execute him without process
of law. Luckily one of them who was less excited than the others urged him to fly and protected his escape. Our good Cévenol peasant
hastened to disappear and profited by the lesson;

because thereafter he was never heard uttering his sentiments aloud in the streets.

The flight of time took those melancholy years away with it. Under the Consulate, Jacques Daudet is found at the head of an important weaving-works, which the large merchants of the city rarely allowed to stand still. At that period the industry of silk-weaving was flourishing in Nîmes. It supplied the stuff for the demand for cravats, skirts, scarfs and other fine lace-like fabrics which in their perfection were quite equal to the finest products of the factories of Lyon. It nourished, throughout the city and the villages round about, a hundred different trades, and it occupied a shining position side by side with that tremendous output of carpets, shawls and scarfs, which carried the name of the commerce of Nîmes as far as the Orient.

Very soon Jacques Daudet became weary of being nothing but a workman. He established a sales-house and was not long in putting together a little fortune. In the mean time he had married, and two sons and three daughters were born of this union. It was his fourth child Vincent who was the father of Alphonse Daudet and myself.

At twenty years a handsome man was that same Vincent, with his Bourbon head, black hair, rosy complexion and eyes well forward in his face, pinched into his tightly-fitting frock-coat and wearing a white cravat like a magistrate — a custom which he kept up throughout his life! His

education had not passed the first smatterings in
Latin, because his father had "harnessed him to
business" as early as the age of sixteen. But he
had moved about the world, namely, Normandy,
la Vendée and Brittany, which was the world at
that time, driving with his own hands a wagon
crammed full of the output of his father's looms,
which he sold in the towns to the larger merchants of those distant lands. He travelled night
and day, winter and summer, with two pistols in a
little green bag to defend himself against high-
waymen.

The commercial customs suited to an epoch
which knew nothing of the telegraph or of rail-
ways are entirely transformed to-day. But they
had the merit of forming a man quickly when in
contact with the difficulties, adventures and responsibilities which they engendered. So, then, at
twenty years of age Vincent Daudet was a fellow
all fire and flames, but prudent and cautious —
very Catholic and Royalist, it is hardly necessary
to say! — and in every respect worthy of the
excellent people who had brought him into the
world; besides, he was extremely fascinating,
which does no harm!

CHAPTER II.

AT that time, about 1829, the house of Daudet
was in constant business relations with the house of
Reynaud, from which it bought the hanks of silk
thread needed for the fabrication of silks. That
was a famous stock, too, was the Reynaud stock —
as we shall soon see. Its cradle can still be seen in
the mountains of the Ardèche in the shape of an
ancient and comfortable house called La Vignasse
which is built on a heap of broken crags among
chestnut and mulberry groves, overlooking that
valley of Jalès, where, from 1790 to 1792, the
Royalist assemblies took place which were called
together by the Abbé Claude Allier and the Count
de Saillans, who were the agents for the exiled
princes.

La Vignasse had been bought the 10th of June,
1645, by Jean Reynaud the son of Sébastien Reynaud of Boisseron. At that time it was a little domain whither Jean Reynaud went to establish himself after his marriage; on it he built the dwelling
which still belongs to his descendants. From 1752
to 1773 one of his descendants, our great-grand-
father, had six sons and three daughters. Of the
latter, two married, the third entered the convent

of Notre-Dame de Largentière, where her grand-
aunt on the maternal side, Catherine de Tavernos,
was at that time the Lady Superior. As to the six
sons, one of whom was our grandfather, for the
most part they had adventures which are worth
noting here.

The eldest, Jean, remained in his father's house
and produced a stock of excellent people; his
grandson, Arsène Reynaud, resides there still, full
of life and health in spite of his great age, honored,
highly esteemed and giving to all about him an
example of the most masculine virtues.

The second, William, "the Russian uncle," went
to London at the Revolution and established there
a fine business in Parisian articles. The French
exiles having been expelled from England, he left
for Hamburg, whence he pushed forward to Russia
and transferred his business to St. Petersburg. By
the use of tact he succeeded in having himself
named as a furnisher to the Court, and he had
quickly put together a fortune reckoned at 300,000
francs, which was a very considerable sum for that
time.

Through what causes did he find himself mixed
up with the first conspiracy against Paul I.? We
have never been able to learn. That conspiracy
having failed, our uncle William had to listen to a
verdict against himself which confiscated all his
property and ordered his banishment to Siberia.
Thither was he led on foot and in chains with the
greater number of his accomplices. At first he
was luckier than the others and succeeded in es-

caping by mingling with the following of an am-
bassador whom the Russian Government was sending to China. Unfortunately he was recognized at
the very moment they were crossing the frontier
and sent back into Siberia. There he would probably have died but for the success of the second
conspiracy against the Czar Paul, who, as will be
remembered, was strangled in 1801; this put an
end to his exile. Alexander I. signed his reprieve
and returned his fortune to him.

Our "Russian uncle" returned to France after
the Restoration and settled in Paris where he died
in 1819, leaving all his property to his house-
keeper, a certain Catherine Dropski, who lived
close to him for twenty years; she disappeared
suddenly without giving time to the plundered
family to make demands on her for the property.

The third son of Jean Reynaud was called
François. He it is that we still designate under the
name of "our uncle the Abbé." A fine type of priest
and citizen was that Abbé Reynaud, concerning
whom his great-nephews have a right to speak with
no little pride. Rarely does a man unite in himself
more natural gifts. Those who knew him never
pronounce his name without a tone of respectful
admiration.

Wishing to enter the Church, he took his first
studies with the Oratorians at Aix, intending to
remain with that famous congregation and devote
himself to instruction; but soon recalled by his
bishop, who wished to keep him among the clergy
of his diocese, he continued his studies at the sem-

inary of Valence, whence he departed in 1789 to occupy a modest curacy in the Vivarais. Having refused to give his adhesion to the civil constitution of the clergy, but wishing to take no part in the plots which were being woven by others round about him, he left in disguise for Paris, intending to live with his brother Baptiste, of whom I shall presently speak.

Very soon after his arrival in Paris he was present at a meeting of the Convention in which very rigorous measures were voted to prevent suspected men from leaving the capital. Without waiting for the close of that meeting, he walked off and took the stage coach to Rouen. A few days later he was in London, whither he caused his brother William to come over after him.

During the long stay which he made in England our uncle the Abbé lived apart from the society of the exiles, whose attitude and proceedings he always disavowed. Having exhausted his means and become a teacher, he entered as instructor the family of a scientific man who was educating a small number of young people belonging to the aristocracy of Great Britain. He gave that finish there to his own studies which was lacking to them, and studied especially the English language, with which he soon became so familiar that he was able to teach it in London itself. During that stay he was the hero of an adventure concerning which he never spoke except with profound emotion.

He had thought it his duty to conceal his profession of priest from the people with whom he entertained social relations. There was a young, beautiful, distinguished and rich girl in one of the families in which he was received. Touched by his natural grace, his gentle look and particularly by the dignity of his life, she took a liking to the exile. As he did not seem to understand the sentiments which he had inspired, she begged her father to make her avowal to him, offering to follow him to France whenever he should return thither. Everything that could be presented to flatter the imagination of a young man, vistas of a brilliant future, the delights of a deep love, all were put in motion to persuade François, but his conscience dictated other duties to him and without betraying his secret he refused the happiness offered him. In that simple episode is there not a delightful subject for a novel? At last his term of exile was at an end.

Under the Consulate, Abbé Reynaud was struck from the list of exiles. He returned to France resolved to continue that career of instruction which his exile had opened for him. Called to take charge of the College of Aubenas, he stayed there a while. In 1811 he was named as principal of the College at Alais. He lived there to the day of his death, that is to say, for twenty-four years more, always a fervent university man, deeply attached to the college, which he had reorganized and rendered flourishing, and, rather than to leave it refusing the highest positions, even the episcopate. One of his biographers has said that he caused to live again the picture of good Abbé Rollin.

He was sweetness and urbanity in action. His tolerance was equal to his liberalism, and in a country where religious differences have engendered so many evils he practised this maxim: In matters of faith, constraint can never produce anything but bitter fruit.

During the Ministry of Villèle he had to undertake a long campaign against the Jesuits, who wanted to take his college away from him. In order to make him leave his post, they had recourse to the most unworthy manœuvres; but his unconquerable energy was equal to their greatest efforts and victory perched upon his banner. An heroic end was fore-ordained for such a life as his. On the 1st of July 1825 an epidemic of cholera sprang up in Alais and became so violent that it was necessary to close the college. At that time Abbé Reynaud was 71 years old. Before they left the college the professors came to him and begged him to leave Alais.

"It is my duty to stick to my post since I am a priest," answered he, "where there are afflicted people to console and wretched ones to help. If I went away I should dishonor myself; I should cover myself with dishonor no less than an officer might who before the battle should abandon his flag and soldiers."

The very next day he entered the hospital and settled himself there; for two months he gave himself up to nursing with the most admirable devotion. On the 10th of September he was suddenly stricken by the disease in his turn and died two days after, victim of a duty which his age might have permitted him to evade, instead of fulfilling it with so courageous an ardor.

The name of Abbé Reynaud has continued popular at Alais, and if I have been somewhat prolix concerning the reasons for that popularity, this comes from the fact that it recalls the kindly man who opened the gates of a college to his grand-nephew Alphonse Daudet, when, long afterward, hardly 16 years old at the time and yet obliged to earn his own livelihood, the latter went to that college to beg for a place as schoolmaster. Read again an account of the sufferings of Le Petit Chose when he became an usher at the college of Sarlande.

I have still to speak of the other three Reynaud sons and will do so briefly.

Baptiste, one of them, left at an early age for Paris. Having entered a shop as apprentice with the hat-maker for the court, the celebrated Lemoine, his intelligence and handsome appearance caused him to be used for "outside." It was he who went to the Tuileries to try on the bonnets for the queen and princesses, and in the same way he went to the social queens in fashion at the moment and to the fops of the period. In such surroundings he quickly acquired a most varied store of information and was soon thoroughly acquainted with the gossip of the fashionable society of the day. And, indeed, how many recollections did his memory not preserve concerning that famous time!

Uncle Baptiste is the only one of our great-uncles whom Alphonse and I have known. He was already an old man, but as clean, fresh and rosy as in the days of his handsome youth, speaking little however of his past in our presence, since we were only children. What we know about him is derived from the stories told to the family. He liked to talk about his sojourn in Paris and the people with whom he was more or less intimately acquainted, amongst others Collin d'Harleville, as well as about his campaigns as a volunteer in the army under Dumouriez.

There is mention of uncle Baptiste in *Le Petit Chose.* But this character in a novel had nothing in common with our ancestor save the name. Alphonse Daudet built him up out of bits and pieces, that is to say, out of various characteristics borrowed from the family.

The two younger brothers of Baptiste who were called Louis and Antoine were far from having a destiny so adventurous as their elders. Both of them took wives in the Vivarais not far from the paternal mansion. Louis stayed there, but Antoine, he who was our maternal grandfather, having become a widower, left the country toward the end of the century in order to go to Nîmes, where he established himself and created an important house for the buying and sale of silks.

At that time the growers of silk-worms in the Cévennes and the Vivarais and the little silk-spinners went to Nîmes and offered their products there. For several days at a time they might be seen wandering about the town in their raw-silk coats with very short tails, their thick stockings of black wool, their heavy iron-bound shoes, and their hair in a cue, doing impromptu business on this moving market. In such cases every operation was done in solid financial fashion with fine big silver pieces, and, since a kilogram of silk was worth from 50 to 80 francs, there used to be a clinking of gold and silver pieces in the shops where the mountaineers bought their goods which would have made Harpagon rub his hands with delight. Then, the sales finished, these sturdy fellows set out upon their return, bowed down beneath the weight of their parcels, this one to Vigan, that one to Largentière and the other to Villefort.

This industry, which for a long while enriched the inhabitants of Languedoc, Provence and the Comtat, is quite dead to-day, killed by the silkworm cholera. The crisis which was the ruin of the south of France had its origin there. Then there came various chemical discoveries that put a stop to the production of madder, which was such a flourishing one in the department of Vaucluse, and finally the phylloxera gave it the last blow. The most firmly established fortunes were not able to stand the strain. But at the moment concerning which we speak people were very far from foreseeing such catastrophes, and the South, like all of France, allowed itself to be carried along by the profitable commercial movement which reached its greatest development under the Restoration.

Antoine Reynaud was one of those in Nîmes who knew best how to profit by it. He had become one of the most important silk-buyers in the South. He then sold again to the large weavers of Nîmes, Avignon and Lyon, supporting the rivalship of similar products from Lombardy and Piedmont in all these different markets. In this trade he accumulated a fine fortune, assisted by my grandmother, for toward 1798 he had married again and this time with a young woman born like him in the Vivarais, whom he had met when going to visit his elder brother at La Vignasse.

CHAPTER III.

OUR grandmother died several years before my birth, but I have heard her spoken of often enough to assert that she was not an ordinary person. A plebeian with warm blood, and a convinced Royalist who had been tried by the harsh suffering under the Terror, she recalled by her beauty, her sculpturesque forms and her eyes widely carved in their sockets some of the portraits of the painter David.

When Antoine Reynaud knew her he was twenty years old; she too was a widow, her first husband having been shot in one of the tumults in the Lozère, to appease which the Convention sent thither one of its members, Châteauneuf-Randon.

One son remained from the first marriage. She had undergone most frightful perils with him. Denounced as a Royalist at the same time with her husband, she had fled for safety to Nimes, where a part of her family lived, whilst he escaped the other way. She lived there in utmost quiet and hidden away, awaiting the end of the black days of Terror. One morning she had the imprudence to go out with her child on her arm, and destiny fore-ordained that she should come across the march of the Goddess Reason, who was being carried in solemn procession through the streets; moreover, fate must needs decree that the citizeness to whom this lofty but transitory dignity was awarded should recognize our grandmother in the street! As far off as she could see her she began to call to her, screaming out: —

"Françoise! On your knees!"

My grandmother was hardly seventeen years old at the time and was gifted with quick repartee and a turn for irony. To this order on the part of the Goddess Reason she replied with a gesture fitter for a street boy. The mob rushed upon her crying, "Zou! Zou!"

She took flight through the town, pressing her child to her breast and reached a suburb where she managed to return to her house by way of gardens, but only by passing along the narrow rim of a cistern at the greatest risk of falling in. As she said later in life: "No cat could have done what I did that day!"

For the moment she had saved her life, but too many perils were about and her safety demanded that she should not remain longer in Nîmes. That very evening she left for the Vivarais.

She had to make part of the trip on foot, marching by short stages and finding refuge at the end of her heavy tramps in some farm or in the house of one of those curates of the constitution to whom kindly souls recommended her. It was during this march, whilst shaken by the most cruel fits of

anguish, that she heard of the death of her
husband.

The night before she had arrived at a wretched
village called Les Mages and asked for a lodging at
the priest's house; on entering the bed-chamber
which had been set apart for her she had been impressed by a presentiment of sorrow. The cemetery lay immediately beneath her windows and the
moon outlined the crosses on the tombs in black
against the gray. It was impossible for her to sleep.

Then the child she was suckling was seized by
terror in its turn. Red in the face and with strain-
ing haggard eyes, the poor little wretch grieved
and cried the whole night, moving about continu-
ously in the arms of its mother, who in vain tried
to quiet it.

A few hours later my grandmother learned that
her husband was dead, having been shot not far
from there, at dawn, by the republican soldiers.
She never ceased to believe that her son had a
vision of the execution of his father during that
frightful night.

As a result of these emotions she lost her milk
and the child was turned over to its grandparents
and was brought up on the milk of a goat. As
to my grandmother, her appearance had been
carefully described and spread throughout the
countryside and the rural police were on her track.
Then she began the roving existence of a fugitive,
roaming hither and thither under various disguises
and only returning to the house to sleep.

Through a very singular circumstance the only

person who knew the secret of her concealment
was an ardent republican patriot, the mistress of
one of the men of the Convention who was acting
as commissioner in the Vivarais and the Gévaudan.
This woman conceived the greatest sympathy and
pity for the proscribed one; she kept her informed
of all the measures taken to seize her, and every
morning my grandmother would absent herself
from the places where her liberty was more than
commonly menaced.

Nevertheless, one day that she was seated on
the edge of a road, broken by fatigue and clad like
a poor goatherd, she saw two policemen appear,
who asked her whether she had not seen "the
woman called Françoise Robert" pass that way,
that being her own name. As you may well believe, she answered in the negative. The policemen having asked her to which village she was
bound, she mentioned one in the neighborhood
haphazard.

"That's just the place we're going to!" answered one of them twisting his moustache in the
most gallant fashion. "Jump up behind me, and
we will take you there."

Weeping copiously, she protested that she was
a good girl, and the policemen, pitying her case,
left her after making excuses for their conduct.

Another time, having caught sight of the rural
police at the end of a road on which she was, she
rushed into a meadow where a shepherd was feeding his sheep; thrusting a piece of silver into his
hand, she seized his hat and cloak, put the hat

on her head and the cloak about her shoulders, saying:

" My dear man, do not betray me; I am your herd-boy."

The shepherd kept silence and the policeman passed without the slightest idea that the little herd-boy whose tattered felt hat covered his face and hair completely, who seemed half asleep as he lent on his shepherd staff, was no other than that Françoise Robert whom they had been seeking in vain for so many days.

Four years had passed after these events when Antoine Reynaud met Françoise. He took a great fancy to her, married her, adopted her son and took her to Nîmes. Our grandmother was the owner of an uncommon mind and possessed unusual courage. These qualities became all the better in her new husband's house and produced excellent results. She raised herself socially along with him and on no occasion did she find herself below that station in society which he had been able to win little by little. She proved a loving and faithful comrade in life as well as a discreet and safe helpmeet. She contributed her full share to the establishment of that fortune which unhappily was not destined to survive her long, but which she had the merit of having to a large extent built up.

A big volume might be filled with interesting traits of our grandmother — the courage she showed one evening when her husband was the victim of an attempt at assassination; her exhibitions of hatred against Napoleon; her joy at the return of the Bourbons and all the episodes of an honest and energetic life of a citizen. At the same time she had the very deuce of a "go," a decisiveness of mind that is rarely found in women, a singular knack of overcoming difficulties, the boldness of a man, a vigorous temperament and a health which flourished notwithstanding the wearing fatigues of successive childbirths.

It was under the Restoration that the fortune of our grandparents reached high-water mark. At that time they had six children, including the one by the former husband, who was treated like the others: three sons and three daughters. All these little creatures grew up in easy circumstances. Trade carefully managed caused the waters of Pactolus to flow through the house. Mme. Reynaud held a fine place in society, where her views of things were the law; she had her box at the theatre and a good property several leagues from the city.

She was present at every social gathering and more especially those which followed the return of the Bourbons. Toward 1829, when the Daudets held close business relations with the Reynauds, this prosperity had only increased and it seemed as if it were not possible that its spring should be weakened.

Such was the family into which young Vincent Daudet dreamed of entering. The oldest of the Reynaud girls was called Adeline. She was a thin and frail-looking body with an olive-brown complexion and big mournful eyes; her physical development had been delayed by some childish malady. She was a dreamy, romantic nature, passionately fond of reading and loving better to live with the heroes of her imagination and their delightful stories than with the realities of actual life, yet all the same she had the soul of a saint and an infinite kindliness and urbanity. She it was whom Vincent Daudet had dared to reach with his love, without fearing the distance that separated them.

At first his project seemed rather ambitious to his parents themselves. The Reynauds were at the head of the business in Nîmes; the eldest son had just made a matrimonial alliance with the Sabrans of Lyon, and the second managed an important commission house in that city. It meant a great deal of audacity merely to be what Vincent Daudet then was and to endeavor to make an alliance with them. Nevertheless he stated his demand and friends intervened to plead his cause and overcome the resistance, which was particularly aroused by the two brothers of Mdlle. Adeline settled in Lyon, for they hoped for a far more brilliant marriage for their sister. Luckily, when Mdlle. Adeline was consulted, she cut the matter short by declaring that she was well pleased.

The marriage took place near the beginning of 1830 at the very moment that Vincent Daudet, who had become a person of importance through his entrance into the Reynaud family, entered into partnership with his brother to continue the business of their father.

The earlier years of the new marriage were sad-

dened by a long list of domestic troubles. My
parents lost their first children one after the other,
with the exception of the first-born, a boy whose
feeble health caused them a thousand disquiets.
Grandmother Reynaud died very suddenly, carried
off by an affection of the lungs. One of her sons
in Lyon squandered a large part of the common
capital intrusted to his care in imprudent speculations. And finally my father was not able to get
on long with his brother. Their partnership was
dissolved and replaced by a rivalry in business
during the course of which my uncle, who was
luckier or cleverer, built up a fortune which his
children have inherited in peace, whilst my father
compromised his own in inventions which rarely
came to any sound results.

Alphonse Daudet came into the world just ten
years after this marriage, the story and beginnings
of which I have thought it necessary to relate at
the same time with the story of our family.

CHAPTER IV.

"I WAS born the 13th of May 18 — in a Languedoc town, where, as in all the towns in the
South of France, a great deal of sun and no little
dust may be found along with two or three Roman
monuments." These are the words in which
Alphonse Daudet tells of his birth on the first
page of *Le Petit Chose*, that one of his novels into
which he has placed the most of himself, at least in
the early part of it.

The town which he describes in this way is
Nîmes. He was born there on the 13th of May
1840, three years after me, in the second story of
the Sabran mansion which our parents inhabited
from the time of their marriage. At the moment
he was the third of the living children.

The oldest was called Henri — a fine artistic
soul, high-strung and mystical, and a musician to
his very marrow, who died at twenty-four years as
a professor in the College of the Assumption at
Nîmes, just on the point of entering into orders.
Memory of this sad recollection has inspired one
of the most eloquent pages in *Le Petit Chose*,
that moving chapter entitled "He is dead! Pray
for his soul!"

The younger brother was the one who tells this story.

In 1848 the family was increased by the arrival of a girl who is married at present to M. Léon Allard, brother of Mme. Alphonse Daudet; he has contributed to various papers romances written in a refined style that reveals a rare talent for writing.

That Sabran mansion where we came into the world still stands on the Petit-Cours almost opposite the Church of St. Charles, behind which the Enclos de Rey extends, that terrible Royalist suburb, whose inhabitants, taffetassiers (silk-weavers) or laborers in the fields, have for a century furnished a noisy and rude contingent to all the revolutions and riots in the old Roman city.

At one of the ends of the Petit-Cours is the square of the Carmes, at the other the Ballore square.

All the political life of Nîmes was condensed in the past between those two points; they are convenient for popular assemblages and are connected together by a wide avenue planted with a double row of plane-trees, trees which each summer powders with a fine white dust down to the smallest leaf, filling with cicadas their crackling branches on which the bark is all burned by the sun.

The bloodiest episodes of the Revolution and the tragical scenes of the "bagarre" were played out upon the stage of the Petit-Cours.

There in 1815 it was that Gen. Gilly, flying to Nîmes the day after the battle of Waterloo in

order to throw himself into the hills of the
Cévennes, marched in procession at the head of his
chasseurs, rage in his heart, anger in his eyes, his
bridle between his teeth, a pistol in one hand and
a sword in the other, and abandoned the Bonapartists to the horrors of a criminal reaction, which
was all too easy to understand in view of the
treatment which the Catholics had undergone
during the Hundred Days.

There again in 1831 it was that the Catholics
met together in threatening groups when the
authorities "dropped the crosses"—a recollection to be kept in mind, since it recalls to the witnesses of scenes in those distant times the exaggeration natural to Southern temperaments and
their violence, the spectacle, namely, of men savage
in their appearance ranged in the lines of a procession, men who sang the Psalms of Penitence and
at the same time uttered frightful oaths against the
"usurper"; of women with dishevelled hair, their
arms folded over their heads, uttering cries of distress; of priests running about through these
groups with the manner of martyrs and preaching
resignation with their lips yet with revolution in
their eyes, all the while that under the protection
of armed forces the authorities were most respect-
fully causing to be deposited within the churches
the crosses that had formerly stood upon the public squares! These crosses had been raised during
the missions which took place under the Villèle
ministry, when the Congregation was all-powerful.

Episodes of local history in Nimes have found

other stages, for instance on the Esplanade, on the
Cours-Neuf, in the Arena and at the Carmes; but
nowhere did they take on a more dangerous
appearance than along that same Petit-Cours,
where the Enclos de Rey debouches by five or six
streets and where for two years after my birth,
during the long July days, Catholics and Protestants gave themselves up to one battle more with
stones as weapons.

How many a time during our infancy, while
breathing in the cool evening air before our house,
have we not been suddenly hurried indoors by our
nursemaid, whilst all about us men and women
were flying hither and thither, and from afar,
uttered by mouths rude in voice, rose the cry of:
"Zou! zou!" the ordinary signal for rows in
Nîmes! It meant that the battle had begun. It all
ended, however, merely in bruises and scratches
and broken panes. The police let things go and
the battle ended through lack of fighters.

It is scarcely unknown that my brother, along
with a good deal of truth, put a good deal of fancy
into *Le Petit Chose.* It was fancy when he wrote:
"I was the evil star of my parents. From the day
of my birth incredible disasters fell upon them from
twenty directions."

On the contrary, it would be more exact to say
that at that very moment there was a respite in the
worries of our family; the business outlook appeared more prosperous; fresh catastrophes did
not occur until later, in 1846 and 1847 and 1848,
the epoch when the general ruin was finished. At

first we know nothing but domestic well-being;
we grew up side by side in an atmosphere of tenderness and an intimate relationship, hour by hour,
which created between us that indestructible friendship which has always been just as lively as ever
and has never been a single day denied.

At that epoch the old Sabran mansion was
filled with our games. The shops of Vincent
Daudet were on the first story and on the same
floor those of one of the cousins, a maker of shawls.
Children were severely exiled from the Vincent
Daudet part. If they showed their rosy faces and
bright locks at the door, one look from the father
caused them to fly at the swiftest pace; but on the
cousin's side they were more friendly.

There was an old clerk there who adored little
children. He made beautiful paper hats for us all
decked with plumes; he fabricated epaulets from
the remains of fringes of shawls, he armed us with
wooden swords, and just above our lips he drew
terrible moustaches with burnt cork. In such guise
as this did we ascend to show ourselves to our
mother, whom we oftenest found plunged in some
book.

A passionate love for books which she com-
municated to us has been one of the consolations
of her life. As a child she used to seek a refuge at
the back of her father's shop, where she would
hide herself between the bales of silk in order to
read without being interrupted. Later it was to
reading once more that she consecrated all her
leisure hours. It is undeniable that we get from

her that vocation which has caused us later to
plunge into literary life.

When I examine my memory in an attempt to
recollect what my brother looked like as a child,
I see a handsome little boy three or four years
old with large brown eyes, chestnut locks, a pale
complexion and features of exquisite delicacy. At
the same time I recall most terrible angers and
half tragic revolts against the punishments which
they brought upon him.

One day, in consequence of I know not what
naughtiness, he was locked up alone in a bedroom.
He beat about in it with such extraordinary violence that it was necessary to open the door of
the improvised prison. He came out all bruised by
the hurts that he had voluntarily given himself by
throwing himself head-foremost against the walls.

He inherited from our grandmothers and especially from our father that tendency to anger
which he has overcome by a tremendous effort of
will since he has grown up; but as a child that
was the dominant trait of his character and it was
hard enough to bring him up. He was the most
extraordinary mixture of docility and lack of discipline, kindliness and wrong-headedness; and along
with that went an inextinguishable thirst for adventures and the unknown, a thirst which his short-
sightedness, increasing with age, aggravated to the
point of danger.

This short-sightedness has played my brother
the vilest tricks; turn and turn about, he has
drowned, burned, poisoned and got himself run

over; even at the present day (1881) it obliges
him to ask the help of a friendly arm in order to
cross the boulevard at the hour when it is crowded
with carriages, and it has often caused people,
whom he has passed close by without seeing them,
to believe that he pretended not to greet them
through indifference or disdain.

But at the same time it has rendered him an
important service: it has forced upon him the
necessity of living within himself; it has gifted him
with the strangest and most precious faculty which
I have met with only in him, a sort of inward look,
or, if you prefer, an intuition of extraordinary power,
in consequence of which it has happened that when
he cannot see with his eyes the face of any one talking to him, he divines the features of his interlocutor and at the same time divines his thought.
Such an intensity of vision in a short-sighted man
is a matter which I cannot explain to myself. He
is like a blind man groping about through life, and
yet in every one of his books he gives a proof of
the most minute and attentive observation, almost
as if with the aid of an enlarging glass.

These qualities seen in the grown person were
still slumbering in the child, who was dominated
by a liveliness and turbulence and boldness which
made our mother tremble whenever she did not
feel him fast to her skirts, or directly within the
sight of our maid. But at the same time his
nature was the most direct, his heart the most
generous and his mind the most active of any.
Oh! what a delightful little comrade I had there!

CHAPTER V.

AMONG the very keenest of our delights in this world must be reckoned our family excursions on Sunday. Generally they were toward some village in the neighborhood, such as Marguerites or Manduel, Fons or Monfrin. At the last mentioned lived our foster-parents, honest people living very comfortably, who were tenderly in love with the child that had been nursed under their roof and always delighted to see him again in company with his own parents. After the death of my grandmother the property Font du Roi had been sold. So it was necessary to go in search of the fine air of the country somewhere else, and that is why we were taken to the farms of our foster-parents, first to one and then to the other.

Early in the morning we set out in the big coach into which we piled, big and little, with a half dozen handsome uncles and male and female cousins of our age, and after a fine journey in the sunshine over turnpikes white with dust, between vineyards and olive orchards, our stop at last made pleasant by rich meals and long walks through the fields, we returned at nightfall by the light of the moon, we children half asleep, but listening to

the ballads and romances which our elders sang
in chorus.

Another goal for long walks was La Vigne,
a little property which lay near the gates of the
city among the small *mazets* (cabins) scattered
about among the *garrides* (stony, sterile fields)
all baked by the sun, where no other protection
from the heat could be found save an arbor covered with vines; there we often took our supper
during the summer evenings after having passed
many an hour devouring grapes — œillades and
clairettes — which our little hands plucked from
the upright stocks crowded with leaves and clusters, vines raised with difficulty above a soil hardened by the long droughts of the summer.

That modest property was not more than a few
acres, yet it possessed a monumental gateway in
iron which helped to make it seem as big to us
as the whole country. Down the centre ran a
path edged with box and dwarf rose bushes; to
the right and left were the vines, and they shared
the territory with almond and olive trees; at the
bottom of the plot was a clover-field where our
father used to hunt larks with a mirror; a tumble-
down wall ran about it composed of stones placed
one upon the other without cement like all the
walls in that part of the world. What delightful
days have we not passed in La Vigne!

On returning from the vineyard we would stop
at the factory where the scarfs were colored which
the Daudet house at that time despatched throughout France, into Italy and Spain, and even as far

as Algiers. Beyond the workshop there was a
decidedly nice garden; there we were apt to call
a halt before entering the town itself and take the
occasion to pluck a few hatfuls of fruit.

Whilst considering these distant recollections I
cannot pass over in silence the season for the fair
at Beaucaire which returned with great exactness
every year. At such times the Daudet house
transferred itself with merchandise and all its older
members to that little town, one that for many
centuries was among the most important markets
of Europe. You will find a very picturesque
description of this fair at Beaucaire in *Numa
Roumestan.*

" It was the holiday of the year in our Southern
provinces, the one attraction for all those shrivelled
lives; a long while before it occurred people got
ready for it and a long while afterwards people
talked of it. It was a reward which a man would
promise to his wife or children, and if he could
not take them with him he would always bring
back from it some piece of Spanish lace or a play-
thing which they would find at the bottom of his
packet. The fair of Beaucaire, making business its
pretext, meant also a fortnight or a full month given
up to the free, exuberant and unexpected existence of a Bohemian encampment. People slept
here and there in the homes of the inhabitants, or
on the counters in the shops, or even in the street
under the canvas of the carts, beneath the warm
light of the July stars. How delightful was business transacted without the boredom of the shop

and matters of finance effected whilst dining at the
door in shirt-sleeves! Then, all the booths set up
in a line along the meadow on the banks of the
Rhône, the river itself being nothing but a moving
fair-ground where boats of every shape bobbed
up and down — *lahuts* with lateen sails coming
from Arles, Marseille, Barcelona and the Balearic
Islands laden with wines, anchovies, cork and
oranges, all adorned with gorgeous banners and
streamers slapping and snapping in the lively
wind and all reflected in the swiftly-flowing water!
And then such an uproar from that many-colored
crowd of Spaniards, Sardinians, Greeks in long
tunics and embroidered slippers, Armenians in
furred caps and Turks in their befrogged waist-
coats, with their broad fans and wide breeches of
gray linen, all of them crowding into the open-air
restaurants; and then the lines of tables covered
with toys for children, canes, umbrellas, silverware,
pastils of the harem, hats and caps, etc."

Although Nimes was hardly six leagues distant
from Beaucaire we little ones were not taken to
the fair; we were left at home. But the house
was turned over to us; we ruled there like little
sovereigns, and God knows with what a noise we
filled it! Then, when they came back, our father
brought us a souvenir which constituted the crown
and culmination of the period of loose discipline,
of spoiling and a free and easy life — a whip or a
box of geographical blocks, a sword or a trumpet,
things of little value which delighted us beyond
measure.

Rarely did children ever have more playthings
than we. During his sickly infancy our elder
brother Henri had been overwhelmed with them,
and when his studies began he turned them all
over to us, and then the mass grew still larger by
the addition of those which were given to us.

Grandfather Daudet, however, was not much of
a bestower of gifts. Economical to the rigor
point throughout his life, his largess to his grand-
children never went further than a box of pepper-
mints, which he thrust into each one's pocket on
New Year's Day after they had presented him
with the compliments of the season.

Grandfather Reynaud was entirely different.
His only pleasure consisted in making us happy
and enjoying our surprise and delight. Christmas-
eve or New Year's Day, or the Day of the Magi,
were just so many pretexts for luxuries and gifts.

Oh what memories of New Year's Day in our
childhood! — meetings at grandfather's house at
noon for dinner, the recitation acquired with such
difficulty and mumbled over with impatient lips,
whilst little eyes rolled round to stare at the side-
board crammed with eatables and playthings —
jumping-jacks, accordions, wooden horses and
sheep, dolls and I know not what more! Then
the distribution of the presents accompanied by the
wild excitement of desires set in liveliest motion;
the dinner composed of the most delicate tidbits,
pastries made by old Sophie, brandade of codfish
from Cadet's kitchen, "estevenos" (cakes) from
Villaret the pastrycook, nougats from Barthélemy

the confectioner, sweetmeats in shapes of people and sugarplums in paper crackers! Then our dances down the big blue drawing-room, which was never opened except on that day, whilst our elders continued their discussions among themselves.

So it was that, thanks to our elder brother and Grandfather Reynaud, Alphonse and I possessed enough playthings to sell. Before he made away with them all, owing to his terrible craze for knowing what they looked like inside, we had filled an entire room with them at the Vallongue Street house into which we moved in 1844.

About that time we were already fitting up theatres with the actors all of wood or cardboard and were already inventing plays. I was very skilful in dressing our actors. One day when I had just finished dressing a little articulated doll as a page, Alphonse arranged a fine scene in order to make use of this masterpiece from my hands; I regret very much that I did not keep it, for it was his beginning as a dramatist.

Among other playthings which we possessed there was an entire furniture for a chapel suited to children of our size; nothing was lacking, neither altar, candlesticks, tabernacle, chalice, pyx, nor host. Our mother had cut the cloth for the altar from an old embroidered gown and sewed the alb and surplice, while one of our uncles at Lyon had sent us chasuble, cross and mitre.

The materials for this little church had remained a long while unused and in reserve, but one fine day they were presented to us outright. Then only began our religious ceremonies, salutations, benedictions and processions through the great garrets where our father had placed the working benches for the women who carded the silk.

These *ourdisseuses* or carders of silk, five or six in number, were good girls and for the most part very devout ones, who took great pleasure in hearing us sing the canticles. Very often our girl cousins, Emma and Maria, with their brother Léonce, a fine boy who was killed at Pont-Noyelles in the war of 1870, and a few of our friends came in for the purpose of taking part in our games. It was at that time the episode occurred which we still call in the family the story of the Virgin Mary.

On that day we had draped with the white alb our cousin Emma, a pretty brunette of our own age and had crowned her with roses and placed her seated in a big basket for silk bobbins lent us by the carding girls, and so we carried her solemnly in procession just as the Virgin Mary is borne along above a reliquary; and so we went through the house, chanting religious songs such as our memory was full of. We had divided all the other ornaments up among ourselves, one carrying the chasuble, the other the mitre and the third the cross. Dressed in the proper gown, Alphonse played choir boy and marched at the head of the procession with a bell in his hand.

Bad luck willed it that at that very moment my father was receiving an important customer from Lyon.

Bothered by our noise, he sent us word to be quiet, but we neglected to take much notice of the warning. Patience was not exactly Vincent Daudet's virtue, and when he did get angry it was no light matter. All of a sudden he appeared on the threshold of the workshop where the procession was just about to end before the brilliantly lighted altar; with the back of his hand he sent the choir boy and the bell rolling over the floor, and then, as every one tried to escape, he seized the reliquary just as one would an ordinary coal-scuttle, and grabbing the Virgin Mary on the fly, he tore the white alb from top to bottom and made her crown skip through the air. That evening he notified my mother, in whose absence this tragi-comic scene had passed, that he had had enough of those ceremonies and canticles in his house!

We children therefore returned to the little room where the playthings were and passed our recreation hours there. Later on we were admitted to a larger room at the end of the apartment and there under Henri's direction a theatre was arranged in which he rehearsed one of Berquin's plays with several comrades. Although they were simply scraps of boys their services were accepted. We had our part in a representation before the family, which was given on a Thursday and in good truth only obtained a " success of esteem."

About that time our dear father brought us one day on his return from the Fair at Beaucaire a

Robinson Crusoe in two illustrated volumes, a *Swiss Family Robinson* and the *Journal des Enfants* bound in six big volumes, full of stories signed Jules Janin, Frédéric Soulié, Louis Desnoyers, Ernest Fouinet, Édouard Ourliac and Eugénie Foa. Then it was that for the first time we read the *Aventures de Jean-Paul Chopart* as well as the *Aventures de Robert Robert et de son Compagnon Toussaint Lavenette*, and the *Théâtre du Seigneur Croquignole*, the *Mystères du Château de Pierrefitte* and *Léon et Léonie* and a hundred other stories written for children of our age, veritable little masterpieces for the most part, which have left an ineffaceable trace upon our memory and exercised so lively an impression upon our childhood that even to-day, when one of these volumes, all worn and torn, happens to come across our path, a crowd of memories of the distant past rises from its dog-eared pages.

CHAPTER VI.

IN the month of September, 1846, our parents resolved to have me begin my Latin studies. Up to that time our education had been left to the Brothers of the Christian Doctrine to whom those families of Catholic faith who were best to do, did not scorn to send their children — as an example. They taught me to read and write and gave me some few ideas of sacred history and religious instruction. Alphonse was left with them for still another year. Our elder brother finished his classes with an old professor named Verdilhan who long before had started on his career as instructor under the auspices of our uncle the Abbé.

As for me it was decided to send me as a day scholar to the College of the Assumption, which a vicar-general of the diocese was directing, namely Abbé d'Alzon, who caused himself to be talked of a great deal later on.

There it was that I took my first communion in 1848, the day before that on which the Archbishop of Paris was killed on the barricades; there I lived two years under the charge of masters whose high-strung opinions I have sometimes been compelled to disavow later, but who were almost all of them eminent, affectionate and paternal men, extremely able in molding the mind and soul of the children confided to their charge.

What decided my father to send me to the Assumption was the relative lowness of the charges for day scholars. But in 1848 his fortune, which had been receiving severe blows for two years past, was completely undermined.

Successive failures of several of his clients carried off one part of it, and then came the commercial crisis and stagnation of business which followed the Revolution, and lastly, to put a final touch to all this list of catastrophes, came the death of Grandfather Reynaud.

That exposed the depth of the abyss into which his sons had allowed his fortune to disappear. Our parents had been counting on that inheritance in order to face difficulties which became every day more inextricable. But they got nothing from it.

It gave the signal for deep and wide divisions in the family. The blackest sadness lay upon our house and our dear mother never ceased from weeping. Under the urgency of his cares my father had become irritable and cranky; he wanted to start a lawsuit against his brother-in-law and flew into a rage with any one who attempted to defend him or talk about a reconciliation.

The clearest point in the whole trouble was this, that it was necessary to reduce expenses and live with the strictest economy. I was taken away from the Assumption and went in turn to learn from Father Verdilhan. Alphonse had entered some months before the Canivet Institute, a modest establishment where he penetrated little by little into the secret recesses of the Latin grammar.

One justice must be given to our excellent father, that, notwithstanding his disaster, he never dreamed of economizing to our disadvantage nor of interrupting our studies under the plea that he could only pay the cost with great difficulty.

One of the family, who was a very practical man and extremely rich, to whom my father was in debt, mingled many counsels with incessant demands for repayment. He loudly declared that the firm intention to give us a solid education in the absence of a fortune was the act of a man filled with absurd pride. His opinion was that we ought to be taught a good trade. If he had been listened to, probably I should be a locksmith today, and Alphonse would be handling the plane and saw.

But Vincent Daudet did not hold to this opinion at all; he persisted in trusting to the star of his sons. It was one of our delights that we had never betrayed that confidence. He therefore looked another way for the means to economize. We left the fine apartment in Vallongue Street to establish ourselves in the factory, that factory on the Avignon road, the remembrance of which, ever vivid in Alphonse Daudet's mind, suggested to him the first chapter of *Le Petit Chose*.

There were big rooms there and plenty of air and space; we were very comfortably installed. There we met together every evening and my brother came in too, after his return from school; there we passed our Thursdays and Sundays running about the courts upon which great empty workshops opened, making mysterious robber dens for ourselves in the steam-engine which was reduced to immobility and rolling about on the grass in the garden under the fig-tree behind the wall of lilacs. Cousins of both sexes come to share our games and our noisy laughter made a strange contrast with the agony of our parents caused by the sickly silence of that vast factory, where the sudden stoppage of all movement merely hastened the complete ruin of the family.

Still, there were some bright clearings in the darkness of our distress. In the first place there was the marriage of our youngest aunt who had come to live with us after the death of Grandfather Reynaud, and the birth of our sister, which sent a warm ray of sunlight through the whole house, and finally the arrival of one of the Lyon uncles who took up his abode under our roof.

In consequence of I know not what arrangement he was to have the direction of the factory and the color-room on the day that business should start up again; but what I am sure of is, that whilst waiting for this rousing up from stagnation, which, by the way, never occurred, he was practising his future functions at a furious rate. He had brought with him a great number of volumes, for the most

part with illustrations, and he occupied all his time
in coloring these pictures. It was a regular craze;
he colored everything that he could get hold of
and even illuminated a Spanish grammar.

This dear man adored my brother and lent himself to every one of his fancies; he pushed his
weakness to the point of being an accomplice of
his naughtinesses by helping him to conceal them
and even went so far as to accuse me of them.
One fine morning, tired of coloring pictures, he
disappeared and we never saw him again. I really
believe that without knowing it he posed as one of
the characters in *Le Nabab*. In that novel there is
a certain cashier in the Caisse Territoriale who has
a terrible likeness to him.

CHAPTER VII.

ANOTHER memory of this period is that of the clubs. Our father had always taken great interest in politics, but of course theoretically and without the shadow of a personal ambition, although like certain others he might have been able to obtain an election as Deputy. At all times during our meals, when the subject of business was worn dry, the usual subject of his talks with our mother consisted of politics, or rather, to speak more exactly, the subject of his monologues. He viewed public matters from the point of view of his Royalist prejudices and would scarcely admit any one to hold a contrary opinion.

In the little Cornand Club, whither he went every day, he met with excellent fellows who were filled with the same ideas, and particularly an old judge who exerted a great influence on his mind, an eloquent talker who explained events with no little ingenuity and occupied himself in forecasting what was to come.

He it was who, taking advantage of the presence of one of the sons of the King at Nimes, went to his hotel and left a card on which he had written these verses : —

" Prince, ne croyez pas que le Français oublie
  Les bienfaits dont il fut redevable à ses rois ;
  Ils sont, quoiqu'exilés, présents à la patrie
  Plus que l'usurpateur qui lui dicte des lois ! "

And the excellent fellow was proud of what he considered an act of boldness and courage. Observe that he was a judge, who could not be removed; such characteristics depict a whole race!

Our father came back from the club to his family filled with all he had been hearing and repeated it to us whilst mixing in his own personal reflections. His entire political faith may be summed up as follows: The Revolution of 1830 was a crime and France will always be unhappy as long as the Bourbons have not reconquered their throne; therefore people ought to long for and hasten on the Restoration of the rightful king.

Whilst expounding these political views he generally added a few harsh truths concerning " those rebels " to whom he was pleased to attribute his own financial ruin. From the earliest days we can recall we have heard much talk concerning Genoude and Lourdoueix and Madier-Montjau, the man who " begged the pardon of God and of men " for his conduct in 1830, and of Guizot, Thiers and Odilon Barrot — God only knows with what bitterness some of them were treated! Under such views and ideas were we brought up!

When the Revolution of 1848 had forcibly arranged a great deal of leisure for our father, politics absorbed him, and indeed that had be-

come the sole preoccupation of all the French.
Nothing was talked about in our presence except
local rows, reviews of the National Guard, night
patrols, cares aroused by the mutinies in Paris and
the uncertainties of the morrow.

Our father constantly met the chiefs of the
Royalist party. At the approach of the elections
they made a demand upon him to open his workshops to assemblages in which their own candi-
dates might be able to appear and be heard. He
met their desire half-way and for several evenings,
whilst playing in the garden, we enjoyed the spectacle of noisy meetings whose cause and object,
however, we did not in any way understand; for
us they simply consisted in tumultuous discussions, violent interruptions and especially in broken windows. After the elections it was necessary
to replace about a hundred panes of glass in the
windows. It is true that the list of Royalist
nominees had been elected. After that, silence
fell again and our life took on its usual features,
but it was for a short time only. A few weeks
after, the factory was sold to a congregation of
Carmelite monks who took up their abode there
and are living there to-day.

"It was a frightful blow," my brother has
written; "heavens, how I wept! You may believe
that I no longer had a heart to play. Oh! no indeed!.... I went and seated myself in one place
after the other and looking round at all the objects
about me I talked to them as if they were human
beings; I said to the plane trees: 'Farewell, my

dearest friends,' and to the water-pools: 'All is at an end, we shall never see each other again.' "

The imagination of the novelist evokes memories of his youthful years when he has come to man's estate. And that which is most sincere in these recollections is the expression therein contained of the sadness which befell him as a child. We had bitter sorrow in leaving the places where the better part of our childhood had flowed happily and peacefully along. We went to live in a little apartment in Séguier Street whilst our father left for Lyon, where he hoped to retrieve his fortunes. In Séguier Street we did not delay long before we re-established much the same life that we passed at the factory. We had there a garden also, but a real garden with trees and flowers and an abandoned hothouse. Alphonse found there once more his cabin and caves and Robinson Crusoe's island, whilst a little girl, the daughter of the landlord, served him in place of a man Friday. But after all he began to take less pleasure in these games. He preferred the noisy recreations at the Canivet school, rough play with comrades and tricks at the expense of neighbors.

Among the latter was an old fellow who lived quite alone like a savage in a house with a mysterious look, which was always shut. My brother and one of his comrades thought it funny to go at night after school hours and pull the bell of the hermitage and then suddenly disappear, so that when he came to open the door no one was there. This conduct lasted eight days, but on the ninth the exasperated man lay in watch, and when, that evening, the little fellows came up as usual to pull his bell, he opened the door and appeared to them with a frightful visage; he sprang upon them, red in the face and almost blind with fury. They fled at the top of their speed and slipped into the side street by our house which the night had filled with darkness. Then, clambering swiftly up the stairs, they rushed for refuge among us, almost crazed by fear. The old man followed them into the dark alley, but he did not know who they were and instead of going to the left, he turned to the right and fell with loud cries of distress down the steps which led into the cellars. People ran up and raised him almost motionless from bruises and carried him back to his house.

This little adventure had no consequences except that, as one may imagine, the bell was left alone from that day onward. I had been the witness of the anguish and terrors of my brother and thus I became a confidant of his schoolboy monkey-tricks and aided him to conceal them from our parents.

This episode is the last I remember from that period of our childhood. In the spring of 1849 we left for Lyon, where our father had discovered a lucrative place.

My mother could not leave her family and her dear Nîmes without a heart-break and her sorrow threw a veil of melancholy across the whole trip, through which, however, I can still see various circumstances which were likely to impress the minds

of children of our age — our journey in the coach
as far as Valence, the monotonous trip up the
Rhône in the steamboat, the arrival at Lyon, our
drive in a carriage along the quays with their high
black houses and our installation in a fourth story
on Lafont Street. Like Le Petit Chose I also am
able to exclaim: "Oh! scenes and objects of my
childhood, what an impression have you not left
upon my mind!"

CHAPTER VIII.

To-DAY that I am separated by more than thirty years full of labor from the time which I describe, turning the eyes of my memory back across that long period, I ask myself what epoch of my life was the most sorrowful, and all my past declares that it was the time of our stay in Lyon. And indeed that is exactly the impression which I find in this passage from a study written by my brother: "I recall a low sky the color of soot and a fog perpetually rising from the two rivers. It does not rain, it oozes with damp fog. And in the enervation of a soft atmosphere the walls of the houses weep, the pavement sweats and the balustrades of the stairways stick to the fingers. The appearance of the townspeople, their gait and language correspond with the moistness in the air."

But beside these purely physical causes for the sadness which the memory of Lyon always awakes in me there are others entirely moral and personal which I should be very sorry to conceal here. I was approaching youthful manhood, and my mind, which had been matured early by the spectacle of the unhappiness of my parents, was, to use the only word which would exactly describe

my thought, "precociously virilized" and at the
same time rendered melancholy. The perplex-
ities of my father and the tears of my mother falling upon my heart were far from making me well
disposed to the recreations natural to my age.

They developed in me a sickly sensibility, the
germ of which I got from my mother. I burst
into tears at the slightest thing, at the least bit of
reproach, or for some question which it embarrassed me to answer. Nobody understood what
was the matter and I understood nothing myself,
for I would have been considerably dashed if I
had had to explain the reason for my tears. In
Le Petit Chose, when my brother traced the
touching protrait of Jacques, he remembered this
trait in my nature. Jacques resembles me more
especially in that point, much more so than in the
various adventures, for the most part purely imaginary, through which my brother makes me move
whilst endeavoring with the eloquence of a grateful heart to depict the solicitude of an older for a
younger brother. Still, I will say and not return
to it again, there is one among all these adventures
which is rigorously true, the scene of the "jug."

We were so poor and wretched, our enterprises
were so unlucky that nobody thought of procuring pleasures for us. The only enjoyments which
were permitted us, because they were within reach
of our almost empty purse, consisted in a few
excursions into the surrounding country, to Char-
pennes and the Tête-d'Or and into the woods of
La Pape.

These forests, which I have never seen again and which I am told a line of railway has destroyed, rose in terraces and showed their splendid green tints upon the banks of the Rhône; they revealed the beauties of meadows, waters and woods to us little Southerners brought up under the burning sun in fields that never are watered, but are ever burned by the fierce sunshine. Alphonse and I took long walks together and we imbibed from these impressions of nature a love of the country which both of us have preserved in equal strength.

On Sundays I accompanied my older brother to Notre Dame de Fourvières. He had infected me with a certain share of his religious fervor; he dragged me to all sorts of pious ceremonies at the church of the Jesuits and of the Capuchins, and he urged me toward the doors of the monastery. Our conversations related almost entirely to the lives of the blessed, their mortifications and their virtues whilst they were toiling up the steep roads of the holy mountain.

We used to stop at the trays of the sellers of pious objects, where ivory crucifixes, gold and silver medals and chaplets displayed upon beds of cotton were crowded together with scapularies, prayer books and a hundred eccentric pamphlets, the product of a sickly illuminism.

Along the fronts of the booths garlands of immortelles and jet and bunches of holy candles swung to and fro in the wind, striking against walls covered with prints very coarsely colored. These prints represented scenes from the New

Testament, portraits of saints and mystical allegories, likewise a collection of all the fungi known, whether poisonous or not; a chart of all the possible accidents, such as burns, stings, poisonings, which was finished up with a statement how to remedy them; then the "Mirror of the Soul filled by Sin," a title which was expressed by the picture of a heart in the centre of which a devil was seated upon a throne, a sceptre in his hand and a lot of pigs at his feet.

We used to listen to mass when we arrived at the chapel, from whose roof hung thousands of votive objects of the most extraordinary kind, grotesque pictures and legs and arms modelled in white wax; and then, quite overcome by tender ecstasy, we went and seated ourselves on the terrace whence the most imposing panorama might be seen: the hundred steeples of Lyon; Bellecour Place and its square overlooked by the monumental portrait of Louis XIV by Coustou; the Saône unrolling its sinuous bends between the fine quays, overlooked on one side by the heights of Saint-Foy and on the other by the rock of the Chartreux, the first buttress of the Croix-Rousse; and then the teeming suburb with its high piled mass of houses, their dark fronts pierced with a thousand windows, inclosing the machines of the weaving guild and yawning like so many crevices opened down into the abyss of misery; the Rhône with its yellow flood which seemed to hurry an entire city of punts, rafts and boats along its swift stream as far as La Mulatière, where it

receives the Saône into its bed ; the tangled and
weather-beaten beams of the Morand bridge, the
pilons in the shape of obelisks on the high portal
of the college, the black and heavy arches of the
Guillotière bridge. Beyond the river lay enormous
plains, here all bare and there wooded, inhabited
and deserted, cut at this point and at that by the
solid mass of forts edged with cannon, or by the
long curtains of poplars above the green pathways ;
and finally at the very limits of the horizon, a chain
of little hills which act as fore-runners to the
higher mountains of the Dauphiné, whose snowy
crests, steeped in the golden vapors of the setting
sun, brighten the horizon with a zigzag line of
silver.

A few months after our arrival in Lyon, on the
advice of my eldest brother, who was just off to begin his ecclesiastical study in the Allix seminary,
we were placed in the *manécanterie* of Saint-Pierre.
On condition that we would do the duty of choir
boys we were allowed to continue our classes in
Greek and Latin there. My poor father had not
found a more practical means than this to continue our studies without opening his purse. But
it was only time lost, for religious ceremonies
occupied all our waking hours and studies were
relegated to the second place.

We had all sorts of disastrous adventures there;
that is the period of my life when I wept the most.
I was awkward beyond words! I never was able
to learn to serve at the mass properly; one day
when I was assisting all alone I got so completely

mixed up in the ceremony that I rang the Sanctus at the Gospels and put all the faithful to flight.

Alphonse too had his own disasters: "One day at mass whilst changing the place of the Gospels the big book was so heavy that it pulled me over. I fell my entire length on the steps of the altar. The reading desk was broken and the service was interrupted. It was during the Pentecost. What a scandal that was!"

The worst of it was that in the complete upset of that strange sort of life my brother became a terribly undisciplined little fellow. What must he do one day, but conceive the idea of digging a mine in the closets for the holy vestments and pouring powder into it! Terrible was the explosion, and it was truly a miracle that no accident occurred.

A little while after, our parents, having perceived that we were not learning anything worth while, decided to put us at college. We were presented to the proctor and after a short examination my brother was admitted to the sixth, whilst I was placed in the fifth form.

CHAPTER IX.

IT may be, reader, that you think I linger over these memories of our childhood; nevertheless you will have to resign yourself to a further march across this melancholy domain with me, for it is the only means by which you can understand in what circumstances the literary vocation of my brother and myself ripened. These circumstances were unfavorable in every respect. We never heard an allusion to things of art and literature, politics, stories of the past, a thousand incidents of our life. Business affairs and the plans which they brought forth, along with the cares and anxieties which they engendered, formed the ordinary topics at our family meetings.

My mother kept to herself the impressions she obtained from her reading, as if she did not dare to avow to us the pleasure which she got from them, the only pleasure in the midst of her trouble which it was possible for her to enjoy.

So it was not the surroundings in which we lived as children that determined our vocation; the only effects they could have would be to re-buff any precocious and accidental manifestations. But it is probable that the influence of these surroundings was attacked and overcome by the influence of a mysterious heritage: it is probable that from some one of our grandparents, a Reynaud or a Daudet, we inherit that thirst for intellectual sensations, that necessity to express them with the pen which is common to us both, and it was from this source my brother received the gift of observation which characterizes his talent, that delicate sensibility and that art of writing he possesses which give his pen the power of a brush. Whence came the fertile treasure of which he had complete possession the very day when for the first time he performed the author's part? which one of those from whom we descend possessed that quality in the remote past? I do not know, but what is undeniable is this, Alphonse Daudet had those qualities, which no one will dream of denying him, all of a sudden, at a single moment and as if by some happy chance he had found them among the frills and laces of his cradle.

Developed later by incessant and grinding labor, they nevertheless exist in his youthful work, with less grandeur undoubtedly than we see in those of his manhood, but ever there; they even exist in the only romance from his hand which has never been published — he was fifteen years old when he wrote it — to which I shall return presently.

College life did not open to us any vistas more smiling than those which had shut in our horizon up to that day : "What struck me at first on my arrival at college," wrote le Petit Chose, "was the

fact that I alone was there in a blouse. At Lyon
the sons of rich people do not wear a blouse, only
the street children, the *gones* wear them, as the
word was used. But I, yes, I had one, a little
blouse with checks that belonged to the days of
the factory; I wore a blouse, I had the look of a
gone."

That was indeed our first sensation and our first
torture when we entered the wide courtyard of
the college exactly in the same guise as we
arrived from our Southern home, being clad as
children of our own age and condition were used
to being dressed in Nîmes, a town somewhat backward in such matters. At once we were classified
by our fellow pupils with those poor wretches
whose parents sweat blood to pay the cost of
their studies. The more elegantly clad among
our comrades disdained to have anything to do
with the new arrivals and affected airs of haughti-
ness or protection with us. A little later we were
given less humiliating clothes, but the effect had
been produced and the impression remained.
My brother overcame it victoriously by gaining
the first places in his classes at the very beginning; from that moment on he was one of the
most brilliant students at the college.

But a queer sort of student, I can promise you!
In a very few months the "school of the hedges"
had become a regular habit with him. During
the week we had ten classes, but it was very seldom that he did not miss five or six and this
lasted for many years. He became so bad that

he did not appear at college save on composition days, a fact, however, which did not prevent him from being always classed among the first, particularly in exact proportion with his advance toward the higher studies.

His intelligence astonished his professors. From the third form on he treated subjects in French composition in verse. Indeed one day he was placed "hors concours" with special praises. His professor having asked him for an apology for Homer, at the end of two hours he gave him an ode which constituted a real event. Here is the conclusion—I have forgotten the rest:

Et dans quatre mille ans,
Au milieu des tombeaux et des peuples croulants,
Comme un sphinx endormi, colosse fait de pierre,
Tu pourras soulever lentement ta paupière,
Regarder le chaos et dire avec orgueil :
Au vieil Homère il faut un monde pour cercueil !

The following year he tried his hand at another sort :

Rito, beau capitaine au service du doge,
Était un gai luron, l'œil bleu, le poil blondin,
Qui lorgnait gentiment une belle en sa loge.
Et qui portait toujours des gants en peau de daim.
Mainte fois, il avait tiré l'épée, et même
Il avait fait, dit-on, gras pendant le carême.
Dieu sait si les maris le redoutaient ! Rito
Leur rendait fort souvent visite incognito.

I am inclined to think that this poem, the beginning of which was written in shorthand dur-

ing the class hour, in order to conceal it from his
professor, was never finished.

I have never yet been able to explain to myself how it was, notwithstanding the disorderly
existence which my brother continued at that
time, that he was able to climb with so much glory
the steps of his studies.

At frequent intervals a printed warning signed
by the censor was left with our house-porter to the
effect that M. Vincent Daudet was notified
that the pupil Alphonse Daudet, his son, had not
appeared at his class on such and such a day.
Thanks to my precautions these were always faith-
fully remitted to me, and I overcame their evil
effects by very crafty excuses which I boldly signed
with the name of our father!

And what a lot of those excuses did I not compose at that time, in order to let my brother escape
well-merited scoldings! I did indeed attempt to
make up for such scoldings by bringing forward
timid counsels, which Alphonse always met by a
promise never to do it again.

The trouble was that he always did do it again.
He was caught in the trammels of a life entirely
outside the family and school, as it were without
watchers or bounds.

There were boating parties on the Saône, or
flights across the green fields which surround
Lyon, stops at taverns — what more can I say?
— a thousand adventures, fitted to reveal his
extraordinary precocity. Without knowing it
himself, he was gathering there impressions that

would never be effaced and with whose aid he should write out accounts of so vivid a sort later in life.

He came back to us worn out and pale, his features all drawn, drunk with weariness and the country air, his eyes filled with visions of waters whirling and sliding through a morning fog. As he always came in too late, I was always anxiously watching the door in order to forestall his return and open it without noise, and then help him to arrange an explanation for our parents. As soon as he appeared I would let him know in a whisper what effect his absence had appeared to make on them; so he knew whether they were angry or his absence had passed unnoticed; thus we hastily improvised some acceptable excuse according to the gravity of the case.

One day he came in all feverish, staggering and with a troubled look, for they had made him drink absinthe. Greatly terrified, I pushed him up against the wall of the vestibule and looking him straight in the eye I said to him:

" Look out now, papa is in there! "

He made an effort, succeeded in gaining command of himself and appeared as usual before our parents. In order to justify his tardy return, he alleged that he had been kept at the college by the visit of an inspector-general of universities.

" But, my dear child," said my mother, " you must be dying of hunger! "

My father was touched and observed that they made boys work too hard. Meantime in a jiffy we

had arranged a plate and cover on the corner of
the table, and though he was sick at his stomach
and could hardly hold up his head, the wretched
boy had to pretend to have a voracious appetite
and eat and drink everything that was given him,
whilst our parents, who were seated by his side,
looked upon him with an air of pity and spied out
every movement with the deepest solicitude.

Hardly thirteen years old and thrown into such
a life with children of his own age, whose influence and example led him on, how was it that he
did not leave right there his fine and intellectual
qualities, the vivacity of his intelligence, the freshness of his soul, the delicacy of his mind and his
native uprightness, that flower of his honor? In
a similar case almost any other would have been
lost. But in his case the trial, which, to be sure, I
would never advise any father to place before his
son, has furnished results contrary to those which
it was logical that he should fear.

The same phenomenon occurred again some
years later when, free and without restrictions
in the streets of Paris at the time that he was
only seventeen, he marched unharmed through
all the caves of Bohemia among the lazy and
enervated and vagabonds of every sort, whose
only sign of activity consists in adding to their
own number, in order that they may find in others
a justification for their own shame — fit at most
to calumniate a conscientious and fruitful talent
and to revenge themselves upon him by low abuse
for the humiliations which are the result of an

incurable necessity to wallow in the most abject laziness.

Such experiences have in two cases given my brother the same result. Nothing of that which is good in him remains sticking to the briers on those perilous paths which he traversed. It is even far from bold to affirm that his talent has profited in a large measure by the discoveries and temptations that met him there. They hastened the ripening of his mind, and far from blunting him, on the contrary refined him and made him more sensitive, until they gave him the nervous reactibility of a violin string.

Whilst turning over in his mind these years full of desperate wretchedness, dangerous escapades and unwholesome distractions, which reappear to him as in a mirror across the lapse of time, it came to him to place like an epitaph on the title-page of one of his books the famous phrase left by Mme. de Sévigné: "One of my worst troubles consists of the memories which *places* fix in my mind; I am affected by them beyond all sense and reason." It is with these words that he came to express the painful impressionability, through which, unwillingly, he preserved the slightest episodes of his childhood and youth deeply engraved on his mind — the most sorrowful ones even more living than the others!

Although he passed in triumph through so many dangerous experiences, the reader would be in error if he supposed that the episodes of his harum-scarum life left me without apprehen-

sion. Along with the anguish of waiting which
overcame me when he did not come home at the
time the classes of the college were discharged,
there was always the fear of accident. He was
so brave and disdainful of danger; and then his
short-sightedness greatly increased the risk!

More than once he succeeded in getting his
boat under the wheels of a steamer, and since,
when he came back from this adventure, I was
the confidant of his sensations at the time, when
in the least behind the hour I began to see him
being tossed into that cursed Saône, whose stream
as it passes Lyon has quite as much movement as
a populous street.

And then there was also the fear of carriages
and of blows received in some quarrel. Oh,
what sorrowful hours I passed! But when I
perceived him coming I forgot everything; as
long as our parents could be kept in ignorance,
my only thought was the happiness of having
him back again safe and sound. I did not even
have courage enough to scold him. Our existence was so terribly monotonous that I understood why he sought distractions outside.

True it is that sometimes he turned to veritable
monkey-tricks. Among our comrades was a boy
of good education but somewhat weak character
who allowed himself to be dragged like him into
adventures such as I am about to tell. He was
the son of a well-placed lawyer of Lyon. He
was of a sympathetic nature to all of us and since
that time has made his way courageously through

the world without allowing the memory of the miseries to which he was victim when a child to leave any bitterness in his heart. But at that time his figure, that had shot up to uncommon height, his long nose and round, staring eyes, a defective pronunciation and his natural naïveté made him the butt for the pitiless raillery of those whose comrade he had become.

A party to all their tricks, it was seldom that he alone did not bear the responsibility. After some escapade which was too noisy for an echo to fail to reach the parents, when it was necessary to find a scapegoat, it was he whom they accused, or it is better to say, who unconsciously and without intending to, accused himself. And when circumstances seemed to prove all the others innocent, they always turned to his detriment; when all escaped, he alone allowed himself to be caught.

Later on it grew far worse. His comrades organized a veritable conspiracy against his father and thought it vastly funny to have him as an accomplice. Most decidedly that age is absolutely without pity! One morning the highly honorable attorney perceived the arrival in his kitchen, which was placed on the same floor with his study, of a long procession of little cook-shop boys, each one bringing a vol-au-vent. Some of them came from the neighborhood and others from distant parts of the town. They jostled each other on the stairs, pushed and reviled each other, each greatly surprised at finding so many others present. The cook received the first vol-au-vent,

though she herself had not ordered it, and then a
second and a third; but when this flood of white
aprons and caps set in she went to find her master.
The tableau may be imagined.

At that time we had left the apartment in Lafont
Street because of the cost of the rent. We were
living in the second story of an old house in the
Pas-Étroit Street, which comes out upon the quays
of the Rhône; it is a badly paved street along
which the college raises its blackened walls, and
these kept all the light away from us.

Our stairs were dark and damp. Every time
the river rose the water came up into our street
and reached at least a meter up our stairs, so that
for three days at a time we were not able to leave
the house except by means of a boat. On its
lower face the house showed the traces of many
inundations; we had two floods in three years.
The big front door was covered with dank spots;
the alley was full of greenish tones from mildew
and the plastering was tumbling everywhere.

That was just the spot arranged for poor people
and such wretched beings as we were at the time.
The apartment was a decent, spacious and com-
modious one, but the proprietor leased it at a low
price because of the lamentable appearance of the
property.

We were living there when the *coup d'état* was
made. We were too young to foresee all the consequences of such an event as that, and judged it
only from the point of view of such amusements
as it might bring us in its wake. Crowds gathered

round the white placards containing proclamations
and the decrees of the Prince-President. As a
usual thing the mob was very sober in its utterances, for the times were not very healthy for
critical remarks. Marshal de Castellane, who was
in command of Lyon, had put the city in a state
of siege. Many arrests had been made and troops
were encamped before big fires in the streets all
along the quays of the Rhône. At the entrances
to the bridges were cannon deployed for work,
for in that direction an army of " hungry ones "
was expected to arrive from the Swiss border, and
steps were taken to meet them.

The season was very severe; when night fell
the soldiers were shivering round their fires, and
since, after all, the population of Lyon considered
them as defenders against dangers which were said
to threaten, they were treated as friends and the
people beat their brains for something which
might add a little pleasure to their ordinary diet.
To please a detachment of chasseurs de Vincennes
which was encamped in front of the gateway of
the college, a fine leg of mutton with string beans
was prepared expressly for their delectation in our
kitchen, and Alphonse and I sallied proudly forth
to bring it to them, along with several bottles of
wine, all of which was accepted with the most joy-
ful gratitude.

But the *coup d'état* was a sore disappointment
to our father, for up to that moment he had cherished the hope of a speedy return of the king.

Called to Paris by business a little while before,

he had been presented to the chiefs of the Royalist party. One of them, invested with due powers by " Monseigneur," had solemnly inscribed in his note-book the name of Vincent Daudet and those of his sons, promising him in reward for his lifelong fidelity places for him and for them, when the hour for the legal and loyal revenges should sound.

A little while afterwards a memento reached us from Frohsdorf, namely a seal in red wax composed of three flowers de luce on a sheet of white paper, with these words round the circumference: " Fides, spes," and underneath, this simple line of mention : " Presented to M. Daudet. HENRI."

It was necessary now to give up all hopes of the brilliant future which so many promises allowed us to expect.

One morning we found in the newspaper the facsimile of a protestation from the Comte de Chambord which began thus : " Frenchmen, they 're deceiving you ! " With a quivering voice I read it aloud to my father who was still in bed. My mother wept a few tears — barren tears ! We had crossed the threshold of the Empire.

CHAPTER X.

THE memory of some of our most cruel misfortunes is associated with that apartment in Pas-Étroit Street. After the deception we experienced, which I have just related, came a long sickness of my father, then the departure of Annette, an excellent maid-servant, who had been in our service several years and adored us. She knew all the secrets of our distress and labored with the courage of a heroine to make it less bitter to us by economizing our outlay. She had followed us to Lyon in order not to part from us; and although the climate was murderous to her health, she remained faithful to us. During his sickness my father conceived a hatred for her and it was necessary to send her away. When he got well he deplored his unjust attitude and wished to bring her back; but she had seen her country's brilliant sky once more and would never return.

Two years before, finding that I was doing nothing of any account on the school bench, and tormented by I know not what yearning for independence and emancipation, urged, moreover, by a powerful desire for some paying labor, I had requested permission to leave college to study business and obtained my parents' consent. My father, needing some one to help him, kept me with him; so I passed my apprenticeship in business under his direction.

Continuing to fabricate scarfs, he had established a salesroom in the largest chamber that our apartment afforded. I can see it still, that melancholy shop where I lived so sad a life for many long months! To the right and left were long planks on trestles; for a desk there was an open board let into the wall under the window; and hung from the ceiling were gigantic balances on which silk was weighed. Along the walls were four chairs and stands in white wood, where the scarf stuffs were ranged; in one corner stood an old iron-bound coffer studded with enormous nail-heads, a survival from the splendors of the past — that was all of this somewhat primitive installation!

How many hours I have passed in that room, folding up the merchandise, writing letters, making out bills and doing up parcels! We labored hard, my father and I, just like two diggers of the soil. With the exception of lading our boxes on our own shoulders, I hardly see what there was that we left to the porter who helped us. Still, neither one nor the other dreamt of complaining: we were well paid when a client appeared.

Clients would not have been lacking, for the output of our house had the reputation of being beautiful, "carefully made and cheap;" but what was lacking was money, capital, the possibility of supplying the advances which our business demanded. At any moment it was necessary to cut short fabrication when it was absolutely necessary to increase it. At other times, when with great effort we had filled the shelves with merchandise, sales suddenly stopped, owing to the prevalence of some accidental crisis, and we were left without any receipts, after having exhausted all our resources in advance payments.

Oh, what burning cares in that march which staggered on between failure and protested notes! How can I relate the anguish of the days when notes fell due? They always came too soon. The little note-book in which the bills to pay were inscribed recalled them ever to our minds. With beating hearts we saw the day approach and reckoned on some buyer, who never came, in order to meet it. Often we were taken unexpectedly. Then we threw two or three hundred pieces into a box in a hurry. A porter took the box on his shoulder and off we went to merchants whose entire business it was to take advantage of the difficulties of the silk-weavers when at bay. Shame on one's brow and anger in one's heart, enough was sold to them at the lowest price in order to meet the note falling due that day. People scarcely become wealthy at a business of that sort.

After a multitude of ruinous operations had opened the gulf into which we were about to fall, the protests arrived — protests and their humiliating sequels. One morning — I can remember it as if it were yesterday — about seven o'clock, three men, obsequious in their manner, entered the shop. It was a bailiff and his assistants. They came to make a seizure in consequence of a verdict pronounced by the tribunal of commerce because of an unpaid draft.

My mother, who was ill that day, was still in bed; my father was shaving himself before the window in the shop; I was writing a letter and my brother was putting a last touch to his lessons before leaving for the college. One may imagine, without the necessity of describing it, what an effect the apparition of the men of law in our home, so peaceful in its monotony, produced!

On that day for the first time I had a manly idea of taking the initiative. Whilst my poor father was parleying, very pale, half his face covered with soap and his razor in his hand, hoping to defend his threatened hearth, I flew off like an arrow to look for help.

Among the merchants of Lyons with whom we had had business connections was one who had known us during more fortunate years. Our misfortunes had not destroyed his sympathy for us. All of a sudden his name presented itself to my memory. Half out of my mind, I reached his house.

"Oh, sir," said I to him, "do come to our house right away!"

I was so upset and so pale that he did not ask any questions, but took his hat and followed me.

On the way I related to him what had happened to us and told him what I hoped he could do for us. He was the friend of our creditor and his intervention might save us.

When he reached the house he sent the bailiffs packing; to the great despair of my mother, they had begun to take an inventory of our furniture; then he had a talk with my father. At the end of an hour we got an assurance that further action should not be taken against us, but our creditor would consent to give us time to clear ourselves of the debt.

The kind man to whom I had appealed rendered us the service with a discreet simplicity which greatly increased its value. He kept our secret absolutely, even as regards his own family. Many years after, in January of 1871, whilst passing through Geneva on the day after the armistice was signed, and at the time that the army of the East had just retired into Switzerland, I met in the streets of that town a poor little soldier of the line, hollow-checked, ragged and dragging his bruised feet with difficulty one after the other. He recognized me and calling to me gave me his name. It was the son of our savior. I took him to my hotel and lavished on him all the care which his condition of health demanded; but the dear boy had no idea that, in addition to the pleasure of helping this French soldier, there was for me the further satisfaction of paying a sacred debt.

Alas, would that our misfortunes had been

limited to such touching trials as these! But
they went on growing more complicated and involved, so that the chapter may be called actually
endless.

After the departure of the good, kind Annette,
who had been sent back to the South as I have
related, her place was taken by a solid, hard-
working woman from Auvergne. But little as the
expense was which she involved, it was necessary
to renounce even that. Then a woman was hired
to do the coarse work of the household and our
dear mother employed her white hands in the
kitchen and installed me as purveyor.

Every morning, after a short talk with her, I
started off for the marketing, a basket under my
arm. I was somewhat humiliated by my part and
attempted to put on the airs of a little rich boy
who was playing at being a servant; and it seemed
that I knew how to buy very well. Before I left
I went to the iron-bound coffer to get the money.

Ah, that old coffer, I see it ever in my mind!
It might have contained in its depth and width a
whole fortune; but, through the acrid irony of
fate, it was always empty. The key remained in
the lock; they even neglected to shut the door.
On one of the boards within my father placed
from time to time a pile of silver pieces. I took
money thence, full of perplexity; a cold sweat
bathed my forehead just in proportion as this
slender pile grew less and less.

One day the last piece in the last pile was gone
and its place remained empty. It was necessary

to turn to any expedient possible, to the pawn-shop for example, whither I carried in succession every piece of old silver, the jewels belonging to my mother and everything which we had saved from former shipwrecks. At my first visit to an official at the government pawn-shop I had interested him in our misfortunes by proudly insisting, contrary to the truth, that our dilemma was only for the moment. In that way I obtained permission to come to him through a door apart and wait for him in a little room, without being compelled to mingle with the mob of poverty-stricken wretches that pushed about his wicket.

Oh, days of blackest misery, what wrinkles you have carved in our memories! What a precocious ripening did you not cause our souls to undergo! Yes, indeed, we became men at a very early hour, through having lived with adversity. Much less would have produced the same result! The soul of a child steels itself quickly under such harsh trials.

But experience which is bought at that price, by the sacrifice of the illusions and joys of youth, is so painful that I would wish no one to gain it so dearly. The anxieties and tears of those whom you love, the despairing pursuit after money, profound and hidden distress, shame at urgent begging prayers, early morning visits to the priest of the parish, the first and only person to whom one dares tell everything, the anguish of hours of waiting which follow demands, the answers which never come, the uncertainty as to the morrow, the whole horizon without a bright point — reader, God keep you from such trials!

Owing to this persistency of bad luck, the con· clusion was come to that there was no place for me in my father's business and that it would be prudent to leave me free to gain my livelihood in some other direction. So I was permitted to look out for work and I found a place at first in the government pawnshop of Lyons.

The place owed us that at least! As a super-numerary I earned the bread which I ate at my parent's house to the extent of three francs a day. Seated between two appraisers behind a wicket, I made investigations under their orders. Ah, how many sad looks and long faces, how many poor, thin hands holding out a little parcel of wretched clothes in shame, have I not seen through the narrow square opening of the grille which separated us from the public!

The evening of the day on which, for the first time, I was a spectator of this heart-rending scene, I said to our mother:

"There are people more unhappy than we are."

At the end of a few months I left the pawnshop, sick, as it were poisoned by the pestiferous air I had inhaled between walls impregnated with all the unwholesome odors which disengage them-selves from these pledged objects. A more lucra-tive place had been offered me — the position as a clerk with Descours, a man who let car-riages and wagons. As a beginning they put me

to work on the carrier's letters. I have filled up
hundreds of those leaflets bearing the Imperial
stamp, at the head of which can be read, printed
by lithography, the old formula: "Under the
hand of God and in the charge of So-and-So,
public carrier. . . ."

My work was hard; it kept me at the office,
very often, to a very late hour of the night. But
at any rate the remuneration was proportionate
with the work and the surroundings were more
human, healthier, less sorrowful than those at the
pawnshop.

M. Descours was an excellent man and showed
me kindness; whilst my comrades treated me as
a person superior to my condition, who had been
accidentally thrown amongst them, but was destined to leave them some day in order to rise
higher.

CHAPTER XI.

My brother was then fifteen years old and was just finishing his "humanities," whilst I was eighteen. All the spare time which his studies allowed him, for his life was at once full of excitement and work, and all that my office work permitted me were absorbed by our literary dreams.

Neither one nor the other of us had stated in so many words that we proposed to give our life to letters. But it is worthy of note that the more our circumstances persisted in separating us from that career into which we afterward embarked, the more a mysterious call made itself heard in us and prepared us for it.

It dated from as early a moment as our arrival in Pas-Etroit Street. On the same floor with us there lived with his parents a certain young man about our own age; we knew him at the college before we were aware he was our neighbor. When we had become close friends, he confessed to us that he was a poet; already he had composed several hundred verses and he made a collection of poems with the greatest fastidiousness, copying them in fine, round script into an album with black morocco covers and broad gold edges.

Since he was brought up upon the *Orientales* and
the *Odes et Ballades,* his productions consisted of
scarcely anything better than more or less suc-
cessful imitations of Victor Hugo. But our admiration could not be killed by such a slight thing
as that; we knew his verses by heart and spouted
them in chorus with him.

> En avant! en avant! Déjà la blonde aurore
> A, de ses doigts rosés, entr'ouvert l'Orient!
> En avant! en avant! Le ciel qui se colore
> De ses premiers rayons déjà jaunit et dore
> Le faîte ardoisé du couvent.

My brother had already made verses and,
encouraged by his neighbor's example, he continued to make them. You may still read some
of them dating from that period in *Les Amoureuses,* in which, three years later, he thought
them worthy to figure. I fell into the same vein
and beneath the sway of my mystical aspirations
which, for a long time, left a deep trace in my
spirit, I sketched a poem on religion. The solitary stanza which I wrote is given complete in *Le
Petit Chose* and it is so delightfully made fun of
there that I have won the right to talk of it without laughing.

Then, after having devoured the poems of
Ossian and the tragedies of Ducis in imitation of
Shakespeare, I also desired to write tragedy. I
arranged a plot. It began in a forest of Corn-
wall, the evening before a combat. My brother
lent me the first line:

Du sang! Partout du sang! Chaque arbre, chaque feuille ...

But I was never able to supply the second line and my tragedy stayed where it was. I dropped verses and turned to prose. Alphonse turned the same way, but without abandoning rhymes. It was at that time he composed *La Vierge à la Crèche :* —

Dans ses langes blancs, fraîchement cousus,
La Vierge berçait son enfant Jésus ;
Lui gazouillait comme un nid de mésanges ;
Elle le berçait et chantait tout bas
Ce que nous chantons à ces petits anges !
Mais l'enfant Jésus ne s'endormait pas !
Estonné, ravi de ce qu'il entend,
Il rit dans sa crèche, et s'en va chantant ;
Comme un saint lévite et comme un choriste
Il bat la mesure avec ses deux bras,
Et la Sainte Vierge est triste, bien triste,
De voir son Jésus qui ne s'endort pas.

To the same period belongs, moreover, *Les Petits Enfants :*

Enfants d'un jour, ô nouveau-nés !
Petites bouches, petits nez,
Petites lèvres demi-closes,
Membres tremblants,
Si frais, si blancs,
Si roses !

Enfants d'un jour, ô nouveau-nés !
Pour le bonheur que vous donnez
A vous voir dormir dans vos langes,
Espoir des nids,
Soyez bénis,
Chers anges !

Pour tout ce que vous gazouillez
Soyez bénis, baisés, choyés.
Gais rossignols, blanches fauvettes,
    Que d'amoureux
    Et que d'heureux
        Vous faites!

That is the way my brother made his prelude to the vast number of pages written, later, amid the tumult of those ardent battles in which he was engaged for life and for glory, all in the thick of Paris and in the full tide of modernity.

Things of this sort occurred to him on his return from a trip in his canoe, or coming out of his classroom, or else after some feverish evening in a room hired in secret along with some of his comrades in order to practise at Lyon their apprenticeship to the Quartier Latin of Paris.

To the renown of their author, the verses have survived the period which caused them to appear; but where are those who, along with me, were the first to hear them read? Whither have they flown, those companions of our youthful years, those witnesses to the upspringing of a poet's soul and the unloosing of our budding passions, over-excited by the precocious and unhealthy labor of our youthful imaginations, driven toward the most flattering ideals? We have found some of them again; but the others, are they dead? are they living? And if they are alive, have they preserved the recollection of our fantastic preparations for the accomplishment of the solemn duties of life?

24

Prior to this flight toward literature, that taste
for books which we had whilst still children, just
as our mother before us, had developed itself with
a singular power within us.

At the old factory, coincident with the first
dawning of his intelligence, my brother never
closed his *Robinson Crusoe* except to revive in
his games the adventurous epic of his hero; recollections of a *Swiss Family Robinson,* read and
re-read again and again, were also inspiration for
our imaginations. Then a strip of turf became a
desert island, the peaches and figs against the
wall were transformed into guavas and bananas
and our dog Lotan became a famished and bloodthirsty lion. All the books we read were turned
into action and our minds became accustomed to
absorb and retain everything. And when we began to write we did not stop reading, but quite the
contrary. Only we passed from *Le Collège In-
cendié* and *Petits Béarnais* and the *Journal des
Enfants* to *Han d'Islande* and *Les Mystères de
Paris* and *Les Burgraves.*

At that time, within the buildings belonging
to the college on the Quay de Retz was an old
bookseller named Gaspet, who lived at the ex-
tremity of a narrow shop. Long hours were
passed in his place, standing before the shelves
crammed with all sorts of worn and dusty volumes. He had books of every period, ancient and
modern, good and bad, the old classics, the liber-
tine authors of the eighteenth century, novels,
medical and scientific books; we turned every-

thing over, standing up and in a hurry, quickly whisking over the leaves to ferret out the interesting passages.

Then we made a few purchases and exchanges — quite a bookseller's business — by means of which we got by turns Buffon, Ariosto, Shakespeare, Boccaccio, Piron, the Abbé de Chaulieu, Vicomte d'Arlincourt, Lamartine, Chateaubriand, Pigault-Lebrun — works of the greatest variety that were bolted rather than read in pursuit of our boyish curiosity, which was eager to penetrate the secrets our studies had not revealed to us.

Later, when my brother had left me, as I shall soon relate, I continued to read and buy books with the savings laboriously brought together — works of modern authors in editions illustrated by Bertall, Riou, Janet-Lange, Philippoteaux, Gustave Doré, who was a master at twenty years, and a hundred others. That is the way I learned to know Balzac, George Sand, Frédéric Soulié, Eugène Sue, Léon Gozlan, Méry, Charles de Bernard, Alphonse Karr, Henry Murger. Then came the time of *Le Journal pour Tous*. That opened the English novels to me — Dickens and Thackeray, whom my brother was to know later in Paris, along with Champfleury, who initiated me into the methods of realism, a far from modest forerunner of naturalism and a not less noisy one.

And finally through the *Revue des Deux Mondes* and the *Revue de Paris*, which I found in the reading-room, I became acquainted with Octave Feuillet, Amédée Achard, Louis Ulbach and the

master Gustave Flaubert whilst at the same
time in the midst of indecisions and gropings
my literary ideas were fixed by Sainte-Beuve,
Gustave Planche, Armand de Pontmartin, Fioren-
tino and Jules Janin.

As a final touch to this unconscious preparation for our entrance into the field of letters the
biographies by Eugène de Mirecourt, the success
of which was so great in the provinces, introduced me to the world of writers; despite the fact
that they contained much that was untrue and
calumnious, they filled my mind with a thousand
characteristics which familiarized me with the
personalities of those men whose works we had
admired.

What a lot we did read in those distant years!
Of an evening, when everything was quiet about
us, a lamp, placed near the bed which we occupied
in brotherly union, lit up our long night watches.
The family thought we were asleep; and from
her distant bed-chamber our mother would call
to us again and again in order to make certain
that our light was quenched. But we took good
care not to answer; we held our breath and
turned the leaves noiselessly and, thanks to our
precautions, we plunged freely into long conversations in place of sleep, talks which stimulated,
little by little, the fertility of our minds.

My father's political connections had opened to
us the editorial office of the *Gazette de Lyon.*
This newspaper, consecrated to the defence of the
legitimacy of the Bourbons, was managed by

Théodore Mayery, a journalist with no great intellectual culture, but of a forcible and acrid temperament. He wrote in a tumultuous, tormented, bellowing style. His writing being filled with slag and savage as his own soul, his articles were of the hurrah-boy sort, but full of new vistas and striking from their uncommon originality.

Under his orders stood Paul Beurtheret, a noisy and kind-hearted fellow from the Franche-Comté, who was as cultivated a literary man as Mayery was lacking in that particular; under a broad joviality of a fine sort he concealed a sensitive nature, an honest heart, a proud independence and an energetic sincerity in his convictions.

Called to the management of the *France Centrale* at Blois, Paul Beurtheret came, later, to Paris, drawn thither by Villemessant, who employed him as secretary in the editorship of the *Figaro*. But his taste for a free and independent life could not accommodate itself to the needs of Parisian journalism and the demands of an enslaving trade. He was taken with home-sickness for his province. He left and went to Tours to establish the *Union Libérale*, one of the most brilliant organs of the opposition toward the end of the empire. In that city he was killed during the war on the day the Germans entered, his head being carried off by a bomb-shell. He was a faithful friend to us; he had foreseen the budding talent of my brother and felt no little pride in it.

The notabilities of the Royalist party closed in

about the *Gazette de Lyon* — Léopold de Gaillard, who was made Councillor of State by the National Assembly, Charles de Saint-Priest, the friend and agent of the Comte de Chambord, Pierre de Valous, curator of the library at Saint-Pierre Palace, the two Penins, father and son, both of them steel and copper engravers, and the sculptor Fabisch.

There we also met with Claudius Hébrard, a Lyon citizen transferred to Paris, where he had become the titulary poet of the meetings of Catholic working men. A bard quite solitary in his kind, toward whom the Royalist party has shown ingratitude, he went to religious meetings of the people and recited there various verses which he improvised with too much facility and which have not survived the circumstances that inspired them.

Although he lived in Paris, he edited a monthly periodical which appeared at Lyon under the title of *Journal des Bons Exemples:* it was that which very often brought Hébrard back to his native town.

At the time he was in all the splendor of his passing notoriety and, owing to our ignorance of degrees and classifications in literature, he realized in our eyes the finished type of the man of letters.

We were very grateful for his natural kindliness, which made him treat us, young, timid and obscure as we were, like comrades. And then he brought with him that fragrance of Paris which we inhaled with vast delight.

CHAPTER XII.

INTRODUCED into these surroundings of Royalism and literature, we met a kindly welcome and as much encouragement as if we were about to become the hope of the party. When I was a clerk with Descours, I had written in secret some articles of literary criticism, penning them in a fragmentary way between two carriage blanks to be filled up. The *Gazette* received them and printed them; from that time on I became quite one of the staff. At the suggestion of Claudius Hébrard, I wrote in the same fragmentary way a novel which I have absolutely forgotten, even to its subject. I sent it to the *Journal des Bons Exemples* which did not publish it and neglected to send it back. Notwithstanding these attempts, my family scarcely believed in my vocation. During the few moments which my office work left me I heard my father and mother exclaiming without cessation: "Stick to money figures." Alas, those miserable sums! My brother was luckier, because under pretext of study he could devote himself freely to his natural bent. He took advantage of it by writing a novel in his own turn. His work was called *Léo et Chrétienne*

Fleury; it was the story of a young soldier whom
a strong devotion to his family had led into an
adventure which was considered a criminal lack of
discipline by his superiors. He died under the
guns of a patrol and almost beneath the eyes of
his mother and sister, who had come too late to
save him.

The story began with a dozen letters exchanged
between his brother and sister. Whatever there
lay of grace, brightness, freshness of heart and
originality of style in Alphonse Daudet made its
appearance in this correspondence. The story
which forms the second part was saturated with
emotion and entirely impregnated with the sweet
perfume of youth and tenderness.

One evening my brother read this novel to the
assembled family. We wept as we listened and,
wild with enthusiasm, I ran to offer the manuscript to Mayery. He was thunderstruck. What!
a collegian fifteen years old had written such
exquisite pages? It was not to be believed!
Nevertheless he was forced to give way before
the proofs and promised to publish the romance
in the *Gazette de Lyon* as soon as the author had
made a slight change which he thought necessary
for the interest of the story.

From that moment to this, what has happened
to the masterpiece? I have forgot. Undoubtedly
Mayery kept it among his papers; but we were
prevented from getting it back from him by certain incidents which intervened and hurried forward the course of our destiny. And since the

Gazette was suppressed soon after, it is probable that the manuscript was lost.

Though twenty-five years have elapsed since then, the impression left upon my memory by *Léo et Chrétienne Fleury* has remained vivid enough to give me the right to say, that if that novel had been published it would have been entirely worthy of a place in a collection of my brother's work. This is a fact that one may properly insist upon, for it is a confirmation of everything that is known concerning Alphonse Daudet's talents, among the high qualities of which, when its origins and first manifestations are examined, an extraordinary precocity must be noted.

Other studies in verse or prose which date from the same time may be found in his books. If one considers the age at which they were written, they are the productions of a child; but judged by their intrinsic merit they are the work of an able craftsman who has acquired the knowledge of his trade without an effort and possesses it in a certain way as a natural gift. This privilege of destiny has been worthily used by my brother; he has earned it by the ardor of his constant struggle for better work, by a self-criticism which urges him to carve and model his inspirations with the most tenacious patience and by the respect he shows his reader and his own talent — a respect which makes him sufficiently master of himself to refuse to permit a page to leave his hands before he has expended upon it the full force of his genius for improvement. And it may be said that he has nothing to regret in what he has written.

The authorized edition of his lifework, the publication of which has just begun (1881) in a form seldom employed by writers during their lifetime, will include everything which he has published — everything, without exception.

When he came to prepare it, there was nothing for him to prune away; everything was considered good enough to be included. In this epoch of hasty productions, improvised under the spur of necessity, how many are there among us whose works could undergo such a trial as that?

How many are there, and I am speaking now of the most illustrious among those whose talent has crowned their vogue and consecrated their success, who in their early life have not written books which were too quickly conceived and too rapidly finished — books they would like to have effaced from the list of their published works?

How many are there who are not bent upon dating their works from a relatively recent period, prior to which they wrote volumes which they would not dare to avow any longer and which they would absolutely refuse to reprint to-day? Few are they who, helped by a lucky fortune, or far-sighted enough at the very threshold of their career, have been able to guard themselves from these dangers. Alphonse Daudet is one of them.

But that is not the only example of the lucky chance which mounted guard about his literary cradle. He did not have any "high-water book"

— that is to say, any book by means of which, with a reference to its great success, critics are able to crush the volumes which the same author publishes later.

In their character as novelists the Goncourts, who are so important because of their historical work, have always remained the authors of *Germinie Lacerteux;* many as have been the charming novels which have come from their bold and innovating pens, none have equalled the memory of that one, which is forever recalled when their name is thought of and their character described.

Let Émile Zola write as many masterpieces as he chooses, people will always bring forward *L'Assommoir*, the book which made his reputation, defined his manner and exhausted his literary procedures — after the production of which he could not astonish the world any more!

Gustave Flaubert is dead, crushed in a literary sense beneath the weight of the very proper success of *Madame Bovary*. Indeed that itself was the great sorrow of the end of his life. It reached such a pitch with him that he became irritated when one spoke to him concerning the resounding success of that novel. When Ernest Renan wrote to him a long and eloquent letter after the publication of *La Tentation de Saint Antoine*, authorizing him to publish it in the newspapers, Flaubert neglected to give it publicity for the sole reason that the letter ended with the wish to have him return to the methods and manner of writing which had brought him glory. And when Renan was astounded at such touchiness :

"My dear fellow," responded Flaubert, "I dislike poor jokes very much; and I have had rather too much of that kind of joke! Always and always *Madame Bovary!*"

"That sort of a joke," as poor Flaubert said, "has never been made and never will be made" on Alphonse Daudet. All the chapters he has written have obtained, pretty equally, the favor of the public. Those who contested his power in fecundity, while doing homage to his talent, when he had only published his *Lettres de Mon Moulin* or the *Contes du Lundi,* place at present in the same rank, whatever their preferences may be, *Le Petit Chose, Tartarin de Tarascon, Fromont Jeune et Risler Aîné, Jack, Le Nabab, Les Rois en Exil* and *Numa Roumestan.* They do not dream of using one of these books, so varied in their inspiration, to depreciate the other. For each one in succession reveals a new effort and a constant progress in the author.

This literary conscience, so powerful and severe toward itself, was aroused in my brother along with the growth of his talent. It affords a clew to his processes, his stern determination to render perfect the expression of his thought and his hourly battles with words, which he grinds and kneads and renders subtle in accordance with the flow of his imagination.

"Style is the fragrance of literary work," cried he one day; and in fact every one of his books represents an almost superhuman labor. There is many an easy-flowing, harmonious page, over which the sentences march with majesty, like some river that rolls across its bed fine scales of gold; but on that page there remains not one trace of the effort which it cost him; and yet that admirably gifted artist, who was never satisfied with his own work, has perspired and suffered and turned pale over it, to the point of feeling broken in health for several days through the mere excess of labor.

Let us therefore not be astonished that he has conquered fortune and glory. Glory and fortune represent the well-earned reward of a tremendous worker who, at the very beginning, had the courage to reject gains easy to obtain and never sacrificed anything to improvisation, even when, being still a boy, he was struggling with the material difficulties of life; as a man at forty years of age he can flatter himself to have made the cultivation of letters the highest aim of his life.

CHAPTER XIII.

THUS it was that the inborn love for letters broke the clouds upon our gloomy horizon; it opened up a luminous point and gilded the threshold of our youth, taking the place of all those pleasures of which we were deprived. But it was none too much to outbalance the anguish of mind which befell us as soon as our family affairs were borne in upon us again.

Things went from bad to worse every day in that respect. During the course of 1856 our father had to abandon entirely the enterprises which he had begun. After seven years of ceaseless labor there was no result except a deficit which was simply crushing us. Strangled by debts, he had turned every way to find some resource. After having struggled desperately against ill luck Vincent Daudet was at the end of his rope. Poverty benumbed him. There was a moment when he had hoped to find some lender of capital who would aid him to carry on his business; but his search was in vain and he gave it up.

One morning he sold in a single parcel all the merchandise which remained in the shop, balanced his accounts and demanded and obtained

from his creditors extension of time. Then he
entered as partner a wine business, where he
would have gained the bread necessary to his
family and a good deal more, if he had known
how to bend to the demands of his new situation.
But a long habit of commanding others made the
place very soon intolerable to him. Resignation
also was not long in reaching its limits; then he
left Lyon for Paris, where his friends had caused
him to hope for a position in closer conformity to
his taste.

From that moment until the day when Fate
permitted his sons to grant him the repose which
he had so cruelly and laboriously earned, our poor
father was like a swallow fluttering about within
bounds that impede its flight and weary its wings
and eyes — a bird striking against those walls
beyond which it knows the wide atmosphere and
open space exist, and ending by falling and dying,
worn out by its despairing efforts. He tried ten
different businesses and looked for employment
in commerce and in government offices. One
moment he thought he had fortune in his grasp
with a certain discovery in industrial matters
which has enriched others since. Then his hopes
vanished and his strength was used up by the
weight of his disasters. Discouragement took
hold of him and he was forced to throw upon our
shoulders the care of rebuilding his ruined hearth.
He has enjoyed the happiness of seeing it rebuilt.
Notwithstanding the long malady which finally
took him from us, his last years have been

serene, peaceful and beautified by the happiness
of his children, which became his own personal
happiness.

When he had decided to quit his trade we left
the mournful house in Pas-Étroit Street and settled down in a modest *entresol* on the Rue de
Castries in the middle of a wind-swept and smiling quarter between Bellecour Place and Perrache
Allée. At that time Alphonse and I were in the
liveliest effervescence of a literary life and most
delighted to begin to give free vent to our aims
and aspirations. It seemed to us that we had
recovered some independence in this new apartment, away from the neighborhood of the shop
with its bales of silk and piles of scarfs and
everything else that recalled the causes of our
ruin to us. My brother finished up his studies
by one vigorous effort ; and, for my part, I undertook to complete mine by giving to my education
all the leisure that my office work allowed me.

Both of us worked pretty solidly at that time,
happy as we were in our voluntary labor, so that,
notwithstanding the wretched ending of our stay
in Lyon, this epoch of our lives seems less sorrowful when we look at it through the memories
that remain about the Rue de Castries.

Still, it was there we learned of the death of our
elder brother Henri.

I said before that he wanted to enter into
orders and had begun his ecclesiastical studies at
the seminary at Allix. He did not stay there
long. When he reached the sub-deaconship, just

before pronouncing the final vows, his soul, ill and troubled by the excess of a devotion pushed beyond measure, had conceived scruples and doubts concerning the sincerity he was bringing to his vocation. So he had returned to us, to the great disgust of my father, who could not understand at all what such hesitations meant.

For several months he had lived near us, trying to teach piano lessons and, in consequence of some chance, playing the organ in one of the parishes of the city. Then, weary of a life that had no aim, he left for Nîmes, where the Abbé d'Alzon offered him a position on the staff of instructors at Assumption College. I have kept most of the letters which our poor Henri wrote to us at that time. They are full of tender counsels for Alphonse and me, but they reveal the greatest lack of experience of the world and show a way of seeing life through the veils of a somewhat narrow mysticism which fitted ill those inexorable demands upon us which we were about to experience in the near future.

But they revealed at the same time a soul full of endless kindness and thoroughly penetrated by the ideal. I have always thought that if my elder brother had lived, his spirit, whilst it grew more manly, would have shaken off the prejudices and doubts which weakened it, and that, having cast aside the hankering after the priesthood, his actual talents as a musician and pianist, while developing themselves, would have helped him to find the true path of his career, that of art.

25

One day a letter from Assumption College suddenly announced to us that he had been attacked by brain fever. My mother left at once, but she reached Nîmes too late to find her son alive. Her only and supreme consolation consisted in the privilege of pressing her lips to the forehead of that young Levite, transfigured by death and lying white and fair upon a pillow in its flood of black hair. She had already suffered so much that this catastrophe found no place on her heart for a new scar. Those wounds which had been open and bleeding this long time only grew a little deeper, and that was all. *Mater dolorosa!*

The news of this disaster arrived in a despatch which my father and Alphonse received one evening just at nightfall, and which I read a few minutes later as I returned from my office. We wept together till a late hour of the night; then our mother returned and life took us up again, a little more sorrowful and wounded in soul than before.

Our solitary amusement at that time consisted in going on fine days to listen to the music in Bellecour Square. There we met Mayery, Beurtheret and Ludovic Penin. We walked about together, talking oftenest of literature and art, already grave and attentive little men and filled with a feeling of pride in the precocious brilliancy we showed as men of letters — a brilliancy which did not fail to flatter our vanity somewhat. Since writing *Léo et Chrétienne Fleury* Alphonse was a person of consideration in those surround-

ings. When he left us to go back to the comrades
of his own age, they talked of his verses and his
talent; brilliant hopes were attached to his future
and for a moment our parents felt their miseries
assuaged when I repeated to them what our friends
had said of their young son.

While speaking of Lyon and Bellecour Square
it is impossible for me to refrain from saying
something about Marshal de Castellane, who was
one of the most vivid impressions of our youth.
It was at the "music hour" that he showed himself to the people of Lyon. A thousand anecdotes of his present and past existence passed
from mouth to mouth and let loose about him an
amount of curiosity which reached the point of
mania. He was one of the grand attractions of
our walk. All of a sudden we heard the drums
beating to quarters; the detail of soldiers on the
square shouldered arms, whilst the marshal on
horseback came down the street and turned the
corner of Bourbon Street, always in full uniform,
wearing in brave show his military chapeau wav-
ing with white feathers. After having saluted
the guard, he mingled among the people, walking to and fro, a single eyeglass stuck in his eye.
He had most singular and eccentric sides to his
character. But what an admirable soldier he was,
and what a splendid military life was his!

My brother left college in August of that year
and had nothing further to do than to present
himself for examination in order to obtain his
baccalaureate. Unfortunately a difficulty only

too well foreseen was about to rise in this direction and the impossibility of solving it was about to determine our parents to take a very great resolution in a matter which touched my poor Alphonse profoundly.

At that time the course for examination for the bachelor's degree amounted to a relatively important sum. However manfully my father might bleed himself, he could never succeed in procuring it and still less in abstracting it from his household expenses, which were rigorously limited to the most pressing needs of our family life. It is true that his son was quite young enough to wait and defer his examination for a year. But in the meantime what should he do with himself?

This being the condition of things, a singular proposition reached us from the South. One of our relatives advised my father to beg the admission of Alphonse to the college at Alais as a teacher; he had ascertained that the gates of that college would open wide in welcome before the grandnephew of Abbé Reynaud and that his youth would not be an obstacle. The child — for he was still a child — might prepare himself there for his examinations, live a whole year without any cost to his family and even put some money aside, no matter how small his salary might be.

At any other time my father and mother would have resolutely rejected this proposition, being quite upset at the thought of separating themselves from their youngest son and delivering

him up to the harsh experiences of a humble and
almost disdained profession; but in the situation
where we then were our future preoccupied them
less than the immediate necessities of our life
from day to day.

After all, it was as good an entrance as another
into the profession of teacher! The sweetest
memories of the youth of my mother were attached
to that college at Alais. In memory she saw it
again, always just as she had seen it long ago,
when the intelligent and paternal management of
"our uncle the Abbé" kept it flourishing and
made a delightful spot of it in which to live.

These considerations, joined to actual necessity, swayed the lot of my brother and his departure was decided upon. He accepted his new
destiny courageously, happy to be able to assist
his family and enchanted first and foremost at
his maiden voyage into an unknown land, the
adventures of which he was very far from sus-
pecting.

As for me, although I understood the wisdom
of it, this resolution confounded me. The idea
of separating myself from my brother broke my
heart. I considered how young he was, how poor
in experience and how badly armed for the trials
which he was about to undergo!

Sixteen years of age, with a tender soul and a
sensitive imagination, having all the weakness of
his youth and a signal awkwardness when confronted by material difficulties, added to a dis-
tressing shortness of sight — how could he put

such a matter through? But, alas, my own
powerlessness was equal to my sorrow! it was
absolutely necessary to be resigned.

"In this family the members had begun to get
used to misfortune. The day following that
memorable affair, the entire family accompanied
le Petit Chose to the boat. . . . All of a sudden
the bell rang — it was necessary to part — le Petit
Chose, tearing himself from the embraces of his
friends, stepped bravely across the landing-plank.

"'Be a good boy!' cried his father to him.

"'Don't get sick,' said Madame Eyssette.

"Jacques wanted to speak, but he could not;
he was crying too hard."

Yes, indeed, Jacques was crying; but they were
not the snivelling tears of childhood, they were
the fertile weeping of his precocious manhood,
dragged from his eyes by the acute sorrow of that
separation, which was the bitterest sorrow he had
yet been called upon to suffer. He saw the future
through his tears. And the more sorrowful the
present hour was, the more he clung to that future
with confidence, forming beneath the very blows
of defeat new projects with a view to revenge for
present ills, with which that comrade was closely
associated whom the swift flood of the Rhône
was carrying far away.

"Le Petit Chose did not cry, not he. As I
have already had the honor to inform you, he was
a grand philosopher, and, really, it will not do
for philosophers to yield to weakness. . . . And
nevertheless, God knows how he loved them,

those dear people whom he left behind him in
the fog! God knows whether he would not have
gladly given for their sake his entire blood and
flesh! But what would you? The joy of leaving
Lyon, the movement of the boat, the intoxication of making a voyage, the pride of feeling that
he was a man — a free and complete man, jour-
neying alone and gaining his own livelihood —
all that intoxicated le Petit Chose and prevented
him from dreaming, as he ought to have done,
about the three darling persons who were sobbing
back there, standing on the quays of the Rhône."

CHAPTER XIV.

My brother's departure made us a little more sorrowful. Several months elapsed without bringing us anything else save successive aggregations of our misfortunes, which were so many witnesses to the severity with which bad luck hounded us. The clouds which had been heaping up so long upon our horizon grew darker day by day and a catastrophe grew imminent. I felt it approaching and prepared for it.

After all, in the wretched situation where we found ourselves, would it not be better that Fate should exhaust its furies on us in a final storm? When it had finally beaten us down and had dispersed the very fragments of our hearth, it would doubtless move elsewhere to strike its blows and give us a free moment to build up that which it had destroyed.

Besides, a supreme disaster would take us out of the harassing uncertainties among which we were battling. Then it would be necessary to make a resolution; I could go to Paris — that unknown Paris, where so many others before us had arrived obscure, unhappy and disinherited and found there the end of their misery. Decided

to imitate them, I often talked to my mother of
my plan, but she feared for me, having lost the
very power to conceive of hope. What would I
do if I went to Paris? It would have been something if I had even had some certain employment!

"I will get a position in the telegraph offices,"
said I to her one day, recollecting that we had
an old friend of the family in the administration
of that government department.

On hearing this she regarded my project with
greater tranquillity and talked to my father about
it during one of his infrequent stops at Lyon, for
he was then much away.

"There is nothing to do but to let him follow
freely his own inspiration," answered he.

From that moment I dreamed of nothing but
the trip and especially of the means to effect it,
for it was exactly the most wretched part of our
condition that any project, however advantageous
it might be, could not be carried out if any advance of money, even a small one, were necessary.
Fortunately, and it is with intention that I employ
that word, a catastrophe did arrive, which allowed
me to realize the idea which I had been caressing
with such perseverance.

During the whole year we had been inhabiting
the apartment in the Rue de Castries the landlord had not known, as the vulgar saying runs, the
color of our money. He had begun by showing
a great deal of patience. What he knew about
us had interested him in our fortune; and when,
again and again, the bills for rent presented by

the janitor had come back to him unpaid, he had contented himself with sending a courteous demand to my father.

But that patience could not last always. Now we owed him for three quarters and the bill for the fourth was approaching. At his own request his business agent came to demand payment. He clothed this demand in the most polite forms; but one felt the hand of iron beneath the glove and under the smooth words of the man of the world the insistence of the creditor. He had been glad to accord delays to us because we were honest people and especially because he believed that our lack of funds was merely temporary. But he could not wait any longer for the payment of the debt already contracted, nor allow us to remain longer in the apartment if our inability to pay the rent should continue. This notification to quit left us without any resource. In the absence of my father I counselled with my mother how we might be able to face the trouble and we came to an agreement and recognized that it could only be done through the sale of our furniture. The furniture sold and the most pressing debts paid, my mother could leave with her daughter for the South, where one of her sisters offered her a roof, whilst I could go to seek my fortune in Paris and hasten our reunion.

I had so lively a faith in my own star and in that of my brother, I uttered my hopes in such a tone of conviction that the dear good woman was not able to prevent herself from sharing them and thus received a certain relief from the bitterness of those cruel hours.

Hardly conceived and approved by my father, to whom a long letter set forth the whole matter, when this heroic plan was put into execution. I notified Descours of my near departure and bravely announced to him that I was going to "do literature" in Paris.

"I always thought that you would end in that way," answered the good-natured man. "Good luck to you."

Then I went to see the agent for our apartment house. I imparted to him our resolution and begged him to spare us the judicial proceedings and permit the sale of our furniture in a kindly spirit. He entered into my views of the case and together we made an inventory of the objects that filled our apartment. He permitted me to set aside a certain number, the sale of which would have broken poor mamma's heart; she was already on her way to the South. I took three days to pack them up, in order to send them after her and did this business with joy in my heart and a song upon my lips, convinced that this unhappy hour would only bring us together again in luckier days.

Thus was the dispersion of the ruins of our hearth accomplished. This time it was all up with the family centre. There was nothing for it save to build it up again somewhere else. On the evening of that day the bills were all settled; and when the part for the creditors and that for

my mother had been set aside, there remained for
me only a few louis-d'or; these at least owed nothing to anybody and permitted me to reach Paris
eight days afterward with fifty francs in my
pocket.

During the last week of my stay in Lyon I
lived with Paul Bourtheret, who had in the most.
paternal way offered me half his room.

That week was consecrated to the preparations
for departure. I had been often told that in
order to succeed in Paris it was necessary to
show one's self well clad and exhibit no trace of
wretchedness whatever. "Make yourself envied,"
Bourtheret kept repeating; "never allow yourself
to be pitied!" Filled with such counsels, I had
ordered an entire wardrobe of clothes from my
tailor, because, notwithstanding my lack of money,
I did have a tailor; not a poor devil of a janitor
who stitches new cloth on old, but an elegant
tailor, high-priced and of great repute with the
fashionables of Lyon, who had opened a credit
for me on my general good appearance, promising
to continue it to my brother and me just as long
as we should find it necessary.

Such a speculation had its dangers; for if we
had died meantime, I hardly know by whom and
how that good fellow would ever have been paid.
Nevertheless he had cause to congratulate himself for having believed in us. When we were in
condition to pay his bills, one may readily imagine that there was no question of demanding the
least rebate. Thanks to his belief in us, we

were able, when we had scarce arrived in Paris
without a penny or parcel, to present ourselves
in certain drawing-rooms where the reputation of
Alphonse Daudet began and where I myself made
many precious friendships.

It would be difficult to pay too dearly for such
genuine services. But is it not a very modern
feature in manners and customs that such a bold
clothier should play at dice for a big pile against
the future of two little unknown fellows, both of
them under age, who had no heritage whatever to
expect and were as obscure as we were at that
time?

And now that the painful sojourn in Lyon is
done with, we shall talk of it no more, if so it
please you. Sorrows and humiliations, deceptions and tears remain down there, sunk within
the fogs of the Rhône, between those high dwellings which make such narrow streets, deep as the
bottom of ditches. From that time forth our sky
continues to brighten with a vivid gleam of hope,
our paths go on enlarging before us and our
prolonged efforts begin to bear their first fruit.

CHAPTER XV.

AFTER a fatiguing journey in a third-class compartment I reached Paris at five oclock in the morning, the first of September, 1857. Having taken a room in a horrible little hotel in the neighborhood of the Exchange, I was marching along the Boulevard as early as eight o'clock in the morning in evening dress, white cravat and varnished shoes, as trig as any young bridegroom on the morning of his wedding. I breakfasted at Tortoni's. A perusal of the bill brought me back to less lofty ideas and I likewise observed that nobody except myself wore evening dress at that early hour in the morning; the very next day I profited by that double lesson of my first day in Paris. I owed a visit to Claudius Hébrard; he had an elegant bachelor's apartment in the Rue de Tournon. It just happened that he was leaving that very night for Lyon, where he intended to stay a whole month. After having taken me about Paris, he offered to install me in his apartment until his return, so that, thanks to him, during his entire absence I dwelt most comfortably established, like the young son of a well-to-do family.

I had brought two letters of recommendation with me — one from Paul Beurtheret for his provincial comrade Armand Barthet, author of *Le Moineau de Lesbie*, the other from Léopold de Gaillard for Armand de Pontmartin, whose books I had presented in a criticism to the readers of the *Gazette de Lyon*.

Barthet received me like an old friend and begged me to come to see him often, authorizing me to profit by his right of entry into the Odéon theatre, whither he never went. I really owe this confession to M. de la Rounat, who was then, as he is to-day, the director of that theatre. For an entire winter I went to the plays there given by negligently throwing down before the wicket-keepers the name of an author whose work the great Rachel had played in her time at the Théâtre Français. Most extraordinary was the fact that my extreme youth did not in any way astonish the gentlemen who kept the wickets, and that later, about two years afterwards, when I obtained the right of entry for myself, they were not astonished at all to see me become Ernest Daudet, after having been for so long a time Armand Barthet.

Having read the letter from Léopold de Gaillard, the Comte de Pontmartin passed his arm under mine and conducted me round into Bergère Street to the newspaper office of *Le Spectateur*, an Orleanist sheet which had taken the place of *L'Assemblée Nationale*, which had been suppressed a little while before. Being presented to Mallac,

the brilliant director of the *Spectateur*, I thought
I was in a dream when he informed me that at the
request of Pontmartin he engaged me among his
editors with fixed emoluments of 200 francs a
month. Two hundred francs! That meant my
livelihood assured; that meant the certainty of
being able to assist our mother; that also meant
the possibility of calling Alphonse to Paris!

And all this had already happened the second
day of my arrival! Had I not good reason to
believe in our lucky star? I took possession of
my employment a few weeks later. I was put to
general city reports on the paper. My task was
easy enough and gave me hours of leisure which
I consecrated entirely to study. And I had so
much to learn!

At the end of the month the return of Claudius
Hébrard obliged me to look for a lodging. There
happened to be a furnished house in that very
Rue de Tournon, a great barrack of students,
entitled pompously the "Grand Hôtel du Sénat."
There I hired a miserable little chamber in the
roof on the fifth story — fifteen francs a month;
that price has its own eloquence! — an iron truckle
bed, a wretched bureau, which served also as
toilet-table, a desk, two chairs, a broken stove of
pottery, a bit of carpet on the red tiles — such
was my interior. Through my single window I
could see nothing but roofs, chimneys and dormer
windows, and, raising their tiresome architecture
above my narrow horizon, the round towers of
the church of Saint-Sulpice.

On a sombre October evening, when I found myself alone for the first time in that poverty-stricken lodging, after quitting the luxurious apartment of Claudius Hébrard, the transition was so cruel and the feeling of my wretchedness so profound, that my youthful courage, weakened by loneliness, the tension on my nerves and excess of labor, was seized with fear. My father without an occupation; my mother so far away and living in a house which was not hers, and my brother very wretched in his college! these were just so many sorrowful visions rudely brought to bear upon my mind by the forbidding look of the walls of my chamber, on which the paper, meant to conceal its rawness, floated down in long torn pieces. I was frightened at the extent of my task and by the weight of my responsibility and I wept in silence.

But this impression was only passing and it was the memory of my brother, of that brave comrade whose talent I recognized and in whom I had as much faith as in myself, that dissipated these melancholy thoughts.

At that very time he was suffering in quite a different way from me. After leaving Lyon he went to stay a few days with our family, first at Nîmes, where brotherly hearts received him with tenderness, and then in the neighborhood of the Vigan, deep within the Cévennes in the Gard, at the house of some young and pretty girl cousins.

Our sixteen-year poet, who from that time forth began to sing of beauty, of nature and of love,

26

saw the termination of his short vacation arriving all too soon to please his wishes; but it was necessary to leave for Alais.

When he came to the door of the college and knocked to enter, he was so small, timid and slender, that at first he was taken for a scholar. For a moment the principal was on the point of sending him away.

"Why, he is a child!" exclaimed the professor, jumping up and down on his chair. "What do they suppose I can do with a child?"

"For one moment le Petit Chose was seized by a terrible fear; he had a vision of himself turned into the street without anything to eat. He hardly had the force of mind to stutter a few words and to hand to the principal the letter of introduction to him which he had about him."

That letter worked marvels; the reminiscence of "our uncle the Abbé" protected my brother and they kept him. Thus it was that he began to earn his bread — very bitter bread it is true, often moistened with tears of humiliation and rage.

He has related his burning sorrows in various pages which have become famous. Turn to *Le Petit Chose.* He is Le Petit Chose and Sarlande is Alais; in that part of his novel where his imagination has studded with the finest of pearls a groundwork of truth, all that was necessary for him to do was to call up in memory the distant actualities in order to fill his account with a sincere and moving emotion.

His pupils were for the most part sons of

peasants, or badly educated little scions of the
gentry who took a hatred to that small *pion*, so
distinguished-looking, delicate and proud, as
handsome as a young god; one whose look indicated cleverness, whilst all his gestures showed
beneath his rustic garments a native elegance.
His delicacy was shocking to their own coarse-
ness and their brutality made sport of his physical weakness.   Gladly would he have taken part
in their games and he only asked that they
should treat him as a comrade; but they exasperated him by their meanness.

What malicious children they were! One day,
what did they think of, but to drag across the dark
staircase an old trunk all bristling with nails?
Alphonse could not see it and he had a bad
tumble which came very near killing him. Another time, whilst out walking, it was necessary
to engage in fisticuffs with one of them — a
powerful fellow who had rebelled against his
authority.   The worst of it was, that after these
adventures the principal always placed him in the
wrong; he was anxious to keep his pupils and, as
for a *pion*, that sort could easily be replaced!

My brother only escaped from these daily mis-
haps to return to a humble provincial interior,
unhealthy, full of envy, perverted and grotesquely
skeptical, peopled by billiard players, smokers of
pipes, frequenters of tap-houses, forming a completely dense and foolish Bohemia, where at every
moment some trick was played upon his simple-
mindedness.

If this torture had continued, to what desperate resolutions might he not have been moved! The news of my departure from Lyon increased its severity; my brother understood that he had not much longer to suffer and he turned his look toward Paris; for thence it was that he h ped to see the arrival of deliverance and happiness. One day in answer to a letter even more heartrending than the others I wrote to him: "Come!" And, all bruised and wounded, the little bird spread its wings to find a refuge near to me.

CHAPTER XVI.[1]

TWICE over has Alphonse Daudet told the story of his arrival in Paris; for the first time in *Le Petit Chose* and for a second in *Le Nouveau Temps*, a newspaper in St. Petersburg which brought his works to the knowledge of Russia. In the latter he has published, beside other things, some episodes from his life as a man of letters, written in the form of an autobiography. Except in a very slight number of details, the two stories hardly differ one from the other. That one which brings up again the entire reality in pages full of emotion is hardly less attractive than the other, which merely used that reality as a source of inspiration by borrowing from it various features suitable for a romance.

[1] Having come to this point in my account I ought to call to memory the fact that whatever I have tried to say concerning my brother's life relates to that part of it which is common to both of us. As to that which is personal to him, I am bound to be very brief, in order not to forestall the account which he ought to make for himself, either in his memoirs or else in the story of his works. I shall therefore say no more than what I consider the necessary completion of that which I undertook to revive from the past; this ought to show the writer in full possession of his manhood, after the picture of him as the timid child, whose features so delicate and proud have been sketched by my brotherly pencil.

In both cases the scene is the same: A child seventeen years old, unhappy and delicate, arriving in Paris with an empty stomach and a light purse, observant, eager for the unknown, hungering for new sensations and filled with happy presentiments of the future, but made timid by the extreme of his misery to the point of doubting himself and fearing to believe in his own star — a boy still too young and poor in experience to measure the intellectual treasure which he carries in his own mind.

As a framework to this picture there are the first frosts of a very harsh winter — it was the first of November, 1857 — two nights spent on the hard bench of a third-class coach, the pestiferous atmosphere of the coach, saturated with the smell of brandy and tobacco, and then the entrance into Paris at dawn, the comforting brotherly embrace, the drive through the streets of the city just awakening, the banging of the cab on the cobblestones, and then the surprise caused by the appearance of the little bedroom succeeding upon such profound impressions of the arrival — that little chamber where the two were to live thenceforward on privations, hard work and hope.

I shall not attempt to tell the story over again, although the recollection of these things has remained engraved upon my memory forever. I only want to recall a single characteristic, the wretched condition in which my brother reached me.

I can see him still, worn out with weariness and

actual need, nearly dead with cold, wrapped in an old renovated overcoat out of fashion and, lest an entirely original appearance should be wanting to his equipment, shod over his blue cotton stockings with india-rubber socks — those socks of india-rubber which have won no little notoriety in the world since they inspired one of the chapters of *Le Petit Chose.*

Luckily that Lyon tailor was on hand. Thanks to him, Alphonse Daudet was soon thoroughly changed and made to look as a young poet should who does not believe that rags and shoes worn down at heel are necessary equipments for the march toward the conquest of renown.

Even at that period he was handsome, with a beauty altogether impossible to believe: "A marvellously charming head" Théodore de Banville wrote some years later in his *Camées Parisiens.* "His complexion pale, yet with warmth and the color of amber, his eyebrows straight and silky, his eye brilliant yet deep, at once moist and burning — an eye lost in revery and one that does not see, yet is most delightful to see — his mouth sensuous, dreamy and rich with blood, his beard soft and childlike, his hair abundant and brown and his ear fine and delicate — all these come together in a proudly masculine combination, despite the feminine graces."

And now let the reader imagine this boy of seventeen years turned loose in Paris, perfectly free to follow his own bent and a mark for all the dangers which rise up before young people in

a great city — perils intensified for him I speak
of by his ignorance of customs as they made
themselves known to him, where everything was
the subject for surprise, anxiety and embarrassment!

Every morning I left for my newspaper; we
hardly saw each other again till evening and
although about that time some of our new friends
who were acquainted with the particulars of our
common existence had surnamed me "the mother,"
my watchfulness was powerless to protect him as
much as I would have wished.

He has spoken, in the pages of his memoirs
which have already been published, of the first
weeks of his sojourn in Paris with a penetrating
melancholy. "With the exception of my brother
I knew nobody. Short-sighted and clumsy and
timid as a man of the woods, as soon as I left my
bedchamber I walked round the Odéon under the
arcade, delighted and at the same time frightened
at rubbing elbows with men of letters." This
melancholy loneliness did not last; very soon he
had his comrades in the Quartier Latin; later
some of them became his friends, such as Gambetta who was reading law and dwelt in the same
apartment house with us, Amédée Rolland, Jean
du Bois, Bataille, Louis Bouilhet, Castagnary,
Pierre Véron, Emmanuel des Essarts and many
others beside, among whom were Thérion — the
philosopher Thérion — whom one might meet any
minute with some old book under his arm, reading everything, knowing everything, discussing

everything, gesticulating about everything — a scientist of rare merit, but of troubled mind and a lofty soul — that unforgettable type, who was to become, later, Élysée Méraut in the *Rois en Exil.*

My brother was thrown with a number of these men living in the artistic and literary Bohemia of that time, the third generation of that most brilliant set after 1830 — namely with Théophile Gautier, Gérard de Nerval, Arsène Houssaye and the two Johannots — a Bohemia which had already been precipitated from its pedestal about 1850, when Henry Murger described its decadence, and at the time we speak of was absolutely overthrown, having lost all its poetry and its attractions at the period when we reached Paris.

Since that time Bohemia has had two historians. M. Jules Vallès has found therein the subject of a striking book, *Les Réfractaires.* My brother knew there the unsuccessful "down-at-heels" described in "Jack." Nobody has described and no one hereafter will describe as well as he did what impotence, jealousy, narrowness of view and unconscious perversity existed among those poor wretches whom laziness conquered without a battle. Surely it is a species of miracle, as I have already said, that he could have passed through the midst of them without losing a bit of his talent and without leaving behind the flower of his youth, the freshness of his soul and the uprightness of his heart, especially as one remembers that he was only twenty years old.

He has often shared their distress, but never their disorderly instinct. He was always sufficiently in control of himself to study the reasons for their lot, prevent himself from succumbing to the same and visiting that deep cavern where they abode without ever letting go the saving clew which was to bring him back to the light, but, contrary to what might have been feared, bringing back from the trip new powers or those which up to that moment had never been revealed.

From the very winter which followed our installation at Paris, we had connections in other circles also. Claudius Hébrard had taken us to see one of the curators of the Library of the Arsenal, Eugène Loudon, a writer for the Catholic party, who united at his house a few friends once a week in a little circle. All the arts and every opinion were represented in that salon, filled as early as nine o'clock in the evening with the smoke of cigars, which rose slowly along the shelves crammed with books, and where the time was passed in noisy conversations entirely connected with intellectual things.

This modest salon even put on the airs of a conventicle; for women were absent from it and the men who came there flattered themselves that they were bound together by a bond which rested on their sympathy in common and on the desire, dear to them all, of rising higher in the world.

There we met Amédée Pommier, a poet of the fine old style, who was already an old man, a remnant from the literary battles of 1830; Vital

Dubray, a talented sculptor, who expiated under the Republic those favors with which the Empire had overwhelmed him; Jules Duvaux, the military painter; Augustin Largent, a sensitive soul and somewhat simple, who afterwards became an Oratorian monk; the two Sirouys, one of whom painted, some years ago, the frescos for the palace of the Legion of Honor; Develay, "dramatic author," who made a boast of the fact that he had never found a director of a theatre who was bold enough to put his work on the stage, although he had sent in to the theatres of Paris more than thirty dramas in verse, fragments from which he spouted forth with a tumultuous emphasis; Henri de Bornier, timid and obscure, walking about with *La Fille de Roland,* his masterpiece, in his brain; and I forget how many more.

Among these men, who were all our seniors, we were mere children, especially my brother, whose beardless face made him seem still younger than he was. At that time he was getting his first volume ready: *Les Amoureuses.*

It was at the Arsenal that we were able to estimate the effect which the opening of the career of such a poet and author would produce. There, too, we got to know our neighbor the publisher, Jules Tardieu, a poet himself, who wanted to be the bringer-out of the volume; there, too, one evening we saw Édouard Thierry, who, a few months later, introduced my brother's work to the readers of the *Moniteur Officiel.*

Eugène Loudon's drawing-room opened others

to us. At the houses of Mme. Ancelot and
of Mme. Mélanie Waldor and Mme. Olympe
Chodsko and in the drawing-room of Mme.
Perrière-Pilté, who exercised the function of grand
fashionable protectoress of letters, my brother
recited *Les Prunes*, *Les Cerises*, *Trois Jours de
Vendange* and prologues for comedies, generously
pouring out the contents of a portfolio, ever filled
again, before lovely ladies, who were in ecstasy
over his elegant manners, brilliant youth, warm
Southern voice and seductive beauty. The publication of *Les Amoureuses* did not give the lie to
that impression. This charming book, published
by Jules Tardieu under a fine white cover decorated in red, earned for Alphonse Daudet at once
the regard of men of letters and of sensitive
minds.

Within twenty-four hours he was ranked among
those beginners of whom the world says: "He's
somebody." Edouard Thierry devoted a long and
eloquent column of eulogy to him in his literary
feuilleton. "When Alfred de Musset died,"
said he, "two pens were left by him at the service
of the man who could take them up: the pen for
prose and the pen for poetry. Octave Feuillet
inherited one of them and Alphonse Daudet has
just claimed heirship to the other."

The good fellow did not suspect that he would
have to complete that flattering appreciation later
—the spirit, if not the text of which I reproduce
— and that Alphonse Daudet would become one
of the first prose writers of his time.

Nevertheless this brilliant entrance into letters did not bring fortune for us with it. It brightened the future with a ray of hope, without softening the anxieties of the present moment. We made a fine appearance in the social world; at Augustine Brohan's house, where my brother had been asked one evening, he had been taken, even by the mistress of the house herself, for a Wallach prince. But we were still living like necessity students, having hardly anything to support us save that which I made in the newspaper office. We only left our garret in the Hôtel du Sénat to climb up into another one, and there, thanks to the trustfulness of a furniture dealer, furnish our interior beneath the eaves of an enormous structure on the Rue Bonaparte, which was, however, so leant up against Saint-Germain des Prés that we were able to indulge in an illusion and believe that we were living in the belfry. We had good reason to fear being kept for a long time to come in a life full of privations; but we were so young that in sober truth the perspective was not so very discouraging after all.

But a sudden change was about to take place in our life and it is my duty now to tell in what new conditions it was to find me.

CHAPTER XVII.

IT may be remembered that on the 14th of January 1858 I had been attached for more than two months to the staff of the *Spectateur* when the attempt to assassinate the emperor near the opera house took place. The evening of that day our political director Mallac sent to the press for appearance in next day's number an article considering this very serious event; in the course of it he developed the following thesis: Only under despotic governments is it possible for the world to see such crimes as that which has just been committed by Orsini. Despotism calls out and provokes revolution. Legitimate sovereigns, protected by their hereditary right and the love of their subjects and placed at the apex of a rigorously constitutional power, have nothing to fear from assassins.

The two-fold objection to this reasoning is patent to every one: It is contrary to the truth of history and in the circumstances that existed it exposed the paper at least to a warning if not an immediate suppression.

Mallac's comrades on the staff drew his attentions to this, but he would not listen to objections.

The business director who represented the property of the paper succeeded no better. After having engaged in an extremely violent discussion with him, Mallac passed a good part of the night at the printing office in order to be quite sure that his article would be published.

Next morning when I reached the office at the usual hour I found the staff there in full numbers — members of the committee and shareholders — the entire crowd wearing a thunderstruck appearance. An Imperial decree, citing with approbation a report by Minister of the Interior Billault, ordered the suppression of the *Spectateur* and at the same time that of *La Revue de Paris*, which at that time was managed by Laurent Pichat, Louis Ulbach and Maxime du Camp.

That was a hard blow for the fusionist politics which the *Spectateur* represented, but it was a real disaster for my brother and me. I had just succeeded in getting permission that he should be tried for the chronicle of local news and I am not sure but that his first article had already been written.

Luckily the disaster was overcome very soon up to a certain point; *L'Union* fell heir to the subscribers and the editorial staff of the suppressed paper. So it came about that I was turned over to the legitimist paper, with my salary, it is true, very notably decreased. "We are poor," they told me, "but we have enough to procure daily bread for us all."

I stayed there for some months and then I was

asked to go to Blois to replace for a time the editor-in-chief of the *France Centrale.* When I came back my place was taken and they never returned it to me. I felt a very lively indignation at that; I was twenty-two years old and had a great deal of ambition and the strongest will to help reconstruct the ruined hearth. But it was not by dying of hunger in the service of a party which did not know how to keep even young men with it; nor was it by writing the memoirs of an old nobleman, chamberlain to Charles X, whose secretary I had become, that I could make my designs and plans real. The Empire was in full prosperity and inspired no repugnance whatever in me. Not having known the horrors of the *coup d'état,* I was not able to share the rancors felt by the conquered. An entire generation, which has cruelly expiated its error and its inexperience since then, believed at that time the very thing that I myself was thinking.

So it came about that I knocked at the door of Vicomte de la Guéronnière who at that time directed the matters of the press at the Ministry of the Interior. I was received most charmingly by that amiable man, who would have left a deep trace in the history of his country if his character had been equal to his talent. I told him my situation and a few days afterwards he sent me to Privas to take the editorship of the *Écho de l'Ardèche,* promising to recall me very soon.

Privas after Paris! A lowly provincial newspaper after one of the great organs of the French

press—what a fall! And then, what a sorrow at
leaving my brother! Still, it was necessary to be
resigned and I left, buoyed up by the hope of
returning and also consoled because this banishment from Paris was bringing me nearer to my
mother who was still at Nimes, and to another
person very dear to my heart who a little while
after was to bear my name.

It was while at Privas that I heard of the beginnings made by Alphonse Daudet in *Le Figaro.* I
had known Villemessant during my short stay in
Blois whither he often came, and having been asked
to stay a couple of days at Chambon, his fine property, I had talked to him of my brother, whom he
very soon learned to know and whose qualities he
quickly estimated at their worth. It was a great
happiness to all. The *Figaro* was a sort of conse-
cration for an author, a brevet accorded to talent
and the doors of the editors opened wide.

My brother began his fame there, first with
chronicles in verse and prose-studies and dialogue
scenes: *Le Roman du Chaperon Rouge, Les Rossignols du Cimetière, L'Amour Trompette*—then
longer stories there and in other places, continued
for several years, which in their briefness were
impressed with so sweet a charm that they created
for him who wrote them a position quite apart in
contemporary literature, even before he dreamt of
writing books of long-continued effort.

These fine literary bits which are worthy of
standing in some classical collection may be read
to-day in his *Lettres de mon Moulin* and in his

27

Contes du Lundi, as well as in *Robert Helmont,*[1] in *Femmes d'Artistes* and in his *Lettres à un Absent.* They are compounded at one and the same time of imagination and historical fact and bear in the highest degree the mark that reveals his state of mind at the time when they were written.

In one he permits his imagination to flutter hither and thither across fields and gambol according to its caprice beneath the sunshine and through the warm air of the South, all balmy with the fragrance of the pines to which he listens as they sound above the wild rocks of Provence.

In another he recalls the memories of his voyages, in the course of which he has looked upon men and things with that mysterious glance of his and that certainty in his mind, clever to question and observe them; and then in a third he allows his soul, torn with patriotic anguish or bursting with a holy indignation, to explode at the spectacle of the misfortunes of his country. Laughter and weeping — upon that harmonious board the gamut is complete and all the notes are present.

There too are some of the works in their germs which he wrote later: *L'Arlésienne, Le Nabab, Jack;* they will be found there in a thousand scattered parts in their first and summary form, just as they were seen by him at first before the labor undertaken by his mind had drawn their lines exact and arranged their development.

The success of these studies, which hardly had

[1] *Robert Helmont* is now published alone without the other stories.

anything analogous to them in French literature before their day, was very lively. Echoes of it reached me in my distant exile, where my brother corroborated them later on when he came to pass a few weeks with me and where he brought me a great piece of news, as if to prove to me that, after all, life was beginning to smile upon us. Having had the chance of meeting Comte de Morny, that notable person, the most powerful of the powerful at that period, charmed by his talent, had promised him an office in the Bureau of the President of the Corps Législatif, one of those places which the great lords of a bygone day had created for the benefit of poor men of letters and which permitted such men to work freely, unhampered by the vexations of material support. As soon as he returned to Paris my brother was to take possession of it.

"But I am a Legitimist" he had proudly objected when he heard the kindly offer of his new protector; and what should the other do but answer laughingly:

"The Empress is more Legitimist than you!"

That is all I shall say of the relations between Alphonse Daudet and M. de Morny, since I do not care to take the edge off that part of my brother's memoirs which he will devote to it. The certainty of being protected by him aroused our hopes and caused us to look into the future through very rosy spectacles. My brother's stay at Privas was charged with this feeling of confidence; we passed some delightful vacations there and together made long excursions into the mountains; then he left me to go to Nimes, from which town he departed for Provence to stay in the hospitable house at Fontvieille, whence the first of the letters "de mon moulin" might well be dated.

During this trip it was that he learned to know Frédéric Mistral, Théodore Aubanel, Roumanille and all the Félibres, and connected himself with them by a friendship which time has never shaken. Returning to Paris he proceeded to take his place in the office of the President of the Corps Législatif.

From that moment on my looks were constantly fixed upon the Palais-Bourbon; I was dying of ennui at Privas and was resolved that I should not stay there much longer; moreover my brother had promised me to help shorten my stay. Just at that moment an occasion offered itself to him to keep his promise and he seized upon it.

At that time the Imperial Government was preparing the grand reforms which were to be applied at the beginning of 1861; a certain amount of liberty was about to be allowed the Chamber. M. de Morny, as President of the Corps Législatif, occupied himself with an increase of the number of secretaries whose duty it was to edit the reports of the debates. He had two positions in his gift; for one of them he had already chosen Ludovic Halévy, who was giving a prelude in modest essays to his brilliant career as a dramatic author; my brother proposed me for the other and made me

accept it at the very moment when, without waiting for him to call me, I had just arrived again in
Paris, urged on by a presentiment of my good
fortune.

"The President wants to know you," said he to
me one evening; "he will receive you to-morrow
morning at seven o'clock."

You may imagine that I was on time. A cab
deposited me before the wide terrace in front of
the President's palace exactly at seven o'clock.
Having a conviction that the great personages in
this world are not to be approached save in
evening dress and white necktie, I had dressed
myself as I did on the day of my first trip about
Paris. It was November and not very light; my
dress did not produce any effect whatever upon
the presidential vestibule, or rather it produced
a very deplorable one, for it was not until after
I had mentioned my name that the messengers
deigned to be polite. One of them conducted me
into the "Chinese drawing-room" and asked me
to wait.

It was a marvel, that drawing-room, with all its
collections — carved ivories and jades, pot-bellied
bronzes, junks and pagodas in miniature, wonderful monsters, squatted dogs and screens covered
with gold and embroideries! But the trouble was
that they forgot me there. One o'clock arrived
and I had not obtained my reception. My stomach
cried cupboard; I walked from the window to the
chimney and from the chimney to the window,
overwhelmed by impatience, worn out and my

underclothes sticking to me through the exercise
I had had in trying all the furniture for a seat.

Finally, worn out and at the end of my resources,
there came a time when I stationed myself before
a mirror in order to "repair the disorder of my
dress." As I was engaged in this somewhat delicate operation with all the coolness of a man who
knows that nobody is remembering his existence,
suddenly a door opened. Much abashed I threw
my overcoat across my unbuttoned waistcoat —
but I was already alone once more, after having
seen a stream of silken gown, the profile of a
blonde lady and the smoke of a cigarette pass
across my vision. Afterwards I learned that it
was Mme. de Morny. She notified her husband.

He came in hastily in his close-fitting blue velvet
coat, with his black skull-cap upon his bald head.

"Who are you — what are you doing there?"

I gave him my name.

"Oh, my poor boy, I entirely forgot you. . . .
Well, your brother has talked to me about you;
you wish to be secretary-editor and it seems that
political affairs are familiar to you. You are nom-
inated; go and see M. Valette the secretary-
general; he will present you to M. Denis de
Lagarde, your chief. . . ."

My audience did not last three minutes, but I
never forgot my long wait, for it had brought me
good fortune. I only had to go downstairs to the
entre-sol to find my brother and announce the
success of his efforts. He lived there side by
side with Ernest l'Épine, who at that time man-

aged M. de Morny's office, and in the midst of these serious occupations, pleasantly broken by artistic junketings, prepared the future successes for his supremely clever *Quatrelles*. At that very time, along with Alphonse Daudet, he was considering those plans of collaboration which were realized successively in *La Dernière Idole*, *L'Œillet Blanc* and *Le Frère Aîné*.

Notwithstanding the success which these plays obtained, this kind of collaboration could never persuade Alphonse Daudet of the efficaciousness of a combined labor of two persons, when it was a question of literary work. He has remained convinced that notwithstanding the conscientiousness of two writers harnessed to the same book or the same play, when the time comes to reap the moral harvest of their joint work, there is always one who is disillusioned, and therefore since that time he has renounced every attempt with the same thought. It is true he has called upon the kind services of his literary comrades when he has wished to make a play out of *Fromont Jeune et Risler Aîné* in the first place, and from *Le Nabab* afterwards; but in these cases it was only a question of arranging scenes which were already in existence, somewhat after the fashion of " enlargement," a placing of things in the proper focus where the part assigned to the collaborator was too small for a possibility that any doubt could arise concerning the real paternity of the success of the work.

My true existence as a Parisian, a man of letters

and journalist, dates from my entrance into the Corps Législatif. The sessions were short, for they lasted only three or four months, and they allowed me leisure which was entirely devoted to my labors with the pen.

Some day I intend to relate what I can recall from that journey of twenty years through the world of politics and the press. I only want to allude to it here in order to recall one episode in my life which my brother knew nothing about and which I would not have spoken of, had not people associated it with him later in connection with his novel *Le Nabab.*

In 1863 I had been for two years in the Corps Législatif. A correspondent for two big provincial newspapers, I also belonged to the editorial staff of *La France*, which was managed at that time by the Vicomte de la Guéronnière, a paper in which I had just started the "parliamentary echoes." My name had already gained a certain notoriety; a favorable wind filled my sails; the paternal hearth had been built anew and my own was rising; it was one of the happiest moments of my life.

Whilst the general elections which took place that year were being held, I happened to be at Nîmes during the vacation. One of my friends took me to see the Nabob, that is to say, François Bravay. He had just come from Egypt and was presenting himself to the electors in one of the electoral districts of the Gard. In order to make a success of his running he had promised the people of that part of France an irrigation canal which was to render their soil fertile, a soil which is rendered sterile through lack of water.

At a later period this promise was judged by the Corps Législatif to be an electoral trick and the memory of it always cast an unfavorable shadow upon François Bravay, even after he had been elected for the third time in succession and forced the gates of the Palais Bourbon, though his other two elections had been declared invalid. Nevertheless that promise had been sincere. He had given it due effect by spending a million francs in good ringing money to meet the expenses of the first work on the canal. He knew my relations with the Paris journals and asked me to support his candidacy.

Then, when he was elected and borne onward to the chamber by the enthusiasm of the people whom his generosity and reputation as a millionaire had excited, aided as he was by a fervent speech as rude as his own personality, but very well suited to be understood by "the rural," he suggested that I should become his political secretary. I accepted the position and have never had reason to regret it.

I have never known a more upright heart than his. One of my regrets has been that I did not possess the necessary influence to enforce my own advice and make him understand how worthless some of the people were who surrounded him. His constant trips to Egypt and the confusion of his life, forever worried by beggars on the one side

and the need of money created by their demands
on the other, caused my activity in his case to
be too often a mere sinecure. But as long as he
remained a deputy he never drew my attention to
the fact and he always remembered the ardor with
which I had embraced his interests. Among all
my friends he is one of those to whom I am most
passionately devoted and I have never ceased to
believe that he was worthy of inspiring that affection. His misfortune had been, while springing
from a very low origin, to have enriched himself
too quickly by those means which are familiar to
men who have gone to the Orient to make their
fortune, and to have returned to France without
any knowledge either of Paris or of the new
surroundings in which he was called upon to live,
where, for that very reason indeed, he was certain
to ruin himself just as quickly as he had
obtained wealth in the East. The portrait which
my brother has traced of this man in an unforgettable book leaves nothing for me to add, unless it
be that when he speaks of the exquisite kindliness
of that perfectly simple soul, notwithstanding all
appearances to the contrary, the author of *Le
Nabab* exaggerated nothing. In the eyes of those
who have known and loved François Bravay the
novel of which he is the hero is the best work
in the world to raise a monument to his memory
and to avenge him for clumsy calumnies. To convince oneself of this it is only necessary to read
the last paragraph: "His lips moved gently and
his dilated eyes, turning toward de Géry, were filled

before death came with a mournful expression. They looked imploring and yet disgusted, as if he wished to cite him as a witness to one of the greatest and cruellest injustices that Paris has ever committed."

How was it possible, therefore, that a calculated malice should have attempted to make people believe that all those eloquent pages constituted an insult to his memory, so that at one moment the relatives of François Bravay actually shared the unjust belief? I have not yet been able to understand it.

But what is much more serious is the fact that they wished to prove that my brother committed an act of black ingratitude. At the time when he had to defend himself against this charge he begged me not to interfere; that literary quarrel being entirely personal and foreign to the intrinsic merit of his work, it was too wounding to his literary delicacy that he should have wished to complicate it by intervention from my side.

But to-day I have recovered freedom to say that Alphonse Daudet was engaged to François Bravay by no bond of recollection which stood in the way of his right as a novelist. He had hardly seen him more than two or three times, and although that sudden and passing sight of him had been enough to give him an impression of the man and his surroundings, completed as the picture was by what he already knew of him and what he learned afterward, that could not be compared in any way to one of those services which condemns to silence

the man who has received them.   So my brother
could write *Le Nabab*, for even I myself, if I had
had the talent to make it what it is, I would have
written and signed it without thinking that I was
false to any duty.

CHAPTER XVIII.

DURING the year 1861 my brother's health, which
had been shaken by the violent attacks upon the
nerves that life in Paris brings, was pretty seriously
affected. Dr. Marchal de Calvi, a great friend of
letters and men of letters, had him under his charge
and surrounded him with anxious care and attentions just as a gardener would cherish some rare
flower. When winter approached he declared to
him up and down that he must leave the city and
go in search of health to the country of the sunlight, because that was the only means to avoid
compromising the future irrevocably. His verdict
was formal and my brother obeyed, leaving for
Algiers, where he passed several months.

He has often told me of the details of that trip
which left a profound impression upon his spirit
and his works; his stay in Algiers and his excursions into the country parts and visits to Arab
chiefs, his long rides through the mountains upon
a mule which carried strapped to its neck a flask
full of a certain oil made forsooth of the liver of
the cod, powerful doses of which he was called
upon to swallow.

But of all the treatment which had been ordered
for him he observed scarcely a single one except

that. As to the one which ordered him to rest
absolutely, he observed that by over-doing everything and spending his strength by running to the
right and left, seeking sensations, joyous at new
discoveries, observing and writing down every evening his impressions of the day on those little note-
books he has been collecting for twenty years, in
which his entire past and future work will be found
in embryo.

"In these note-books," said he in the preface to
Fromont Jeune et Risler Aîné," there is sometimes
nothing but a skimped line for remarks and for
thoughts — something to recall to me a gesture or
intonation which may be developed and augmented
later to complete the harmony of some important
work. At Paris as well as on journeys and in the
country these memorandum books have become
blackened with lines without a thought, even without thinking of the future work which was piling
up in them; proper names sometimes are met with
there which I have not been able to change because
I find in proper names a kind of physiognomy, an
impress very like the people who bear them."

When my brother returned from Algiers in the
spring his health gave us no more disquiet, although it demanded a good deal of care, but his
note-books were teeming with a multitude of precious memoranda. A charming study of Milianah
which has found a place in *Lettres de Mon Moulin,*
a story called *Kadour et Katel* in the first edition
of *Robert Helmont,* as well as *Un Décoré du Quinze
Août,* and Namoun the little Arab in *Le Sacrifice,*

and finally the immortal *Tartarin de Tarascon* —
all these Alphonse Daudet brought back from
Algiers, a rich booty, as one can see, in which no
account is taken of the visions of the sun, landscapes and blue skies, whose fruitful light has
remained luminous in his memory.

During his absence the Odéon theatre had
played his *Dernière Idole*, that play in one act
which he wrote conjointly with Ernest l'Épine.
Just as my brother left for Algiers the rehearsals
of his play were about to begin; his collaborator
was to have directed them, but he fell ill at the
same time and I had the task of following them up.
Tisserant, who played the principal character, had
undertaken to place it on the stage; Mdlle. Rous-
seil made her début in the character of handsome
Madame Ambroy, and although a one-act piece
was in question, the theatre expected a success.

Our common hopes were indeed by no means
dashed and those who were present at the first
night would be able to recall the fact. If I call
for their testimony it is only to prove that I exaggerate nothing. The old authors tossed their
heads, saying: "It is n't the drama!" But they
applauded all the same; I can still see Paul de
Saint-Victor seated in his box and applauding with
his hands.

The audience was one of the most brilliant. It
was understood that M. de Morny was interested
in the two authors, and there he was, somewhat
surprised at the warm applause from the public,
without understanding very well those scenes re-

plete with emotion, yet such as to draw tears from the most skeptical; but his wife, carried away by delight, broke her fan while applauding. The very next day I sent the news of the success to my brother; it reached him deep in the interior of I know not what far-distant country. Since then he has told me that in the midst of the incidents of his splendid journey the news left him entirely cold, so small, far-distant and forgotten did Paris seem to him at that moment.

The following year Marchal de Calvi insisted again that he must leave at the approach of the frost and this time he went to Corsica. There very different emotions awaited him. Traces can be found in his short stories — read *Marie Anto, Le Phare des Sanguinaires, L'Agonie de la Sémillante* — and last, not least, *Le Nabab*, in which his remembrances of Ajaccio have clearly had their influence on the financial combinations of the rascal Paganetti and the electoral scenes recounted by Paul de Géry.

After two winters passed in this fashion far from Paris my brother was able to take up again his old way of living, for the warm air of the South was no longer indispensable to him. It was merely prudence which suggested the idea of leaving again at the end of 1863. But he stopped short in Provence; his stay there was full of hard work; it is enough to read his books to convince one of that.

From that epoch on belongs more especially the period when the South and Southerners entered into his work, for that was the time when he studied them in their landscapes, their social life and their customs, filling out his daily observations with the recollections drawn from the past, adapting a characteristic found living in some person whom he met there or elsewhere, making himself the historian of the fashions and habits of a race just as others have made themselves the historians of the events of a country.

In pursuance of his method of describing nothing but what he had seen, never relating anything but what had happened to him and of taking everything from reality — stories, descriptions and characters — every new discovery which he made in the course of human adventures, every inner event which played itself off under his own eyes are just so many sources which sooner or later will be sure to enrich his intellectual domain. I am much inclined to believe that it was particularly during the period of his sojourn in Provence that he took the measure of the fruitful power of this procedure and when he definitely laid down for himself the rule which he has rigorously observed ever since.

What literary wealth does he not owe to that severe discipline of his mind! It has given actuality and modernity to his books, which is as much as saying it has given one of the conditions for success in a social fabric carried away by its thirst for enjoyment, burnt as if with fever, which has no longer any time to reflect and turn the mind upon the days which are already past — a society that is all the while tormented by the desire of seeing

itself live again in works of fiction which shall
translate its passions, virtues and vices, which shall
teach people to understand themselves without
ever imposing any obligation of studying themselves or what relates to them.

It is quite true that a special organization is
needed to put this system into action with good
results, a flame of personal energy, a gift from
nature which the most laborious efforts can never
add to one who did not find it in his cradle.
Émile Zola, making an estimate of Alphonse
Daudet's talent, wrote some time ago: "Kindly
nature has placed him in that delightful border-
land where poetry ends and reality commences."
There we have the principal cause of the literary
good fortune of my brother concisely defined.

But in order to understand the long strides
which he has made toward renown since that time,
it is necessary to take some account of that ceaseless labor of his mind of which I just spoke and of
his ambition which ever turned its face toward
betterment. Notwithstanding these natural gifts
he might have lingered on the way, if he had not
constantly stimulated and developed them, refin-
ing them through his tenacious will, never weary,
always ready to exert his strength in order to
make the work of his hand more perfect.

Events that happened at the close of the Empire, the anguish felt at the siege of Paris, the
tragedies under the Commune and all those start-
ling episodes which seem to be part and parcel of
our individual history because they have weighed

so greatly on the destiny of each of us, were sure
to inspire and in fact did inspire more than one
author. Novelists and poets have made use of
those incidents, referring to them in their verses
or including them in the framework of the plots
in their stories. How does it happen that nowhere are they more living than in the pages
which Alphonse Daudet has devoted to them?
Just exactly because he related them as a realist
and as a poet besides. The flame of his talent has
gilded reality and not only clothed it with all the
graces of an original and penetrating style, but
lent it the accent of an infinite tenderness which
starts the tears. And in fact the most ordinary
trait, when it is touched by this master workman,
becomes a jewel rare.

Would you like an example of the effect which
he could produce by the simplest means? Open
the *Contes du Lundi* and re-read *La Dernière
Classe.* The scene is a poor Alsatian village on
the day when, submitting to the conqueror, the
French province is about to become a German
one. The teacher is giving his lesson for the last
time in French — he has asked in the parents of
his pupils in order to make his farewell to them
and at the same time on that day of mourning
call them to witness to his ardent love for the
conquered fatherland, as well as sow in their souls
before he leaves them that seed of patriotism
whose flowers they may leave as heritages to their
children. A little schoolboy who had come to
school that day just the same as every day relates

the scene, and that is all — hardly more than a
trifling event which the newspaper of the adjacent
town perhaps might have placed in its columns of
local news!

Now observe what that unimportant fact becomes under the pen of Alphonse Daudet. Without adding a single thing except the emotion that
fills his soul and the magic of his style, without
uttering a single noisy word or one of those somewhat coarse sayings which are like an eternal
menace of reprisals hereafter in the speeches of
the conquered to the victor, statements which he
would have been very excusable to have used in
the circumstances, he has written eight pages without overstepping the tone of a cool narrative —
eight pages which form the most eloquent protest
which has ever been raised against a barbarous
law that treats a people like so much cattle.

If one desires to look through his works for
other proofs of that so personal a gift of causing
reality to live again in his stories, without allowing
a bit of its power to be lost, but on the contrary
through the art of arranging words giving it the
saliency of life, they can be found by hundreds.

I will take the death of the Duc de Morny.
My brother was present; hour after hour he followed that intimate drama which the important
place held by the dying man was about to transform into a drama of history. He saw sickness
enter the palace and death clinging to the walls
covered with black hangings. He has caught
from the very life the fright of the politicians and

phrase-mongers, in whose eyes the event took on
the proportions of a catastrophe. He listened to
the comments of the lackeys, torn between the
pride of having served so powerful a master, regret
at losing him and haste to find some destiny or
lot elsewhere. He assisted in destroying the intimate papers and a voluminous correspondence,
witnesses to the baseness of human beings, which
the dead man did not wish to leave behind him.
He entered the room of death at the very moment
when the embalmer left it. Every one of those
touches which he collected as they occurred went
into the note-books to enlarge the materials of the
novelist.

Now take the pages of *Le Nabab* in which he
has remolded that striking picture for which there
is a first sketch in *Robert Helmont* (first edition).
Though you had opened the book supposing it a
work of pure imagination, though you were entirely ignorant of modern history to the point of
ignoring the fact that it contains the truth, yet you
would not be able to read that chapter, between
the white of whose lines sarcasm peeps out, sarcasm
aroused in the mind of the story-teller by such examples of the vanity and impotence of men, without divining that the death which he relates was
also the symptom which foreruns a terrible fall,
that it was not merely some imperial duke who
was disappearing from the scene, but the whole of
an enormous edifice which was beginning to crum-
ble to its fall. The exactness with which things
seen are reproduced when not a single political

allusion can be met with, the life which the painter has given them, the art with which he has introduced into his account all those looks of anguish whose trace he has caught upon all those frightened faces, are quite sufficient to reveal that which he did not say. Produced by such simple means, the effect remains most striking. In works of art that is the true mark of talent, by which I mean the talent which assures their lasting quality.

CHAPTER XIX.

THE death of the Duc de Morny decided my brother to carry out a project he had debated for a long time, the project of recovering his liberty. He was indeed actually too much of a man of letters to persist in living otherwise than by his pen when the first difficulty had once been mastered. As soon as it appeared that the independence of his ideas might be compromised thereby he left the Corps Législatif.

Is it necessary to add that during the stay which he made in that office he never either wrote a line or performed an act which could be considered in the light of a sacrifice of that same independence to the demands of his situation? Throughout his entire life he has had the good fortune of living detached from every sort of political bond. "I am a Legitimist" he had said to M. de Morny when he entered his office for the first time. That little bit of a Southerner's boasting was less a truth, even at that time, than it was a manifestation of native pride and perchance the homage paid by him to opinions which had been professed in his father's house. But my brother would not say such a thing as that to-day.

And this, not because he has had time or indeed the will since then to form for himself a very clear feeling of the kind of government which is best fitted to France; it was disdain of politics. He expressed that disdain one day in indignant terms in the epilogue to *Robert Helmont* (first edition).

"O politics, how I hate you! I hate you because you are coarse, unjust, noisy and babbling; because you are the enemy of art and of labor; because you serve as a label for every kind of folly, for all sorts of ambitions and for lazinesses of every variety. Blind and passionate, you separate honest hearts which were made to be united. And on the contrary you knit together individuals who are in every respect unlike each other. You are the great solvent of consciences, you teach the custom of lying and of subterfuges, and thanks to you we see honest people becoming the friends of knaves as long as they are both members of the same party. And in especial do I hate you, O politics, because you have reached the point of killing in our hearts all feeling and idea for our country. . . ."

After having read that virulent apostrophe it might seem rather difficult to classify my brother in one party or another, notwithstanding the friendships which he may have otherwise made to right and left among the admirers of his talent or to believe that he desired to classify himself under any mark or label. Too often had he reason to congratulate himself on that happy independence to be disposed to depart from it.

There is more than one man to-day who regrets he did not follow his example. Without professing as he did a disdain of politics pushed to the point of hatred and whilst recognizing that the misfortunes of the French have their origin especially in an indifference to politics felt in former ages, still, it must be confessed that the farther we get along, the less do men of letters and sensitive natures feel that they can congratulate themselves on having plunged into the hurly-burly of our current quarrels. If one conquers, the harvest is envy; if conquered, injustice. Most implacable of all are political resentments.

I know something about it, I who consider myself a passionate lover of liberty and have never proved a traitor, and yet whom certain men have never forgiven the modest share which I had in the perhaps inexpedient but rigorously legal act of the Twenty-fourth of May. In 1876, when the verdict at the polls proved conclusively to us that we had been mistaken, it was all in vain that I voluntarily resigned the functions which I was performing; it was all in vain that when my friends invited me to take them up again at the Sixteenth of May, I refused the offer; in vain for me to abstain since that time from any systematic belittling of a government whose defenders I had attacked in quite other circumstances — the men I speak of have never laid down their arms, but have continued to treat me as a foe, although I never provoked either their goodwill or their anger.

They have not even spared my literary works, concerning which certain members of their set wrote while speaking of me: " Daudet! — not the one who has some talent, the other — " believing that they were aiming a profound blow at my self-respect through that malicious reference to the successes won by my brother. The serenity with which I express myself to-day may prove to them how greatly they have been mistaken; I only allude to it in order to show the implacability of resentments which are born of politics, from which Alphonse Daudet has escaped.

Left at length entirely to himself, he devoted himself absolutely to letters. Then began that long series of stories, comedies, dramas and novels which have consecrated his fame as step by step they marked the persevering rise of his talents. Successively he published the *Letters from My Mill*, a collection made up of his impressions in the South, *Le Petit Chose*, partly inspired by our childhood, which he wrote in midwinter at a modest farm in Languedoc where he lived alone like a hermit for several weeks, having an old copy of Montaigne as his only companion, the reading of which rested him after his laborious watches. He had *L'Œillet Blanc* played at the Théâtre Français, *Les Absents* at the Opéra-Comique and *Le Frère Aîné* and *Le Sacrifice* at the Vaudeville.

In the course of his halts in the world of theatres he reaped a rich harvest of notes and observations upon actors, filling his barn with the fruitful corn from which later the character of Delobelle in

Fromont Jeune et Risler Aîné was to spring, as well as the critical appreciations which one can still read in a collection of his dramatic criticisms from *L'Officiel,* through which he has scattered the leading chapters of a history of theatrical criticism.

Speaking of this part of his life work, I have often heard people express astonishment that his plays did not meet with the same favor from the public as his books. It is quite true that he has never carried off one of those victories of the boards which afford fortune to an author of a theatre. I am not speaking of the plays which he adapted from his novels; the latter came upon the boards protected by the memory of the resounding success which they had had in their earlier form, though sometimes even this remembrance was a weight upon rather than a service to them, particularly when the public did not find on the stage in their fullness and set within their descriptive framework those individual types which had charmed it the most. As to the others, with the exception perhaps of *La Dernière Idole*, they have usually given their author more expense than satisfaction.

In this undeniable fact I am almost tempted to see a proof of his superiority, or, if you prefer, the inferiority of the scenic art. The books of Alphonse Daudet owe their greatest attraction more especially to the details, to descriptions, analysis of events and the composition of the cast of characters, to I know not what personal, original and seductive quality which theatrical conventions piteously destroy. His best qualities are exactly contrary to those which the modern boards exact, where conversation means little and the fact brought forth is of value only through the manner whereby it catches the observation and interest of the spectator.

On a single occasion only has my brother been tempted to write a drama suited to the taste of the day and in a form which allowed no room for his poetical expansiveness. He allowed himself to be got around by theatrical people and produced *Lise Tavernier* and he came to grief. It may be alleged that the play was put in the most grotesque fashion on the stage; at the Ambigu Theatre we were still under the management of Billion in 1872 — which says everything; but even if it had been put on the stage by a director who was more anxious to uphold the dignity of art, I do not believe that it would have produced a better result.

Toward the end of that year Alphonse Daudet gave the measure of what he was able to do for the theatre with *L'Arlésienne.* This tragic idyl he has clothed in the most brilliant decorations; he has touched all its periods with the hand of love, as if they were the stanzas of a pastoral poem; in the scenery drawn from Provence he has caused the entire gamut of passion to sound. From the very day when he began that work he had a fever, and that fever did not cease until the evening of the first performance in the lassitude and disappointment

which a doubtful victory brought with it. In
every sentence he scattered profusely the finest
pearls his wallet contained; he has written pages
in that work which you cannot read without feeling
your soul oppressed by a poignant emotion.

Nevertheless the effect on the boards did not
answer his expectations. Is it because the action
is too local? Is it because *Mireille* had exhausted
the interest felt by Parisians for things of Provence?
Or is it because *L'Arlésienne* would have had another destiny upon some other stage than that of
the Vaudeville, in some other atmosphere than that
of the corner of the Chaussée d'Antin, so fero-
ciously cynical? I am well disposed to believe it,
for but little was lacking and the uncertain success
of the play, sufficient as it was to do honor to an
author's career, would have transformed itself into
an incontestable triumph.

CHAPTER XX.

I AM editing these notes somewhat at haphazard, just as they come into my mind, without being careful of the chronological order of these intimate events that I am jotting down at present rather than relating. So that the reader will not be surprised if, after talking of plays given in 1872 in order not to have to revert to them, I should go back in time in order to find Alphonse Daudet where we just now left him, that is to say, at the moment when he has just left the only employment that he ever held.

At this time he lived the greater part of the year in the country. He loved the forests which surround Paris, lavishing the tenderness which he has always had for things of nature upon them — waters, forests and mountains — a tenderness which caused him to suddenly leave some village far away in the valley of Chevreuse to make a walking tour through the Vosges and Alsatia.

He has always eagerly searched for sensations which exterior objects bring forth. In the preface of *Fromont Jeune et Risler Aîné* he relates how the mere chance which made him settle in the Marais caused the selection of the neighborhood in which he has framed the action of his novel. Analogous circumstances exercised the same kind of influence on the making of his other books; that is particularly true of *Jack*, in which many pages contain recollections of long excursions made by him into the country about Paris toward Corbeil on the banks of the Seine where his marriage was destined to lead him and make him a fixture for several months in every year.

This marriage took place early in 1867; in the course of the preceding summer we had been installed at Ville-d'Avray in the family circle, but my brother, who was ill, had remained in Paris. An epidemic of cholera drove him out, so he came and settled down with us. One day some friends who lived in the neighborhood called upon us and brought with them one of their relatives, a Mademoiselle Julia Allard, a most charming young girl, highly educated and learned. It had been her good fortune to grow up in an atmosphere of tenderness and poetry between a father and mother passionately stirred by intellectual things who were poets themselves. A few months after that she bore the name of Alphonse Daudet.

Although she had already proved herself a writer by publishing *Les Impressions de Nature et d'Art*, wherein the childhood of a Parisian girl can be read, detached notes, impressions which recall things merely glimpsed and a dozen studies on recent books, yet I would not have talked about it, because I know how scared she is by any noise made about her, if it had not been that my brother himself has publicly acknowledged the influence which she has exerted over his works.

Alphonse Daudet being the man we know him, the partner whom he took for life might have quenched the pure flame of his spirit and killed his talent, if he had made a mistake in his choice. Fear of just this danger had always mastered him and kept him from marriage. An expression of this made after his marriage will be found in *Femmes d'Artistes,* more particularly in the story which opens that volume, *Madame Heurtebise.* All of us shared in this fear for him, but his wife has been the very peace of his hearth, the regulator of his work and the discreet counsellor of his inspiration.

" She is herself so much of an artist ! She has taken such a share in everything that I have written ! Not a page which she has not revised and retouched and on which she has not scattered a little bit of her fine golden and azure powder. And so modest withal, so simple, so little the literary woman ! One day I expressed all this and bore witness to a charming and indefatigable collaboration in the dedication to *Le Nabab ;* my wife has not permitted that dedication to appear, and so I have allowed it to stand only upon ten or twelve copies for friends."

I know of nothing more eloquent than this simple homage which is no less to the honor of him who gave it than of her who merited it. At the time that my sister-in-law, yielding to the urgent requests of her husband, had just published her collection of impressions, after a few hours passed between her and my brother one evening, quite moved by the happiness I found in their house, I wrote a few lines on returning to my home which seem in place for this study, the pretext for them being her book just out. These lines form as it were a precise picture of the lucky household where art is god and where the radiance of the happiness one perceives makes a striking and heart-warming contrast with the harsh beginnings which I have related.

"The working room is broad and lofty. The master of the household is seated before a table piled with papers and books beneath the white rays of the lamp, the brilliancy of which is softened by a shade in stamped paper; he is writing the new book promised to the people, announced by the papers and expected by translators and editors. Between each sentence, after having carefully chosen all the words and carved all the lines, he makes a stop, listening to the promptings of his imagination but disciplining it in order to keep it within the limits of truth, or to drag it back whenever it is tempted to exceed the bounds. The characters whose adventures he describes and whose souls, instincts and passions he reveals to us pass before his eyes.

"With the precision of a painter from the life he reproduces them exactly as he has known them; he is anxious to render them as truthfully as nature itself, employing in the struggle after nicety of expression, elevation of thought, descrip-

tion of scenery and surroundings and purity of
style, that vigor, that gracefulness, that fancy and
all those master qualities which exist in him and
with which he decorates the offspring of his
dreams under the most ardent searchings of conscience, never acknowledging himself satisfied until
he has exhausted all the forms of that effort and
thus proclaiming the respect which he has for the
public and that which he has for himself.

" Over against him at the other end of the table
his wife has come quietly in and taken her seat,
after having watched at the bedside of the children
and kissed their brows good-night. It is a perfect
hour, propitious to that quiet labor which en-
genders fine works of art. The noises of the
streets seem dampened and the whole house slumbers; this silence so deep is wholesome. A log
burns with a merry note on the hearth, the flame
therefrom dances above the glowing embers and
hangs sparks of red on the gilded frames of the
pictures and the copper vases in which green
plants are growing. Never did a sweeter and
gentler eloquence emanate from the intimate soul
of that domestic happiness, never from the
serenity of that family hearth where glory has
been a visitor.

" The young mother lets herself drift at the will
of her dreams; she enjoys the present and tries to
divine the future, and through an involuntary need
of comparing what she knew before with what she
possesses now and what she hopes to have, she lets
her thoughts turn toward the past. She sees once

more her infancy and is at once transported into
another home, warm also, comfortable and peaceful and full of caresses. She sees the days that
are passed. Here she is in command, there she
obeyed, and that itself was very sweet. She regrets
nothing in that past, but on the contrary thinks of
it with joy; her memory is full of its echoes and
recalls its souvenirs, dear to her mind.

"And so, seated at her happy table where talent
is infectious, seated opposite that man who is everything to her and whose pen is writing masterpieces,
she suddenly feels herself seized in short by a
sort of nostalgia, then she lets fall in harmonious
stanzas in prose or in verse these suddenly resur-
rected souvenirs upon the white page lying beneath
her hand. Such happy evenings are often renewed
and when summer comes they are completed by
delightful days of country life in the house among
the fields backing up against the forest, where the
emerald-colored vines and the Chinese glycines
with their blue flowers are mirrored in the stream."

CHAPTER XXI.

Up to 1873 Alphonse Daudet had shown himself averse to works that need long labor. He had written two novels, *Le Petit Chose* and *Tartarin de Tarascon*, but these were his works at the beginning and belong much earlier in his career; he hardly seemed disposed to take up again a series which had been interrupted. After the war he turned his principal efforts to the theatre, whilst, on the other hand, he gathered together recollections of the end of the Empire, the siege of Paris and the Commune into short studies either historical or imaginative, after the manner of *Lettres de Mon Moulin.* No less than three volumes were necessary to include them, namely *Lettres à un Absent, Contes du Lundi* and *Robert Helmont.*

It is true that during this period he had been examining men and things very closely; as early as the beginning of 1870 he had already allowed himself to be turned aside from his preoccupations, which up to that time had been purely literary, by the forerunning symptoms of the hurricane; as an observer he followed all the popular manifestations and incidents of politics.

I remember that one evening, a few days before the *plébiscite*, he wanted to drag me across the

Faubourg du Temple, full of threatening faces and
rumors, to be present at an electoral meeting.
Tumultuous groups which were restrained with
difficulty by an enormous show of armed forces
prevented our reaching the end of our walk; battle
had already begun between the Parisians and the
Bonapartists.

Another evening, a few hours after the assassination of Victor Noir, we went to the Ministry of
Justice to see Émile Ollivier whom up to that time
he had not met. Then occurred the Fourth of
September and the siege, during which he remained in Paris enrolled as a volunteer in the
National Guard, and, notwithstanding his short-
sightedness, a great frequenter of advanced posts,
a fearless searcher after sensations, braving danger
in order to have the satisfaction of seeing everything and of increasing at the end of each exciting
day the bulk of those pages of notes, pages already
charged with his fine and closely set writing. For
nearly two years his literary output was nourished
by these recollections and in that way he has hung
in his life work, as if in a gallery, a hundred pictures which have all the value of historical documents, owing to their exactness and the truth of
the observation behind them.

Perhaps in no part of his work has that powerful faculty of sight shown itself in the same degree
as in these short stories, which are impregnated
besides by an emotion that caused his pen to
tremble, when, hurriedly, for fear he should forget it, he noted down in one line some master

impression which contained all the others. Often a characteristic that struck him lasted several minutes. Often he only had a glimpse of his model; but that was enough for him to paint the picture without falsifying the likeness. The same statement can be applied to all his work.

The Commune obliged him to fly from Paris. When he returned and was able to get to work again he only thought of books in which the events he had taken part in should be engraved just as they remained in his memory.

At the same time, as I have said, he was working for the theatre. The failure of *Lise Tavernier*, the disappointment as to *L'Arlésienne* put a stop to his energies in that direction. During a representation of the latter play the idea struck him to make a novel with scenes in Paris and he wrote *Fromont Jeune et Risler Aîné* in 1873, without foreseeing the immense success which that volume was to bring him, although its prior publication in *Le Bien Public* could scarcely have passed unperceived. With this novel Charpentier the publisher began his series of volumes with immense editions. A few weeks were enough to distribute that novel through the entire world; it was read in foreign parts just as much as in France, either in the original or translations.

This popularity during the first days of its appearance did not exhaust its success; at the time I write (1881) several thousand copies are printed every year. The Académie Française itself wanted to share in the manifestations that took place about the name of Alphonse Daudet and it decreed the most literary of the prizes which it annually awards to his novel.

Owing to the force of events this study of mine has little by little so taken on the character of an apology that at present I feel a certain embarrassment in saying what I think of *Fromont Jeune et Risler Aîné.*

When speaking of Alphonse Daudet I am able to offer an understanding of the man by means of a simple story of the events of his life, just as one imparts knowledge as to an historical episode by the aid of authentic documents, but I could hardly judge his literary work otherwise than by expressing a personal opinion in which admiration would hold the highest place; so that my judgment would be suspected and therefore without value. It would add nothing to the authority of this chapter of literary history and so I renounce the occasion of formulating it.

But what I have the right to affirm is this, that the truth of the characters and the actuality (*vécu*) of the events were the determining cause of the good fortune that befell the first long novel by Alphonse Daudet. No one bothered himself to see whether the plan was very new or whether in one way or another it did not have connecting threads with some other plot which had been already used in books more or less widely spread. What the reader saw above all things and what moved, persuaded and charmed him, was much less the moral of a story which arrayed in contest commercial honor and the honor of the domestic hearth, than the simplicity of the intrigue, the truth of the characters to life, the poetry and emotion scattered with both hands through those altogether charming chapters.

Our older men of letters have often told how in other times an entire generation took the greatest, most passionate interest in some hero of romance — Monte Cristo, Fleur-de-Marie, d'Artagnan — whose unlikeness to nature at last caused the interest of living men for fictitious beings to grow stale. It is a long time now since manifestations provoked by a book have fallen to very quiet lines, but they were seen afresh on the appearance of *Fromont Jeune et Risler Aîné*. Little girl Chèbe, Désirée the lame girl are popular characters, whilst Delobelle has become a classic. His name will remain as an epithet suited to define all those in his profession, fashioned after his image and resembling him, who go out in the world. People say: "He's a Delobelle" just as they say: "He's a Harpagon."

After this novel Alphonse Daudet wrote *Jack*. In that case also the impulse started with a simple story which came to his knowledge and which the chance of neighborhood permitted him to follow through its various episodes as a witness or confidant; this formed the basis of his novel. Faithful to his usual system, he wove in succession about this actual story various characters who in reality never played any part therein, but who nevertheless had actually lived and had posed before him without their knowing it. These characters themselves were completed by characteristics and phrases which belonged to others but could be adapted to their character and nature.

This labor of adaptation and recomposition lies at the root of all Alphonse Daudet's novels — unless it might be of *Le Nabab*, where he has transferred two characters to his pages without changing anything in their historical physiognomy, namely the two principal actors — I do not know of a single person whom he has put in his works without having composed the character in this way out of bits and pieces. After the appearance of *Rois en Exil* there was a veritable craze of curiosity to know which of the living my brother had aimed at and portrayed, a curiosity provoked by the desire to tear away the masks. Well, there is not a single one among the types of that book which is completely and personally real; a number of models were needed in order to compose a single one.

This is even true of *Numa Roumestan*. When this novel began to appear my fellow-countryman Senator Numa Baragnon, after reading the splendid description of the Arena on a day of popular festival, wrote to me at the close of one of his letters: "I have a great mind to sign this letter Numa Roumestan, because people say that it is myself your brother wished to draw, but alas, it is a very long time since the people have taken the horses out of *my* carriage!"

On the other hand there were several people I might designate who were a trifle uneasy, con-

vinced that Alphonse Daudet had published his
book in order to present them in complete life to
the curiosity of the public. They were mistaken,
all of them; the continuation of the novel must
have proved that to their satisfaction. As was his
good right, the author had taken a bit from each
of them; there was not one of them who had
posed to him for the entire figure. It is sufficient
to be acquainted with the list of politicians of our
times to recognize what belongs to one and what
to the other.

But I return to *Jack.* My brother had talked to
me a great deal as to this novel before writing it;
having been placed in the management of the
Journal Officiel, I asked him for the right to publish it in the *Bulletin Français* which we had just
founded, I representing the Ministry of the Interior
in partnership with Émile de Girardin and Witters-
heim, to take the place of the *Petit Journal Officiel,* which had disappeared with the Empire.

Alphonse already had charge of the dramatic
review in the *Officiel.* I had confided it to him,
having with good reason foreseen that his talents
would justify too well the appointment which I
made that any one should think of accusing me of
nepotism. A wish to give a profitable brilliancy
to the newly-born paper placed in my control was
sure to justify in the same way the appearance in
that paper of a novel signed " Alphonse Daudet."

But when he brought it to me I was a little
frightened at the bringing in toward the beginning
of the book of an establishment run by the Jesuits.

The official character of our two papers had already
occasioned me a certain embarrassment and was
about to give me more, all arising from the difficulty of granting liberty to writers without impli-
cating the government. There are certain Deputies
who pick carefully to pieces all the non-official
part of the paper, articles on art, articles on literature and even the chronicle of daily events, from
which I was expected to banish every mention of
crime, suicide or attempted murder. They carried
their complaints to the Minister for every line
which failed to please them. The papers of that
period are full of criticisms and attacks which
sprang from the "liberties" taken by the editor
of the government journals.

I remember especially one circumstance which
assumed the proportions of an event of importance
in our humble family of editors bound together
by the strictest fellowship. My learned comrade
Bouchut, while alluding to I know not what malady of the nerves in an article devoted to a medical book, had timidly insinuated that it would be
easy to explain the ecstasy of Saint Theresa by
physiology. The Hon. M. Keller discovered in
that very simple and very true statement a denial
of miracles; he told me this during a meeting of
the Chamber at Versailles, and after having tried
in vain to drag the promise of a denial of the article
out of me, he marched off to point the matter out
to M. Buffet, the President of the Council and
Minister of the Interior, who had been but a few
hours in office.

Although M. Buffet would certainly be incapable of exacting from an honest man an act which degraded his professional dignity, still, at first blush he insisted, in order to put it through, that I should disavow what my collaborator had said. One may imagine what my answer was. Insistence on one side, resistance on the other. The incident lasted two days and I could only cut it short by declaring that it was true they could take my office from me, but I never would disavow my own fellow-worker. Whether it was kindliness or weakness, M. Buffet disliked extreme measures and the affair came to an end by means of a letter which Dr. Bouchut wrote me, in which with a good deal of cleverness he demonstrated that both of us were above caring for our misadventure.

I have only told this item from our political customs in order to explain the reasons which made me hesitate to publish *Jack.* Having been made acquainted with my embarrassment and troubles, my brother refused to discuss my objections and took his novel to the hospitable office of the *Moniteur*, which is full of illustrious souvenirs and literary traditions. Paul Dalloz hastened to accept it.

This book did not meet at the publisher's the success of the preceding one; which can only be explained by the necessity in which Dentu found himself of publishing it in two volumes and raising the price, for never had the fine qualities of author and poet shown themselves in greater splendor, never in the same degree had he expressed his affection for the small and humble persons of this world, nor shown better his gifts of moving others when brought in contact with his own emotion, his gift of handling irony and describing the scenery in which he causes his characters to live.

Whether he is laying bare the peacock brain of Ida de Barancy or is showing us d'Argenton, the most important of the good-for-nothings, squatting so proudly in the midst of his nullity and folly; whether he takes us in the footsteps of poor little Jack as he escapes from the Moronval academy, overwhelmed by the terror of the dark, of the silent and the unknown, as he wanders lost through the fields wrapped in shadows, or relates to us the martyrdom of the little negro king; whether he describes the quiet landscapes on the banks of the Seine or takes us to Indret to make us laugh with Bélisaire and cry with Jack; whether he opens to our view the still interior of the Rivals or allows us to be present at the last years of d'Argenton's victim — in every case his talent is shown with the rarest power. And although people have pretended that he is lacking in imagination, making of this by turns a fault and a merit, yet, through the arrangement and logical accumulation of events which may perhaps have happened before, he has produced in every respect the illusion of a complete and a personal invention.

Moreover types of humanity follow each other closely, numerous, multifold and original, in a fairy-like setting of descriptions with flesh upon their bones, muscles under the skin, blood in their veins and all the forces of actual life.

Jack is as free from the anxious care for actuality visible in *Le Nabab, Les Rois en Exil* and *Numa Roumestan*, as *Fromont Jeune et Risler Aîné* is, but when considered by itself *Jack* will always be found a species of revelation as a study of manners and yet rigorously exact to life and filled with a vivid sentiment of modernity. Looked at as a whole, this work seems to me a transition, after which Alphonse Daudet came to create for the modern novel a new mold by introducing our social and political history through living characters and inaugurating what I may call his second manner, characterized by that preoccupation for actuality of which I have just spoken.

That preoccupation itself starts from a constant anxiety to reach the truth. Naturally its result was to complete that masterly faculty in his genius which turns the pen into a brush, gives the saliency of a painting to style and causes color to spring up through the arrangement of words; it brings men and things to the eyes of the reader, though fixed on a printed page, with a power of vision quite as intense and tangible in its contours as life itself.

And here it is fitting to add that the quality which gives especial value to the books of Alphonse Daudet and assures serious chances of durability to them is the fact that as a whole they constitute an exact image of his time. Whether stories or novels or even intimate studies like those which furnish forth the volume *Les Femmes d'Artistes*, one of the less known books which I recommend to connoisseurs, all include a "documentary quality" which greatly increases their value. This story found in *Lettres à un Absent* or that episode in *Les Rois en Exil* will be found a page of history which those persons ought to read before they set to work who may undertake to study us, their predecessors, in the future, as to events, as to family life and as to mankind. The death and funeral of the Duc de Mora, the visit of the Bey of Tunis to the castle of the Nabob, the studio of Félicia Ruys, the Levis agency, the watch under arms and the trip of Numa Roumestan as Minister to his native town — there is history in the best sense of the word, not the official history of facts, but that history of passions and appetites and aspirations which help to make them understood! Mérimée was quite right when he said he was ready to barter *Thucydides* for a single page of the *Memoirs of Aspasia.* No less is required to brighten with a luminous ray a vanished civilization.

By giving a commentary on history in that way, by taking possession in such fashion of men and things, the modern novel has made a glorious conquest. Moreover it has imposed new convictions upon the science of history. Among the younger writers all those who occupy themselves with that science have perceived that since the novel has taken something from them, history must also take something from the novel. It has borrowed from the novel its form and analyses, its descriptions and even its dialogues.

Only a little while ago, with rare exceptions, even the most distinguished historians would have thought that they were derogating from the rules of their art and the majesty of the past and from memoirs in the grand style; they would have thought that events were degraded if they departed from a cold and restrained style by placing their characters within a descriptive framework, while showing us their features and adapting their actions to the proportions of daily life and by making them act and talk just as we act and talk ourselves.

The modern school has modified and transformed the procedure; it will modify and transform it still more and that peaceful revolution will have been ocasioned by the transformation of the novel, which itself has been performed through the power of public taste. For what those of us who have any sort of care, lest we drown in the sea of general indifference, should never forget is the fact that it is reality, it is life, that the present generation exacts from artists. The novel for its own sake, that is to say fiction, is dead, very dead. What the reader expects to find in books that demand his attention is himself, his vices and virtues, his own image, everything which by himself he would not be able to see. The art of the novelist, like that of the painter, as well as the art of the historian, consists in showing himself well to himself under the different forms which each of these kinds of literature demand.

That is, and I know it well, or very nearly that,

the doctrine of the naturalistic school. The decisiveness with which that school has made itself the owner of these truths by endeavoring to claim as its own the personality of Alphonse Daudet has not done anything less for its own success than has the energetic temperament which belongs to the most famous of its apostles. But whatever may be the scientific formulas, perhaps a trifle puerile, with which he has clothed them in order to decorate his conception of the novel with a special and personal merit of its own, we can hardly admit that these truths are his own invention or that these rules are exclusively his.

They had been employed before he wrote them on his banner and entered the fight under their name. Without going back to Balzac, when one considers how great the advance is which they have made since his time and the large share which they hold in our preoccupations, it is very difficult not to attribute the chief reason for their progress to Edmond and Jules de Goncourt. There are the two fathers of the naturalistic novel! *L'Assommoir* had its ancestor: *Germinie Lacerteux!* There stand the principles of the school put into practical form by that manifestation of a manly genius which never tried either to make a dogmatic profession of them nor to impose them upon others, and which never cared to demonstrate their power save through the uses which were made of them. So then, if it is not permissible for the most famous disciple of naturalism to proclaim himself its inventor without committing a grave injustice, it is all the easier for him to ally the Goncourts to his school, which is indeed theirs.

But he would not be able to introduce in the same way Alphonse Daudet, whose qualities as poet and author, whose exquisite delicacy and deep tenderness, as well as his repugnance for everything that is trivial or coarse, protest against the use that some people have wished to make of his name in a party which only owes its victories to its chiefs, a party which has not yet founded anything and which would suddenly vanish if it lost them.

No, Alphonse Daudet cannot be enlisted in those ranks any more than others, for he is too little a man of schools and dogmas, too averse to every kind of ostracism, too proudly independent and, to sum up everything in a word, too completely an artist! Whatever effort may be made to put a label on him, that effort will be in vain. Alphonse Daudet is himself. That is the essence of his inborn originality, the personal mark of his life work.

PETITES-DALLES (SEINE-INFÉRIEURE).
August–September, 1881.